Federal Financial Institutions Examination Council

A User's Guide for the Uniform Bank Performance Report

December 2008

Board of Governors of the Federal Reserve System, Federal Deposit Insurance Corporation, Office of the Comptroller of the Currency

December 2008

Prepared by:
Federal Financial Institutions Examination Council
3501 Fairfax Drive, Room D8073a
Arlington, VA 22226

Send comments to: UBPR Coordinator
Phone: 703-516-5732
Fax: 703-562-6446
Via regular mail to above address

For questions regarding content of the UBPR products, or UBPR data on DVD please call John Smullen at:
Phone: 1-703-516-5732
E-Mail: jsmullen@fdic.gov

Table of Contents

Introduction

The Uniform Bank Performance Report (UBPR) is an analytical tool created for bank supervisory, examination, and bank management purposes. In a concise format, it shows the impact of management decisions and economic conditions on a bank's performance and balance-sheet composition. The performance and composition data contained in the report can be used as an aid in evaluating the adequacy of earnings, liquidity, capital, asset and liability management, and growth management. Bankers and examiners alike can use this report to further their understanding of a bank's financial condition and through such understanding perform their duties more effectively.

The UBPR is now available online at no charge at WWW.FFIEC.GOV. A UBPR for any bank in the country may be viewed online, printed or downloaded. The site includes 5 years of history including all intermediate quarters.

A UBPR is produced for each commercial bank in the United States that is supervised by the Board of Governors of the Federal Reserve System, Federal Deposit Insurance Corporation, or the Office of the Comptroller of the Currency. UBPRs are produced for FDIC insured savings banks also. The report is computer-generated from a data base derived from public and nonpublic sources. It contains several years' worth of data, which are updated quarterly. Those data are presented in the form of ratios, percentages, and dollar amounts computed mainly from Reports of Condition and Income submitted by the bank. Each UBPR also contains corresponding average data for the bank's peer group and percentile rankings for most ratios. The UBPR therefore permits evaluation of a bank's current condition, trends in its financial performance, and comparisons with the performance of its peer group.

In addition to the individual bank report, the following is also available:

- A Peer Group report, which presents all peer averages.

- A List of Banks in Peer Group, which presents a list of banks within each peer group.

- A State Average Report, which presents ratio, averages within States.

- A Distribution report is also produced using the peer groupings in the state average and peer group average reports. Selected percentile values are displayed for individual ratios to provide additional insight into the range of bank performance that comprises an average.

- UBPR data, which present all types of UBPR information in bulk format on dvd.

This user's guide contains basic guidelines for using the UBPR, including a suggested method of analyzing the report, technical information, and ratio definitions. The UBPR, related statistical reports and the User's Guide are available online, free of change, at www.ffiec.gov. Questions relating to details in this guide may be addressed to the Coordinator for Uniform Performance Reports, Federal Financial Institutions Examination Council, Arlington, VA. See the Title Page for the complete address.

Summary of Changes to the 2008 UBPR

This information describes changes included in the June 30, 2008 UBPR.

Delivery of the User's Guide

The User's Guide will continue to be made available to all users through the FFIEC website http://www. ffiec. gov/ubprguide.htm as a series of PDF files.

UBPR Available Online

The UBPR will continue to be made available to bankers and the general public at no charge. The UBPR portion of the FFIEC website provides several other analytical tools to support the UBPR including Peer Group Data Report, Peer Distribution Report and a List of Banks by Peer group. Bankers and others may also use the Custom Peer facility to re-compute UBPR peer group statistics based on a custom or user defined group of banks. Please see

http://www.ffiec.gov/UBPR.htm for details.

UBPR Page Layouts

Replaced all UBPR sample pages. See section III for details.

Changes

Several additions were made to the Uniform Bank Performance Report through March 2008. To the extent possible these changes were made retroactively.

Page 7.

Added: Detail on construction loans and loans secured by nonfarm nonresidential properties.

Page 7a.

Added: Detail on construction loans and loans secured by nonfarm residential properties.

Added: Loans Held For Sale and Loans Not Held For Sale to the Balance Sheet Assets and Liabilities and Capital ($000) page.

Page 7b.

Revised: Concentration of credit ratios are computed using total capital from RC-R.

Added: Detail on Construction loans and loans secured by nonfarm nonresidential properties.

Added: Five ratios to the Supplemental section.

Page 8 & 8a.

Added: Current 1–5 Family Restructured Loans, Loans Secured by 1–4 Family Real Estate in Foreclosure, detail on Construction Loan delinquencies, detail on Loans secured by nonfarm residential properties.

Section I: Using the Uniform Bank Performance Report for Financial Analysis

Summary

The Uniform Bank Performance Report is designed to be used by bank examiners and bank management evaluating the financial condition of banks. By analyzing the data contained in the UBPR, the user can obtain an overall picture of the bank's financial health and can discover conditions that might require further analysis and investigation. The UBPR is not designed to replace on-site examination or investigations but to supplement present examination procedures. It also functions as a common point of financial analysis between regulator and banker and can be useful as a part of a bank's own internal bank process. The UBPR presents three types of data for use in the financial analysis of a bank: (1) the bank's data, (2) data for a peer group of banks similar in size and economic environment, and (3) percentile rankings. A thorough understanding of those data groups and their interrelationships and limitations is essential in order to use the UBPR effectively. As a general rule, any analysis should compare the bank to its peer group, consider the bank's trends over time, and also be aware of trends and changes in peer group averages. This user's guide does not present detailed in-depth instructions on ratio analysis, nor does it assign particular value to individual ratios or groups of ratios. Rather, it simply summarizes one way of using the UBPR for analysis; other approaches may be equally effective. Its primary purpose is to explain the calculations of individual ratios.

Availability

All Uniform Bank Performance Reports and related information are distributed online through the FFIEC website www.ffiec.gov. First select Uniform Bank Performance Reports (UBPR) under Quick Links on the FFIEC website. Please review the Schedule for the Online UBPR for information on when the current UBPR will be available.

Uniform Bank Performance Reports —

Select Search for a Uniform Bank Performance Report

To identify a bank enter the FDIC certificate number OR enter the name of one or more of the geographic criteria. For example just entering Los Angeles and California will return a list of all banks in Los Angeles, California.

All Statistical Reports—

Select All Statistical Reports

This section lists all reports available in the online UBPR system. Then choose from the following list of special reports.

Uniform Bank Performance Report—See above.

Bank List Report—This report provides a list of banks by peer group. The list includes core information such as location, assets and net income and it may be resorted by several criteria. An individual bank's UBPR may be accessed directly from the list by clicking on the certificate number.

Peer Group Data Report—This report displays all UBPR ratios averaged by peer group in UBPR format. All peer groups are available.

Peer Group Distribution Report—This report provides a distribution or range of values for all ratios that appear in the UBPR by peer group.

This report can provide valuable insight into the population of banks that are used to calculate peer average data that appears in the UBPR. For example the UBPR calculates a trimmed average ROA for the peer group 9 of 1.18%. Peer group nine is made up of 339 banks with net income to average assets (ROA) that ranges from –2.24% at the first percentile to 5.51% at the 99th percentile. The report displays ratio distribution data in UBPR page format.

State Average Report—Provides summary UBPR ratio data and selected aggregate information averaged by state. A further breakdown of average statistical data is provided by asset size. The information is provided for all states and territories in UBPR format.

State Distribution Report—This report provides a distribution or range of values for all ratios that appear in the state average report. As with the peer group distribution report this report can provide valuable insight into the population of banks used to calculate state average data.

Custom Peer Group Report—This report allows a selected bank to be compared with the composite performance of a user defined peer group of banks. UBPR peer statistics are recomputed based on a user defined group of banks and displayed along with individual bank data in UBPR page format. Banks may be identified as peers by either entering FDIC certificate numbers or using the built-in search engine.

Analytical Considerations

Effective use of the UBPR entails consideration of the level and trend of individual ratios and the interrelationship among related ratios. No single ratio, percentile ranking, or trend is indicative of a bank's condition. Each bank has its own unique operating characteristics that affect both its balance-sheet composition and its income stream. A given bank may be above or below the peer group average for a given ratio, however that information must be considered in combination with other related facts including other UBPR data before its importance can be determined.

For example, if a bank's net interest income (TE) to average assets (UBPR page 01) is 3.03 percent compared with the peer group average of 3.96 percent, placing it in the 15th percentile, the bank may appear to be having profit-margin difficulties. However, if the bank's temporary investments (UBPR page 10) are 49 percent of average assets compared with the peer-group average of 17 percent and its volatile liabilities are 43 percent of average assets compared with 19 percent for the peer group, it can be concluded that the bank's assets and liability composition is substantially different from that of its peers. Thus, a lower net interest income (TE) to average assets ratio may be normal and proper, as would be a lower overhead expense to average assets ratio. Dependence on large time deposits and federal-funds purchased in short-term investments normally produces narrower profit margins and does not require as large a building, staff, or operating budget as engaging more heavily in retail activities.

However, overhead expenses that are not well below the peer group mean for such a bank could be cause for concern, because of the potential effect on earnings. As the above example demonstrates, differences in assets and liability composition must be taken into consideration in order to properly interpret percentile rankings and ratio variations between the bank and its peer group. By employing percentile rankings and peer-group data as general guides or points of reference, rather than as strict bench marks, and by being aware of the interrelationship between the bank's balance sheet

and its income statement, analysis may focus on those areas of a bank's operation that merit concern, thus providing a more complete understanding of the entire bank.

Method of Review

The introductory page of the UBPR describes the bank's current peer group and the name and address of its holding company, if applicable. The primary financial analysis begins on UBPR page 01 with a review of summary ratios.

The Summary Ratios page (Page 01) presents the bank's average assets and net income in dollars; performance ratios, asset and liability management data, capital ratios, and growth rates. It also shows percentile rankings and peer-group averages. This page provides direction for analysis of the other sections of the report. After the summary ratios section has been analyzed, the bank's earnings section can be evaluated using a "Decision Tree" analysis approach. Note that the UBPR is organized so that ratios on page one are supported by details on subsequent pages. This approach is an attempt to explore how ratios are interrelated and how one ratio can affect other ratios, thus allowing the analyst to trace the source of a particular performance characteristic to its root cause.

For example, the interplay of rates earned on assets or paid on liabilities and the volume or mix of such assets and liabilities is segregated in the decision tree analysis.

Each component of a ratio and of each succeeding ratio can be determined by referring to Section III, where the method of calculating each ratio is explained. Exhibit I-1 charts the systematic process a user might follow in analyzing a bank's net income to average assets ratio.

Rather than trace each earning component separately, the analyst may review the earnings page in sequence to analyze the trend and interrela-

tionships of these components while tracing their causes. Concurrently, the analyst may identify conditions that may be cause for concern and find corroborative evidence of conditions noted during the review of the summary ratios. This method allows for an orderly progression of thought and helps the analyst develop a perception of the bank as a whole.

This method of page-by-page review may be extended to the other sections of the UBPR. After completing the review of the last page of the report, the user should have a relatively comprehensive overview of the bank's financial condition and, possibly, a list of causes for concern that warrant further inquiry.

Using Peer Group, State Average and Distribution Reports

The UBPR Peer Group Report and State Average Report present ratio averages for peer groups and States, respectively. These reports are used to analyze conditions and trends in these banking industry groups. The grouped averages do not constitute supervisory targets or ideal values. Rather, they are intended to provide some insight into the performance of similarly sized and situated banks across the country. While individual peer averages may be thought of as representing the composite performance of a group of banks, those values may or may not be an appropriate goal for a given bank. Only a full analysis of all financial data including historical trend analysis and comparison to peer group averages can provide that answer. Additionally, the peer distribution reports, which show several percentiles values for UBPR ratios are designed to show the range of values that compose a given average. As such, they provide additional support to the argument that the averages represent a middle point and that most banks will fall on either side of that average. See Section II for technical considerations regarding averages.

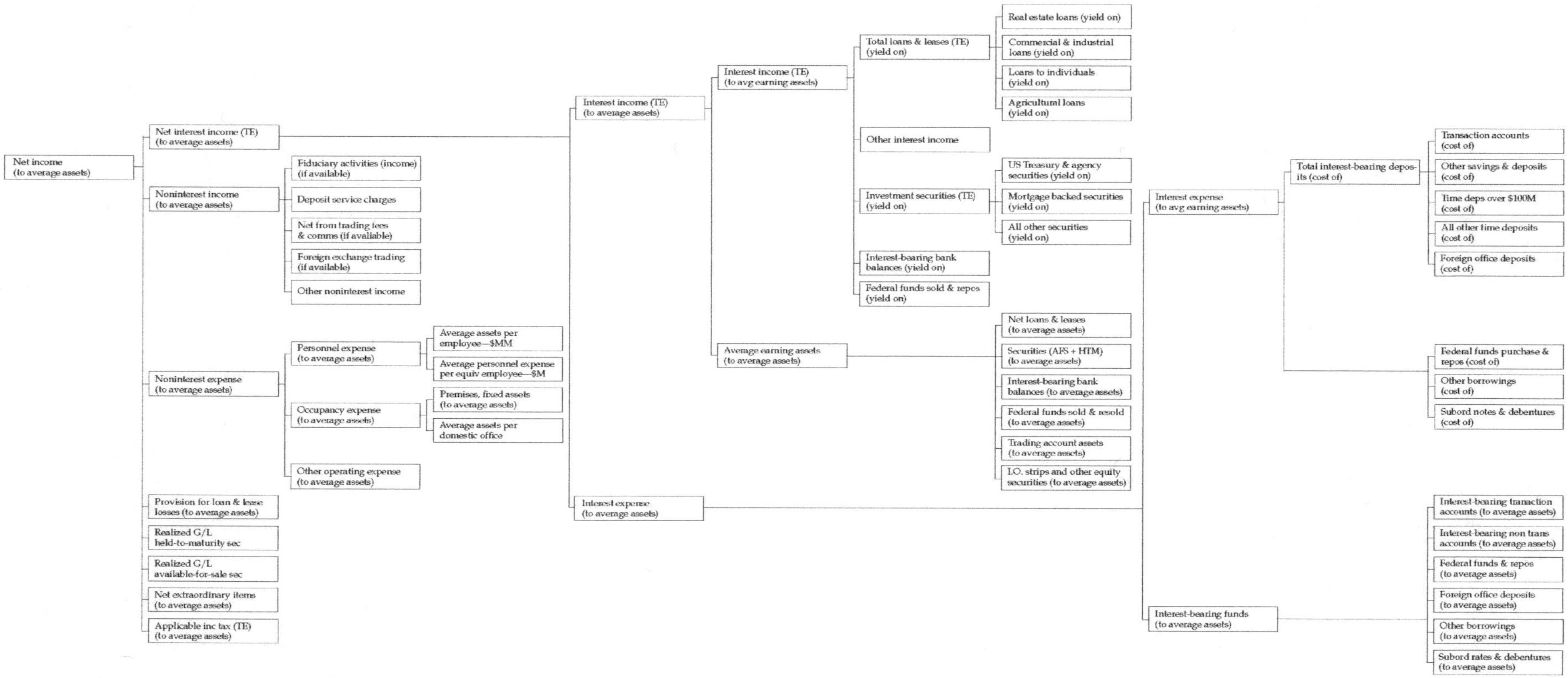

Net income
(to average assets)

Net interest income (TE)
(to average assets)

Noninterest income
(to average assets)

Noninterest expense
(to average assets)

Provision for loan & lease losses (to average assets)

Realized G/L held-to-maturity sec

Realized G/L available-for-sale sec

Net extraordinary items (to average assets)

Applicable inc tax (TE) (to average assets)

Interest income (TE)
(to average assets)

Interest expense
(to average assets)

Interest income (TE)
(to avg earning assets)

Average earning assets
(to average assets)

Interest expense
(to avg earning assets)

Interest-bearing funds
(to average assets)

Total loans & leases (TE)
(yield on)

Other interest income

Investment securities (TE)
(yield on)

Interest-bearing bank balances (yield on)

Federal funds sold & repos
(yield on)

Real estate loans (yield on)

Commercial & industrial loans (yield on)

Loans to individuals (yield on)

Agricultural loans (yield on)

US Treasury & agency securities (yield on)

Mortgage backed securities (yield on)

All other securities (yield on)

Net loans & leases (to average assets)

Securities (AFS + HTM) (to average assets)

Interest-bearing bank balances (to average assets)

Federal funds sold & resold (to average assets)

Trading account assets (to average assets)

I.O. strips and other equity securities (to average assets)

Total interest-bearing deposits (cost of)

Transaction accounts (cost of)

Other savings & deposits (cost of)

Time deps over $100M (cost of)

All other time deposits (cost of)

Foreign office deposits (cost of)

Federal funds purchase & repos (cost of)

Other borrowings (cost of)

Subord notes & debentures (cost of)

Interest-bearing transaction accounts (to average assets)

Interest bearing non trans accounts (to average assets)

Federal funds & repos (to average assets)

Foreign office deposits (to average assets)

Other borrowings (to average assets)

Subord rates & debentures (to average assets)

Fiduciary activities (income) (if available)

Deposit service charges

Net from trading fees & comms (if available)

Foreign exchange trading (if available)

Other noninterest income

Personnel expense (to average assets)

Occupancy expense (to average assets)

Other operating expense (to average assets)

Average assets per employee—$M

Average personnel expense per equiv employee—$M

Premises, fixed assets (to average assets)

Average assets per domestic office

Section II: Technical Information

Banks Covered

The Uniform Bank Performance Report covers all insured commercial banks and FDIC-Supervised Savings Banks, which may be categorized according to their charter types and primary regulatory agencies:

- National banks, which are regulated by the Office of the Comptroller of the Currency

- State-chartered banks, which are members of the Federal Reserve System, regulated by the Federal Reserve Board

- State-chartered banks, which are not members of the Federal Reserve System, and are regulated by the Federal Deposit Insurance Corporation

- FDIC-Supervised savings banks, which are regulated by the FDIC.

Sources of UBPR Data

The source of all bank financial data in the UBPR is the Report of Condition and Report of Income, (Call Reports), and filed quarterly by each insured bank. These Call Reports differ somewhat between banks in amount of detail, depending on the characteristics of the banks. The following "report type" designations refer to the FFIEC form numbers on different Call Reports:

From March 31, 2001 forward:

- 031 Reporters: all banks with domestic and foreign offices

- 041 Reporters: all banks with domestic offices

From December 31, 2000 back:

- 031 Reporters: all banks with domestic and foreign offices

- 032 Reporters: all banks with

domestic offices only with assets of $300 million or more

- 033 Reporters: all banks with domestic offices only and with assets of $100 million or more but less than $300 million

- 034 Reporters: all banks with domestic offices only and with assets of less than $100 million.

The UBPR also uses various items of bank "structure" data from agency files, to categorize banks or to gather additional information. Such items of information include:

- bank name and address

- number of offices

- established date

- whether located in a Metropolitan Statistical Area

- holding company identification

- occurrences of bank mergers.

Format and Content

Each Uniform Bank Performance Report presents pages of bank financial data organized into: (1) summary ratios, (2) income information and (3) balance sheet information. These different formats are illustrated in Appendix A of this user guide. Also, the source items and calculations used for some UBPR items may vary depending on Call Report type, bank class, or other factors. The items and calculations are discussed in Section III.

Primmary Peer Group Criteria

Banks are assigned to one primary peer group to permit average ratios to be calculated. Most banks are assigned to one of the primary insured commercial bank peer groups. In addition several primary

line-of-business peer groups have been established because of the unique operating characteristics of some institutions. Those groups include Savings Bank, Credit Card Specialty, and Bankers Bank peer groups. Peer-group data are included in the UBPR to show the average performance of a group of banks with similar characteristics. This information can be used as a benchmark against which an individual bank's asset and liability structure and earnings may be measured. Users should note that primary peer group data appears on pages 1, 3, 5, 6, 7, 8, 9, 10, 11, 12, and 13. See section III for definitions of individual ratios.

Insured Commercial Bank Peer Groups

Over 7,800 banks are assigned to one of 15 asset-based primary insured commercial bank peer groups. Peer groups are defined by up to three criteria as described in the table below. Banks are first grouped by asset size using 90-day average assets from call report schedule RC-K. This asset-based grouping applies to all peer groups and is reviewed quarterly. Smaller asset groups are sub-divided by the number of full service branches. The number of full service branches is gathered from the annual Summary of Deposits filed with the FDIC. Those groupings are subdivided again by whether a bank is located in a metropolitan area or not. A metropolitan area is a Metropolitan Statistical Area (MSA) as defined by a federal agency, the Office of Management and Budget (OMB). De Novo, or newly chartered insured commercial banks are compared to other banks that opened in the same year for a period of five years. For example banks that were chartered in the year 2006 will be placed in peer group number 2006

Insured Commercial Bank Peer Group Descriptions

Peer Group Number	Average Assets for Latest Quarter	Number of Banking Offices	Location
1	In excess of $3 billion	-	-
2	Between $1 billion and $3 billion	-	-
3	Between $300 million and $1 billion	-	-
4	Between $100 million and $300 million	3 or more	Metropolitan area
5	Between $100 million and $300 million	3 or more	Non-metropolitan area
6	Between $100 million and $300 million	2 or fewer	Metropolitan area
7	Between $100 million and $300 million	2 or fewer	Non-metropolitan area
8	Between $50 million and $100 million	3 or more	Metropolitan area
9	Between $50 million and $100 million	3 or more	Non-metropolitan area
10	Between $50 million and $100 million	2 or fewer	Metropolitan area
11	Between $50 million and $100 million	2 or fewer	Non-metropolitan area
12	Less than $50 million	2 or more	Metropolitan area
13	Less than $50 million	2 or more	Non-metropolitan area
14	Less than $50 million	1	Metropolitan area
15	Less than $50 million	1	Non-metropolitan area
De Novo	Less than $750 million. Each De Novo bank is grouped by the year of opening with other De Novo banks for period of five years subject to the asset limitation. Each De Novo peer group is described by it's year, e.g. 2002, 2003, 2004, 2005, 2006.		

and compared to one another for five years. After five years, banks will be placed in one of the asset-based peer groups. The UBPR will include DeNovo peer groups from 2001 forward.

This structure is used to develop average or composite ratios by peer group. Because similar sized banks operating under similar conditions are compared, the peer group ratios provide a useful benchmark of performance. Consistent differences in peer group performance are apparent over time. For example, the average non-branch bank in a non-metropolitan area tends to have lower overhead, lower noninterest income, higher profitability and higher capital ratios than similar sized branch banks located in metropolitan areas.

FDIC Insured Savings Banks

Over 500 FDIC Insured Savings banks are assigned to one of four primary asset based peer groups as defined in the table below. Banks are grouped by asset size using 90 day average assets from call report schedule RC-K. This asset-based grouping applies to all peer groups and is reviewed quarterly. Savings banks continue to exhibit consistent differences in performance when compared to insured commercial banks. As a consequence

this peer group comparison has proved to be useful.

FDIC Insured Savings Banks Peer Group Descriptions

(Includes FDIC insured savings banks with the following characteristics:)

Peer Group Number	Assets*
101	In excess of $1 billion
102	Between $300 million and $1 billion
103	Between $100 million and $300 million
104	Less than $100 million

*Asset figure used is latest quarterly average assets (from the FFIEC call report Schedule RC-K).

Credit Card Specialty Banks

Approximately 39 banks are assigned to one of three primary credit card specialty peer groups based on asset size. Banks are grouped by asset size using 90 day average assets from call report schedule RC-K. This asset-based grouping applies to all peer groups and is reviewed quarterly. Banks that exhibit both of the following characteristics are considered to be a specialized credit card lender.

1. Credit Card Loans plus Securitized and Sold Credit Cards divided by Total Loans plus Securitized and Sold Credit Cards exceeds 50%.

2. Total Loans plus Securitized and Sold Credit Card divided by Total Assets plus Securitized and Sold Credit Cards exceeds 50%.

Credit card specialty banks are by definition focused on one type of lending. As a consequence many appear as outliers when compared to traditional benchmarks of performance. Credit card specialty banks exhibit very high noninterest income, noninterest expense, interest margins, loan loss provisions and profitability when compared to traditional commercial or savings banks. As a consequence this specialized peer group analysis has proven to be especially useful as a benchmark for reviewing such banks.

Credit Card Specialty Banks

(Includes insured commercial and savings banks with the following characteristics:)

Peer Group Number	Assets*
201	In excess of $5 billion
202	Between $1 billion and $5 billion
203	Less than $1 billion

* Asset figure used is latest quarterly average assets (from the FFIEC call report Schedule RC-K).

Bankers Banks

Twenty banks have been assigned to the primary bankers bank peer group. Bankers banks are a unique type of financial institution that provide services to other banks, bankers and bank directors. They do not provide any banking services to the general public. Because bankers banks are highly specialized institutions, many appear as outliers when compared to traditional measures of balance sheet structure and other forms of comparison. As a consequence the bankers bank peer group data has proven to be an especially useful as a tool for analyzing bankers banks.

Bankers Banks Peer Group Description

Peer Group Number	
301	All Bankers Banks

Supplemental Peer Groups

The UBPR also groups banks into two separate supplemental peer groups. Selected ratios are then averaged. This analysis is provided as an enhancement to the primary peer group analysis available for all banks.

Fiduciary Peer Groups

Trust pages 1 and 1A include peer group average data for banks engaged in fiduciary activities. For the purposes of these two pages, banks are compared to peer group data that is computed using supplemental peer group definitions. Banks continue to be compared to a primary peer group on all other pages of the UBPR.

Over 1,800 Commercial and FDIC Insured Savings Banks engaged in fiduciary activities have been assigned to one of six supplemental trust peer groups. Banks are grouped by total fiduciary assets(managed and non-managed) as reported on schedule RC-T. This grouping is reviewed quarterly.

Data from schedule RC-T is available from December 31, 2001 forward, however several reporting limitations apply. Depending on asset size and the percentage of trust and related revenue to total income, an individual institution may be

Fidcuciary Peer Group Descriptions

Applies only to data shown on trust pages. (Includes insured commercial and savings banks with the following characteristics:)

Peer Group Number	Total Fiduciary Assets*
TRST301	In excess of $100 billion
TRST302	Between $10 billion and $100 billion
TRST303	Between $1 billion and $10 billion
TRST304	Between $500 million and $1 billion
TRST305	Between $100 million and $500 million
TRST306	Less than $100 million

*Asset figure used are latest total for managed and non-managed fiduciary assets from the FFIEC call report Schedule RC-T.

required to report certain items quarterly, annually or not at all. As a consequence peer group data for interim quarters may be based on a much smaller population of banks than year-end data. Please see instructions for the report of condition and income on www.ffiec.gov for details. Because information on fiduciary income and expense is considered confidential, only peer group data for those items will appear on the public UBPR website. See section III for definitions of individual ratios.

State Average Peer Groups

The State Average Page (STAVG) is displayed for all banks as a part of the online UBPR. While it does not display individual bank data, it does provide averages of selected performance and balance sheet data for banks within in the state. Additionally, the same performance and balance sheet data is sub-divided into three asset categories. The state average page is provided as a supplement to the primary peer group data discussed above.

Computing Peer-Group Averages

Peer group averages shown in the UBPR are a trimmed average of the ratios for individual banks. The peer group average for a given ratio is trimmed or adjusted to eliminate the effect of outliers or banks above the 95th and below the 5th percentile. The resulting average in most cases is very close to the median or mid-point value for a given group of banks. Thus the peer group average could be thought of as representing the performance of the-bank-in-the-middle for a specific ratio. It should be noted that the group of banks averaged for one ratio will differ from that used in other ratios. This occurs because the top and bottom 5% of banks designated as outliers will change from ratio to ratio. Consequently averages for separate ratios cannot be added or otherwise combined. The resulting

peer group ratios are very stable over time and are not influenced by outlier banks.

As an example the trimmed average Return on Assets (ROA) for peer group 3 was 1.26%. The 180 banks in peer 3 have an ROA that ranges from –1.60% to 6.35%. After sorting the banks from highest to lowest ROA, eighteen banks were identified as being in the top and bottom 5% and excluded from the group of banks to be averaged.

When an item is reported by only a small group of banks within a peer group, an insufficient number of valid observations can distort peer-group data. To minimize this problem, a floor has been set for the minimum number of ratio values that may be used to calculate the peer-group average. If fewer than five ratio values are available to compute the peer-group figure, a double number sign (##) is displayed rather than the value.

Percentile Rankings

Percentile rankings (PCT) are presented to the right of most of the individual and peer group ratios. The percentile ranking is the position or ranking of one bank relative to all others within the peer group for a given ratio. Thus, if a bank is at the 80th percentile for the tier one leverage ratio, it may be said that 20% of the banks in the peer group have a leverage ratio that is higher and 80% have a lower ratio. A high or low percentile ranking is a simple statement of statistical fact; it does not imply a good, bad, satisfactory, or unsatisfactory condition. However, when analyzed within the context of other related data, an opinion can be formed about the potential relevance of a high or low percentile ranking to an individual bank's financial condition and performance.

Please note that unlike the peer group average methodology discussed above, all banks within the peer group are included in the percentile ranking.

Computations and Adjustments

Calculating Asset and Liability Averages

The UBPR uses three different methodologies for calculating averages.

The first type of average is a cumulative or year-to-date average of the one quarter averages for assets and liabilities reported in call schedule RC-K. The resulting year-to-date averages are used as the denominator in earnings ratios, yield and rate calculations found on pages 1 and 3 of the UBPR. As an example, the average assets used for page 1 earnings analysis in the September 30th UBPR would reflect an average of the quarterly average assets reported in March, June and September of the current year.

The second type of average is a cumulative or year-to-date average of end-of-period balances reported on Schedules RC, RC-B, RC-C and RC-E from the beginning of the year forward. To provide an accurate average, the asset or liability balance at the prior year-end is also included. Averages calculated in this manner are used to determine the percentage composition of assets and liabilities on page 6 as well as selected ratios on page 7.

For example, the September 30th year-to-date average total loans is composed of the spot balances for total loans from call schedule RC-C for the prior December, and current March, June and September divided by 4.

The final type of average uses one quarter average data from schedule RC-K. These averages are as the denominator in the one-quarter-annualized-income-analysis on page 12.

Thus, average assets used in the September 30 UBPR analysis of net income on page 12 would include the quarterly average assets from schedule RC-K for September. That average is divided into the annualized one quarter income or expense item.

Annualization of Ratios Using Interim-Period Report-of-Income-Data

The dollar amounts displayed for most income and expense items in the UBPR are shown for the year-to-date period. However, to allow comparison of ratios between quarters, income and expense and related data used in ratios on pages 1, 3 and 7 and 11 are annualized for interim reporting periods. Thus, the income or expense item is multiplied by the indicated factor listed below before dividing it by the corresponding asset or liability. All income and expense ratios on page 12 are computed from income or expense data for one quarter and are annualized by a factor of 4.

Income and expense information reported on the December 31 call report is not annualized. Since the year-end UBPR represents a full fiscal year, that data does not have to be annualized. The UBPR annualization factors are:

March	4.0
June	2.0
September	1.3333

Special Annualization for De Novo Banks and Banks Reporting Pushdown Accounting

The annualization algorithm reflects the actual number of days a De Novo bank has been open in its first year of operation or the number of days that have elapsed since a push down transaction was reported. The algorithm divides the number of days in the year by the number days a De Novo Bank has been open or by the number of days since a push down transaction was reported. For affected banks the revised annualization factor will replace the standard annualization factor in the effected year.

Missing Data or Extreme Ratio Values

When data is missing from an indi-

vidual calculation the UBPR will display NA.

When a ratio exceeds 999 or is less than -999 then + ## or - ## will be displayed respectively.

If there is an insufficient number of banks (observations) to permit calculation of a valid average ratio for peer group analysis, NA will appear.

Subchapter S Adjustments

For banks that elect Subchapter S status for income taxes, the UBPR adjusts after tax earnings used in Net Income as % of Average Assets (ROA). This adjustment is performed to improve the comparability of those income between banks that are taxed at the corporation level (non S Corp. banks) and those that have shifted income taxation to the shareholder level (S Corp. Banks). Dollar data displayed in the UBPR is not adjusted. In essence an estimated tax is substituted for any reported taxes then deducted from income.

After tax earnings are adjusted as follows:

Estimated income taxes: Federal income tax rates are applied to net income before extraordinary items and taxes plus non-deductible interest expense to carry tax-exempt securities less tax-exempt income from securities issued by states and political subdivisions, less tax-exempt income from leases, less tax-exempt income from other obligations of states and political subdivisions. (See appendix A-3 for tax table)

Net Income adjusted for Subchapter S: Net Income plus applicable income taxes less estimated income taxes.

Tax-Equivalency

Virtually all banks have some income that is exempt from federal or state taxes. The tax benefit derived from this tax-exempt income is a significant element in determining the true return on investment. Banks may differ both in the amount of tax-exempt assets held and in their ability to use tax-exempt income. In order to reduce distortions and allow meaningful comparisons of different banks' income (and of a single bank's income at different times), the tax benefit is added to book operating income so that pretax income figures for all banks are presented on a tax-equivalent basis. The tax benefits from municipal loans, leases, and municipal securities are used in the UBPR to compute the tax-equivalent income. Because interest income from these obligations is normally the largest component of tax-exempt income for commercial banks, the adjustments made using this data normally produce a close approximation of the true tax-equivalent position. In essence the UBPR tax equivalent adjustment "grosses up" tax-exempt income so that it approximates taxable income.

The tax-equivalency adjustment in the UBPR follows this general procedure:

- Determine the amount of tax-exempt income available for tax benefit: If pretax taxable income exceeds tax-exempt income, then all of the tax-exempt income results in tax benefit. In all other cases, taxable income and tax credits may be used to determine what amount, if any, of the tax-exempt income produces tax benefit.

- Estimate the tax benefit: Income tax rates are used to determine what proportion of the available tax-exempt income is to be used as the estimated tax benefit.

- Apply tax benefit to earnings: The total tax benefit is allocated to securities and loans & leases. These estimated tax benefits are then added to pretax income for UBPR purposes.

The computed tax-equivalent adjustment is also added to applicable income taxes to balance the UBPR's income and expenses presentation.

For purposes of the UBPR income and expense presentation, the tax-equivalency adjustment is divided into two portions: (1) the amount of currently usable tax benefit (current tax-equivalent adjustment) and (2) the amount derived from carrying back losses to prior years (other tax-equivalent adjustments).

By adding the tax benefit on tax-exempt assets to both book operating income and applicable income taxes, the net (after-tax) income reported by the bank remains unaffected. Adding the tax-equivalent adjustments to income makes the pretax income figures for all banks comparable.

A Tax-Equivalency Worksheet is provided in appendix A of this guide to enable the user to replicate the UBPR tax-equivalent adjustment.

Mergers

Merger activity occurs frequently among insured commercial banks. The UBPR does not attempt to make a historical adjustment to restate information prior to the date of a merger.

The UBPR does attempt to minimize the effects of a merger on year-to-date profitability, yield and rate calculations (pages 1 and 3) after a significant merger. A significant merger is one where asset growth exceeds 25%. When a significant merger is encountered all profitability, yield and rate calculations are adjusted to include only average assets and liabilities reported after the merger. Pre-merger asset data is ignored in the year of the merger. However, income and expense data is used as reported without adjustment.

The UBPR adjusts 1 quarter annualized earnings ratios on page 12 when pushdown accounting is indicated. The adjustment applies only to income and expense data. Average asset and liability data is not adjusted because it applies only to one quarter. When pushdown accounting is indicated the UBPR does not subtract prior from current income or expense items to develop data for one quarter. Instead the income or expense item is annualized as reported.

Finally, the UBPR will flag the occurrence of a merger with a footnote on page 1.

Section III: Definitions of UBPR Items

General

This section describes the derivation of each of the items on each UBPR page.

Some UBPR pages have more than one set of items, depending on the type of Call Report filed by the bank for the latest period. See Section II for a summary of Call reporter types.

Such UBPR page versions differ in the amount of detail reported by the bank and presented in the UBPR. Also, some page versions differ in the manner of categorizing loans. In addition, some items do not appear on the public version of the UBPR, compared to the bank and regulatory version. Such items involve Call Report data that are deemed to be confidential. This section specifies all of these distinctions between UBPR page versions.

UBPR Introductory Page

The Introductory Page specifies the edition date of the UBPR being presented, identifies the subject bank, provides a table of contents, and presents other notes and information.

Bank Identification

The information presented on the first two lines is repeated on all subsequent UBPR pages. These items are:

- Cert#: bank's FDIC insurance certificate number

- DSB#: bank's Federal Reserve district-state-bank member

- Bank Name

- City and State

- Charter #: For national banks, bank's OCC charter number

This page also provides the bank's mailing address, the name and location of bank's holding company if any, and the name of the bank's primary federal regulatory agency.

The Introductory Page also specifies the banks' current UBPR peer group number and the criteria for that peer group. See Section II of this guide for specification of all peer group criteria.

Note that each UBPR is addressed to the chief executive officer by title, not name.

CERT # DIST/RSSD					SUMMARY RATIOS								PAGE 01	
CHARTER # COUNTY														
	06/30/2008			06/30/2007			12/31/2007			12/31/2006		12/31/2005		
AVERAGE ASSETS ($000)	169,798,208			177,365,349			173,640,242			178,783,017		158,323,556		
NET INCOME ($000)	860,897			1,171,705			1,871,083			2,125,292		2,032,286		
NUMBER OF BANKS IN PEER GROUP	187			193			190			185		183		
EARNINGS AND PROFITABILITY	BANK	PG 1	PCT	BANK	PG 1	PCT	BANK	PG 1	PCT	BANK	PG 1	BANK	PG 1
PERCENT OF AVERAGE ASSETS													
INTEREST INCOME (TE)	5.07	5.39	26	5.80	6.16	28	5.84	6.16	30	5.56	5.95	4.93	5.15
- INTEREST EXPENSE	2.20	2.25	48	3.00	3.00	52	2.96	2.98	52	2.83	2.72	1.90	1.89
NET INTEREST INCOME (TE)	2.88	3.12	32	2.81	3.15	26	2.87	3.16	31	2.73	3.20	3.03	3.25
+ NONINTEREST INCOME	1.91	1.20	80	1.63	1.28	70	1.70	1.23	74	1.62	1.26	1.65	1.49
- NONINTEREST EXPENSE	2.72	2.65	55	2.53	2.56	48	2.72	2.63	56	2.43	2.54	2.66	2.70
- PROVISION LOAN&LEASE LOSSES	1.19	0.79	78	0.18	0.16	64	0.38	0.28	72	0.15	0.13	0.11	0.13
= PRETAX OPERATING INCOME (TE)	0.88	0.95	39	1.73	1.76	46	1.46	1.53	45	1.78	1.90	1.90	1.98
+ REALIZED GAINS/LOSSES SEC	0.58	0.01	98	0.27	0.00	99	0.14	-0.01	98	-0.05	-0.01	0.00	0.00
= PRETAX NET OPERATING INC (TE)	1.46	0.91	64	1.99	1.75	62	1.60	1.49	54	1.72	1.89	1.90	1.97
NET OPERATING INCOME	1.01	0.60	66	1.32	1.13	65	1.08	0.97	57	1.19	1.23	1.28	1.27
ADJUSTED NET OPERATING INCOME	1.47	0.99	78	1.33	1.17	65	1.22	1.07	63	1.20	1.24	1.27	1.29
NET INCOME ADJUSTED SUB S		0.60	N/A		1.13	N/A		0.96	N/A		1.23		1.28
NET INCOME	1.01	0.60	66	1.32	1.13	65	1.08	0.96	57	1.19	1.23	1.28	1.28
MARGIN ANALYSIS													
AVG EARNING ASSETS TO AVG ASSETS	90.10	91.69	36	90.32	92.06	28	90.00	91.66	33	90.24	91.92	90.49	91.80
AVG INT-BEARING FUNDS TO AVG AST	77.67	82.22	25	78.60	81.68	28	78.12	81.70	27	76.44	81.67	75.72	80.89
INT INC (TE) TO AVG EARN ASSETS	5.63	5.90	28	6.42	6.71	32	6.48	6.73	34	6.17	6.47	5.45	5.63
INT EXPENSE TO AVG EARN ASSETS	2.44	2.46	47	3.32	3.28	53	3.29	3.26	53	3.14	2.98	2.10	2.07
NET INT INC-TE TO AVG EARN ASSET	3.19	3.42	36	3.11	3.45	28	3.19	3.48	33	3.03	3.51	3.35	3.55
LOAN & LEASE ANALYSIS													
NET LOSS TO AVERAGE TOTAL LN&LS	0.95	0.57	77	0.23	0.20	68	0.32	0.28	67	0.19	0.16	0.18	0.20
EARNINGS COVERAGE OF NET LOSS(X)	2.75	8.62	28	10.72	36.52	34	7.23	17.37	32	13.62	32.42	15.63	35.22
LN&LS ALLOWANCE TO NET LOSSES(X)	1.35	4.18	19	3.47	11.12	24	3.03	7.24	28	4.24	10.82	5.17	10.50
LN&LS ALLOW TO LN&LS NOT HFS	1.33	1.43	51	0.88	1.13	20	1.04	1.22	31	0.86	1.13	0.89	1.17
LN&LS ALLOWANCE TO TOTAL LN&LS	1.28	1.41	48	0.80	1.09	19	0.97	1.20	23	0.78	1.09	0.80	1.13
NON-CUR LN&LS TO GROSS LN&LS	2.50	1.60	77	0.90	0.62	75	1.54	0.91	80	0.64	0.51	0.50	0.52
LIQUIDITY													
NET NONCORE FUND DEPENDENCE	37.48	38.13	50	42.33	32.73	71	38.62	34.74	59	39.34	33.66	37.91	33.16
NET LOANS & LEASES TO ASSETS	74.96	67.33	72	73.66	65.32	72	74.83	65.83	75	72.47	63.60	71.95	62.05
CAPITALIZATION													
TIER ONE LEVERAGE CAPITAL	7.72	8.04	46	7.70	8.17	44	7.56	8.02	39	7.35	8.15	7.04	7.87
CASH DIVIDENDS TO NET INCOME	74.34	40.17	73	54.62	58.39	48	95.13	62.41	69	49.88	46.72	65.15	47.33
RETAIN EARNS TO AVG TOTAL EQUITY	2.25	0.98	51	5.50	3.67	59	0.47	2.12	36	5.66	5.65	4.74	6.21
RESTR+NONAC+RE ACQ TO EQCAP+ALLL	14.02	10.25	73	4.22	3.50	68	7.80	5.34	73	2.84	2.71	1.60	2.83
GROWTH RATES													
ASSETS	-3.14	15.68	12	-2.41	10.48	15	-4.10	13.08	7	3.02	13.27	35.52	12.92
TIER ONE CAPITAL	-3.47	11.72	14	5.52	10.94	42	-3.84	10.16	17	9.53	14.32	27.86	12.62
NET LOANS & LEASES	-1.43	17.58	9	0.36	12.97	17	-0.98	15.59	9	3.77	13.77	38.27	15.82
SHORT TERM INVESTMENTS	32.95	23.07	67	-61.58	97.25	10	-52.47	38.05	22	39.31	173.78	-36.93	61.14
SHORT TERM NONCORE FUNDING	-16.23	29.59	8	-8.23	10.33	26	-16.90	24.85	6	10.53	23.46	70.10	22.31

##ONE OR MORE MERGERS, CONSOLIDATIONS OR PURCHASES HAVE OCCURRED DURING THE PERIOD.
12/31/2005

UBPR Page 01

Summary Ratios

The earnings and balance sheet ratios and other information presented on this page provide a synopsis of the bank's condition and serve as a guide to more detailed data presented elsewhere in the UBPR. Ratios using after tax income and dividends have been adjusted for assumed tax rates. See Section II Technical Information.

Average Assets ($000)

A year-to-date average of the average assets reported in the Report of Condition Schedule RC-K. Thus for the first quarter of the year the average assets from Call Schedule RC-K quarter will appear, while at the end-of-year, assets for all four quarters would be averaged.

Net Income ($000)

The year-to-date amount of net income shown in the Report of Income after applicable taxes, net securities gains or losses, and net extraordinary items.

 # Banks in Peer Group

Total number of banks in the bank's peer group.

Earnings and Profitability

% of Average Assets

Interest Income (TE)

All income from earning assets plus the tax benefit on tax-exempt loans, leases, and municipal securities, divided by average assets.

Interest Expense

Total interest expense divided by average assets.

Net Interest Income (TE)

Total interest income, plus the tax benefit on tax-exempt income, less total interest expense, divided by average assets.

Noninterest Income

Income derived from bank services and sources other than interest-bearing assets, divided by average assets.

Noninterest Expense

Salaries and employee benefits, expenses of premises and fixed assets and other Noninterest expense divided by average assets.

Provision—Loan/Lease Losses

Provision for loan and lease receivables losses divided by average assets.

Pretax Operating Income (TE)

Net interest income on a tax-equivalent basis plus Noninterest income, less noninterest expenses, the provision for loan and lease-financing receivables losses and the provision for allocated transfer risk, divided by average assets.

Realized Gain/Loss Secs

Pretax net gains or losses from the sale, exchange, retirement, or redemption of securities not held in trading accounts divided by average assets. After December 31, 1993 includes available-for-sale and held-to-maturity transactions.

Pretax Net Operating Income (TE)

Pretax operating income, plus securities gains or losses divided by average assets.

Net Operating Income

After tax net operating income, including securities gains or losses, (which does not include extraordinary gains or losses), divided by average assets.

Adjusted Net Oper Income

Net operating income after taxes and securities gains or losses, plus the

provision for possible loan and lease losses, less net loan and lease losses, divided by average assets.

Net Income Adjusted Sub S

Net income after securities gains or losses, extraordinary gains or losses, and applicable taxes, adjusted for sub chapter S status divided by average assets. Estimated income taxes is substituted for any reported applicable income taxes for banks that indicate sub chapter S status. Estimated income taxes: Federal income tax rates are applied to net income before extraordinary items and taxes plus non-deductible interest expense to carry tax-exempt securities less tax-exempt income from securities issued by states and political subdivisions, less tax-exempt income from leases, less tax-exempt income from other obligations of states and political subdivisions. (See appendix A-3 for tax table)

Please note that this ratio will only be displayed for banks that elect subchapter S status.

Net Income

Net income after securities gains or losses, extraordinary gains or losses, and applicable taxes divided by average assets.

Margin Analysis

Average Earning Assets/Average Assets

Year-to-date average of average total loans (net of unearned income) in domestic and foreign offices, lease-financing receivables, U.S. Treasury, Agency and Corporation obligations, mortgage backed securities, other securities, assets held in trading accounts, interest-bearing balances due from depository institutions, and federal funds sold and securities purchased under agreements to resell, plus a five period average of Interest Only Strips (Mortgage loans and

Other) and Equity Securities divided by average assets.

Average Interest-Bearing Funds/ Average Assets

Average interest-bearing domestic and foreign office deposits, federal funds purchased and securities sold under agreements to repurchase, other borrowed money, and notes and debentures subordinated to deposits, divided by average assets.

Interest Income (TE)/Average Assets

Total interest income on a tax-equivalent basis divided by the average of the respective asset accounts involved in generating that income.

Interest Expense/Average Assets

Total interest expense divided by the average of the respective asset accounts involved in generating interest income.

Net Interest Income (TE) (Percent of Avg Earning Assets)

Total interest income on a tax-equivalent basis, less total interest expense, divided by the average of the respective asset accounts involved in generating interest income.

Loan & Lease Analysis

Net Loss to Average Loan & Leases

Gross loan and lease charge-off, less gross recoveries (includes allocated transfer risk reserve charge-off and recoveries), divided by average total loans and leases.

Earnings Coverage of Net Loss (X)

Net operating income before taxes, securities gains or losses, and extraordinary items, plus the provision for possible loan and lease-financing receivable losses divided by net loan and lease losses.

Loan & Lease Allowance Net Losses (X)

Ending balance of the allowance for possible loan and lease-financing receivable losses divided by net loan and lease losses. If gross recoveries exceed gross losses, NA is shown at this caption.

Loan & Lease Allowance to Loans & Leases Not Held For Sale

Ending balance of the allowance for possible loan and lease losses divided by total loans and lease-financing receivables not held for sale. Available from March 31, 2001 forward.

Loan & Lease Allowance to Total Loans & Lease

Ending balance of the allowance for possible loan and lease losses divided by total loans and lease-financing receivables.

Noncurrent Loans & Leases to Gross Loans and Lease

The sum of loans and lease-financing receivables past due at least 90 days, plus those in nonaccrual status, divided by gross loans and lease-financing receivables outstanding.

Liquidity

Net Noncore Funding Dependence

Noncore liabilities, less short term investments divided by long term assets. See definition on UBPR page 10.

Net Loans & Leases to Assets

Loans and lease-financing receivables net of unearned income and the allowance for possible loans and lease financing receivable losses divided by total assets.

Capitalization

Tier One Leverage Capital

Tier one capital divided by adjusted average assets. See the description of UBPR Page 11A for definitions of tier one capital and adjusted average assets.

Cash Dividends to Net Income

Total of all cash dividends declared year-to-date divided by net income year-to-date. If net income is less than or equal to zero, NA is shown at this caption.

Retain Earns to Average Total Equity

Net income, less cash dividends declared, divided by average equity capital.

Restructured + Nonaccrual + RE ACQ to EQCAP, ALLL

The sum of loans and leases which are on nonaccrual, restructured but 30–89 days past due, restructured but over 90 days past due, restructured and in compliance with modified terms and non-investment other real estate owned divided by the sum of total equity capital plus the allowance for possible loan and lease losses.

Growth Rates

Growth rates on UBPR page 01 are calculated for a 12-month period. The percentage is determined by subtracting the account balance as of the corresponding reporting period in the previous year from the current period account balance and dividing the result by the previous year balance. The following growth rates are displayed:

Assets

Tier One Capital

Net Loans & Leases

Short Term Investments

See UBPR page 10 for definition.

Short Term Noncore Funding

See UBPR page 10 for definition.

Footnotes

Footnotes are printed on UBPR page 01 to indicate the occurrence of certain events.

(***)Bank has elected sub chapter S tax treatment. NOTE: Ratio Net Income Adjusted for Sub S on page 1 and 12.

**A transaction using push-down accounting as of mm/dd/yyyy was reported.

One or more mergers occurred during the period.

This comment appears when a merger or consolidation is reported during the period.

	06/30/2008	06/30/2007	12/31/2007	12/31/2006	12/31/2005	PERCENT CHANGE 1 YEAR
INTEREST AND FEES ON LOANS	3,617,836	4,234,706	8,412,569	8,221,475	6,295,301	-14.57
INCOME FROM LEASE FINANCING	120,694	108,300	234,451	187,195	148,246	11.44
TAX-EXEMPT	90,177	124,135	253,641	148,251	149,272	-27.36
ESTIMATED TAX BENEFIT	46,161	63,263	129,992	74,113	76,050	
INCOME ON LOANS & LEASES (TE)	3,784,691	4,406,269	8,777,012	8,482,783	6,519,597	-14.11
U S TREAS & AGENCY (EXCL MBS)	9,615	5,719	12,850	109,943	91,235	68.12
MORTGAGE BACKED SECURITIES	278,666	193,203	470,439	785,781	773,509	44.23
ESTIMATED TAX BENEFIT	8,818	8,606	17,397	15,586	15,247	
ALL OTHER SECURITIES	51,538	47,545	92,868	176,821	201,176	8.40
TAX-EXEMPT SECURITIES INCOME	17,227	16,88	33,946	31,177	29,928	2.01
INVESTMT INTEREST INCOME (TE)	348,637	255,073	593,554	1,088,131	1,081,167	36.68
INTEREST ON DUE FROM BANKS	130	467	774	837	561	-72.16
INT ON FED FUNDS SOLD & RESALES	26,725	94,190	138,214	245,736	127,483	-71.63
TRADING ACCOUNT INCOME	119,677	362,593	567,954	72,407	34,050	-66.99
OTHER INTEREST INCOME	28,539	26,913	55,343	57,971	48,474	6.04
TOTAL INTEREST INCOME (TE)	4,308,399	5,145,505	10,132,852	9,947,864	7,811,332	-16.27
INT ON DEPOSITS IN FOREIGN OFF	75,878	254,560	405,748	536,098	251,895	-70.19
INTEREST ON TIME DEP OVER $100M	474,085	766,876	1,447,511	1,373,345	593,198	-38.18
INTEREST ON ALL OTHER DEPOSITS	794,238	924,480	1,916,049	1,636,040	1,019,672	-14.09
INT ON FED FUNDS PURCH & REPOS	97,784	327,966	518,755	723,402	391,619	-70.18
INT TRAD LIAB & OTH BORROWINGS	413,112	354,766	810,220	570,021	603,068	16.45
INT ON MORTGAGES & LEASES	NA	NA	NA	NA	NA	NA
INT ON SUB NOTES & DEBENTURES	9,725	28,039	46,753	224,104	149,673	-65.32
TOTAL INTEREST EXPENSE	1,864,822	2,656,687	5,145,036	5,063,010	3,009,125	-29.81
NET INTEREST INCOME (TE)	2,443,577	2,488,818	4,987,816	4,884,854	4,802,207	-1.82
NONINTEREST INCOME	1,624,102	1,445,925	2,944,258	2,901,587	2,606,212	12.32
ADJUSTED OPERATING INCOME (TE)	4,067,679	3,934,743	7,932,074	7,786,441	7,408,419	3.38
NONINTEREST EXPENSE	2,311,178	2,242,279	4,729,242	4,345,095	4,216,410	3.07
PROVISION LOAN & LEASE LOSSES	1,007,212	161,121	664,922	262,536	176,886	25.13
PRETAX OPERATING INCOME (TE)	749,289	1,531,343	2,537,910	3,178,810	3,015,123	51.07
REALIZED G/L HLD-TO-MATURITY SEC	0	0	0	0	0	NA
REALIZED G/L AVAIL-FOR SALE SEC	489,209	236,440	243,124	-98,231	-5,713	06.91
PRETAX NET OPERATING INC (TE)	1,238,498	1,767,783	2,781,034	3,080,579	3,009,410	29.94
APPLICABLE INCOME TAXES	322,622	524,209	762,561	865,589	885,827	
CURRENT TAX EQUIV ADJUSTMENT	54,979	71,869	147,390	89,698	91,297	
OTHER TAX EQUIV ADJUSTMENTS	0	0	0	0	0	
APPLICABLE INCOME TAXES(TE)	377,601	596,078	909,951	955,287	977,124	
NET OPERATING INCOME	860,897	1,171,705	1,871,083	2,125,292	2,032,286	26.53
NET EXTRAORDINARY ITEMS	0	0	0	0	0	
NET INCOME	860,897	1,171,705	1,871,083	2,125,292	2,032,286	26.53
CASH DIVIDENDS DECLARED	640,000	640,000	1,780,000	1,060,000	1,324,000	0.00
RETAINED EARNINGS	220,897	531,705	91,083	1,065,292	708,286	58.45
MEMO NET INTERNATIONAL INCOME	0	0	0	0	0	

UBPR Page 02

Income Statement Revenues & Expenses ($000)

This page presents a summary of the bank's year to date Report of Income. The major categories of income and expense reported on this page are expanded on subsequent pages of the UBPR. The tax benefit associated with tax-exempt income has been estimated and added to total interest income and applicable income taxes. The estimated tax benefit is allocated to municipal securities and to municipal loans and leases. This adjustment improves the comparability of interest income among different banks and among different time periods. Net income is shown as reported. Please note that certain income items noted below are available only from March 31, 2001 forward.

One year growth rates for the various categories on this page are shown in the right most column.

Interest and Fee on Loans

Year to date interest and fee on loans.

Income from Lease Financing

Year to date income from lease financing receivables.

Tax-Exempt

Year to date income on loan obligations of states and political subdivisions and tax-exempt income from direct lease financing.

Estimated Tax Benefit

The estimated tax benefit resulting from having tax-exempt loan and lease financing receivables income. See Section II, Technical Information, or Appendix B, Tax-Equivalency Worksheet, for a discussion of the method used to calculate this item.

Income on Loans & Leases (TE)

Year to date income on loans and lease financing receivables plus the estimated tax benefit.

US Treasury & Agency (Excl MBS)

Year to date interest on U.S. Treasury securities and on other U.S. government agencies excluding mortgage backed securities. This item is available from March 31, 2001 forward.

Mortgage Backed Securities

Year to date interest Mortgage Backed Securities. This item is available from March 31, 2001 forward.

Estimated Tax Benefit

The estimated tax benefit resulting from having tax-exempt municipal securities income. See Section II, Technical Information, for a discussion of the method used to calculate this item.

All Other Securities

Year to date income on all other securities not held in trading accounts, including taxable and tax-exempt securities issued by states and local subdivisions.

Tax-Exempt Securities Income

Year-to-date interest on securities issued by states and political subdivisions in the United States.

Investment Interest Income (TE)

Sum of U.S. Treasury and agencies securities income, municipal securities income, the tax benefit on municipal securities income, and other securities income.

Interest on Due From Banks

Year to date interest on balances due from depository institutions.

Interest on Federal Funds Sold/Resales

Year to date income on federal funds sold and securities purchased under agreements to resell.

Trading Account Income

Year to date interest income on

assets held in trading accounts (excluding gains, losses, commissions, and fees).

Other Interest Income

Year to date other interest income. This item is available from March 31, 2001 forward.

Total Interest Income (TE)

Sum of income on loans and leases on a tax equivalent basis plus investment income on a tax equivalent basis plus interest on interest bearing bank balances plus interest on federal funds sold and security resales plus interest on trading account assets.

Interest on Deposits in Foreign Offices

Year to date interest expense on deposits in Foreign Offices. Reported by banks filing 031 call form.

Interest on Time Dep over $100M

Year to date interest expense on time certificates of deposit of $100 thousand or more.

Interest on All Other Deposits

Year to date interest expense on all deposits except time certificates of deposit of $100 thousand or more and deposits held in foreign offices, if applicable.

Interest on Federal Funds Purchased & Repos

Year to date expense of federal funds purchased and securities sold under agreements to repurchase.

Interest on Trading Liabilities and Other Borrowings

Year to date interest on trading liabilities, demand notes (note balances) issued to the U.S. Treasury and on other borrowed money (including Federal Home Loan Bank).

Interest on Mortgages & Leases

Year to date interest on mortgage

indebtedness and capitalized leases on banking premises, fixed assets, and other real estate owned.

Interest on Subordinated Notes & Debentures

Year to date interest on subordinated notes and debentures.

Total Interest Expense

Sum of all interest expenses listed previously.

Net Interest Income (TE)

Total interest income on a tax equivalent basis less total interest expense.

Noninterest Income

Year to date income from fiduciary activities (when available), service charges on deposits, gains or losses and commissions and fees on assets held in trading accounts, foreign exchange trading gains or losses, other foreign transactions, and other Noninterest income.

Adjusted Operating Income (TE)

Net interest income plus noninterest income.

Noninterest Expense

Year to date salaries and employee benefits, expenses of premises and fixed assets (net of rental income), amortization of intangibles and other noninterest operating expense.

Provision for Loan/Lease Losses

The year to date provision for possible loan and lease financing receivable losses.

Pretax Operating Income (TE)

The sum of year to date total tax equivalent interest income plus Noninterest income less interest expense, noninterest expense, provision for possible loan and lease financing

receivables losses, and provision for allocated transfer risk.

Realized G/L Hld to Maturity Sec

Year to date pretax net gains or losses on the sale, exchange, redemption, or retirement of securities excluding those held in trading or available-for-sale account. Prior to March 31, 1994, gains/losses on all securities are displayed here. For March 31, 1994 and subsequent quarters only gains/losses from held-to-maturity securities are shown.

Realized G/L Avail for Sale Sec

Year to date pretax net gains or losses on the sale, exchange, redemption, or retirement of securities recorded as available-for-sale. Available only for March 31, 1994 and subsequent quarters.

Pretax Net Operating Income (TE)

The sum of year to date pretax operating income on a tax-equivalent basis plus net pretax securities gains or losses.

Applicable Income Taxes

The total estimated federal, state, local, and foreign (if applicable) income taxes applicable to operating income, including securities gains or losses.

Current Tax-Equivalent Adjustment

Reverses the current part of the tax benefit included in interest income on loans and leases and securities. The current tax-equivalent adjustment is an estimate of that portion of the tax benefit that is attributable to current period income.

Other Tax-Equivalent Adjustments

Reverses the remainder of the tax-equivalent adjustment included in interest income on loans and leases and securities. The other tax-

equivalent adjustment is an estimate of that portion of the tax benefit that is attributable to tax loss carry backs.

Applicable Income Taxes (TE)

Applicable income taxes plus the tax benefit on tax-exempt income; current tax-equivalent adjustment plus other tax-equivalent adjustments.

Net Operating Income

Year to date income after securities gains or losses and applicable taxes but before extraordinary gains or losses.

Net Extraordinary Items

Extraordinary gains or losses less applicable taxes.

Net Income

The year to date net income after securities gains or losses, extraordinary gains or losses, and applicable taxes.

Cash Dividends Declared

All cash dividends declared on common and preferred stock year to date.

Retained Earnings

Net income minus cash dividends declared year to date.

Memo: Net International Income

Estimated net income attributable to international operations. Available for banks filing call form 031 only.

Footnotes:

Footnotes are printed at the bottom of Page 2 to indicate the occurrence of certain events.

Note: Bank has elected sub chapter "S" treatment for taxes.

This footnote appears when bank indicates sub chapter "S" treatment on call report.

	06/30/2008	06/30/2007	12/31/2007	12/31/2006	12/31/2005
NONINTEREST INCOME & EXPENSES					
FIDUCIARY ACTIVITIES	221,938	225,389	461,969	465,619	474,354
DEPOSIT SERVICE CHARGES	441,531	386,091	822,493	764,363	773,128
TRADING,VENT CAP,SECURTZ INC	-155,631	48,758	-180,082	86,589	94,256
INV BANKING,ADVISORY INC	36,449	30,770	74,571	38,660	63,854
INSURANCE COMM & FEES	32,206	17,965	39,747	30,115	28,512
NET SERVICING FEES	63,658	69,280	144,200	55,455	317,728
LOAN & LSE NET GAIN/LOSS	-180,474	-274,487	-585,341	-284,916	-222,714
OTHER NET GAINS/LOSSES	5,370	12,337	160,314	70,735	-2,957
OTHER NONINTEREST INCOME	1,159,055	929,822	2,006,387	1,674,967	1,080,051
NONINTEREST INCOME	1 624 102	1 445 925	2 944 258	2 901 587	2 606 212
PERSONNEL EXPENSE	1,187,176	1,170,066	2,263,414	2,220,616	2,050,328
OCCUPANCY EXPENSE	273,875	272,652	553,800	527,979	511,584
GOODWILLL IMPAIRMENT	0	0	0	0	0
OTHER INTANGIBLE AMORTIZ	31 907	39 777	76 435	91 691	107 421
OTHER OPER EXP(INCL INTANGIBLES)	818,220	759,784	1,835,593	1,504,809	1,547,077
TOTAL OVERHEAD EXPENSE	2,311,178	2,242,279	4,729,242	4,345,095	4,216,410
DOMESTIC BANKING OFFICES(#)	1,695	1,711	1,708	1,732	1,688
FOREIGN BRANCHES (#)	5	5	5	5	5
ASSETS PER DOMESTIC OFFICE	101,180	103,487	102,521	105,420	104,994

PERCENT OF AVERAGE ASSETS	BANK	PG 1	PCT	BANK	PG 1	PCT	BANK	PG 1	PCT	BANK	PG 1	BANK	PG 1
PERSONNEL EXPENSE	1.40	1.23	64	1.32	1.27	54	1.30	1.25	56	1.24	1.26	1.30	1.32
OCCUPANCY EXPENSE	0.32	0.33	45	0.31	0.34	38	0.32	0.34	41	0.30	0.33	0.32	0.35
OTHER OPER EXP(INCL INTANGIBLES)	1.00	1.02	57	0.90	0.90	56	1.10	0.98	68	0.89	0.90	1.05	0.98
TOTAL OVERHEAD EXPENSE	2.72	2.65	55	2.53	2.56	48	2.72	2.63	56	2.43	2.54	2.66	2.70
OVERHEAD LESS NONINT INC	0.81	1.32	20	0.90	1.20	28	1.03	1.33	27	0.81	1.18	1.02	1.13
OTHER INCOME & EXPENSE RATIOS													
EFFICIENCY RATIO	56.82	58.30	42	56.99	56.13	48	59.62	57.71	56	55.80	55.30	56.91	55.45
AVG PERSONNEL EXP PER EMPL($000)	82.72	72.96	71	76.48	74.74	64	76.28	71.64	66	71.92	71.45	66.89	66.61
ASSETS PER EMPLOYEE ($MILLION)	5.97	9.75	55	5.79	11.56	58	5.90	10.50	58	5.91	10.74	5.78	6.72

YIELD ON OR COST OF	BANK	PG 1	PCT	BANK	PG 1	PCT	BANK	PG 1	PCT	BANK	PG 1	BANK	PG 1
TOTAL LOANS & LEASES (TE)	5.81	6.31	21	6.67	7.30	20	6.71	7.32	18	6.50	7.15	5.76	6.24
LOANS IN DOMESTIC OFFICES	5.79	6.30	19	6.63	7.30	19	6.67	7.31	18	6.50	7.14	5.73	6.24
REAL ESTATE	5.98	6.28	25	6.79	7.21	30	6.83	7.21	29	6.68	7.06	5.94	6.21
SECURED BY 1-4 FAM. RESI PROP	6.06	6.18	45	N/A	N/A	N/A	N/A	N/A	N/A	N/A	N/A	N/A	N/A
ALL OTHER LOANS SEC. REAL ESTATE	5.80	6.34	20	N/A	N/A	N/A	N/A	N/A	N/A	N/A	N/A	N/A	N/A
COMMERCIAL & INDUSTRIAL	4.55	6.26	6	4.94	7.84	2	4.93	7.67	3	4.97	7.64	4.30	6.48
INDIVIDUAL	5.91	7.46	15	6.39	7.99	16	6.46	8.11	19	6.14	7.77	5.67	7.01
CREDIT CARD	8.40	10.25	26	5.85	11.64	12	3.09	10.40	10	N/A	11.41	N/A	9.77
AGRICULTURAL	4.96	6.43	5	7.23	7.91	24	7.17	7.87	26	6.90	7.77	5.54	6.68
LOANS IN FOREIGN OFFICES	N/A	5.64	N/A	N/A	6.52	N/A	N/A	6.43	N/A	N/A	5.88	N/A	5.08
TOTAL INVESTMENT SECURITIES(TE)	5.91	4.98	92	5.77	5.07	91	5.82	5.11	90	4.72	4.82	4.64	4.35
TOTAL INVESTMENT SECURITES(BOOK)	5.76	4.78	94	5.58	4.88	90	5.65	4.92	92	4.65	4.65	4.58	4.18
U S TREAS & AGENCY (EXCL MBS)	4.58	4.43	56	4.20	4.72	22	4.59	4.74	40	4.55	4.40	4.09	3.63
MORTGAGE BACKED SECURITIES	5.77	5.02	90	5.50	4.97	84	5.61	4.98	88	4.54	4.75	4.57	4.34
ALL OTHER SECURITIES	5.98	4.51	89	6.16	4.86	88	6.07	4.89	85	5.27	4.74	4.86	4.48
INTEREST-BEARING BANK BALANCES	4.13	2.74	81	6.03	4.70	87	6.16	4.58	91	3.52	4.24	2.82	3.05
FEDERAL FUNDS SOLD & RESALES	2.34	2.72	19	5.33	5.30	71	5.10	5.21	46	5.00	5.01	2.75	3.24
TOTAL-INT BEARING DEPOSITS	2.64	2.58	54	3.60	3.43	61	3.59	3.41	60	3.33	3.04	2.11	2.03
TRANSACTION ACCOUNTS	1.50	1.20	67	2.36	1.87	64	2.36	1.83	67	1.79	1.71	1.00	1.23
OTHER SAVINGS DEPOSITS	1.59	1.45	62	2.12	2.35	42	2.20	2.32	49	1.96	2.03	1.26	1.29
TIME DEPS OVER $100M	4.09	4.00	51	5.12	4.81	78	5.14	4.79	79	4.81	4.38	3.48	3.20
ALL OTHER TIME DEPOSITS	4.23	3.97	65	4.47	4.50	44	4.56	4.57	51	3.99	3.98	3.21	2.92
FOREIGN OFFICE DEPOSITS	2.52	2.59	45	5.25	4.52	93	5.09	4.35	90	5.17	4.21	3.47	2.83
FEDERAL FUNDS PURCHASED & REPOS	2.16	2.77	17	4.99	4.74	62	4.74	4.58	55	4.79	4.48	3.06	3.03
OTHER BORROWED MONEY	4.71	3.76	85	4.83	5.00	41	4.98	4.91	51	5.03	4.74	3.87	3.85
SUBORD NOTES & DEBENTURES	0.57	5.47	3	1.63	6.09	5	1.38	5.99	7	6.23	5.74	4.75	5.15
ALL INTEREST-BEARING FUNDS	2.83	2.76	56	3.81	3.71	54	3.79	3.68	54	3.70	3.36	2.51	2.36

UBPR Page 03

Noninterest Income and Expenses ($000) and Yields

This page presents most of the dollar figures that are components of Noninterest income and overhead expense as reported in the Report of Income, together with related information such as number of offices and employees. Key overhead items are also presented as percent of average assets, together with other related ratios. The lower portion of the page presents information relating earning assets, the return or yield on specific earning-asset categories, and the cost of funds. All yields and costs (rates) are annualized.

For more information concerning the methods used to calculate averages for asset yields and liability costs, see Section II, Technical Information.

Noninterest Income and Expenses ($000)

The dollar amounts, in thousands, for Noninterest income and expenses as reported in the Report of Income.

Fiduciary Activities

Year-to-date income from fiduciary activities. Available for all banks from March 31, 2001 forward. Not available prior to March 31, 2001 for banks filing 034 call form.

Deposit Service Charges

Year-to-date service charges on deposit accounts.

Trading, Venture Capital, Securitization Income

From March 31, 2001 includes information from schedule RI Trading Revenue (RIADA220) plus Venture Capital Revenue (RIADB491) plus Securitization Income (RIADB493). For prior quarters includes Trading Revenue (RIADA220) for banks filing call forms 031, 032 or 033.

Investment Banking, Advisory Income

From March 31, 2001 forward includes information from schedule RI Investment Banking, Advisory, Underwriting, Brokerage Fees and Commissions (RIADB490).

Insurance Commissions and Fees

From March 31, 2001 through December 31, 2002 includes information from schedule RI Insurance Commissions and Fees (RIADB494). From March 31, 2003 forward includes Insurance and Reinsurance Underwriting Income (RIADC386) plus Income From Other Insurance Activities (RIADC387).

Net Servicing Fees

From March 31, 2001 forward includes information from schedule RI Net Servicing Fees (RIADB492).

Loan and Lease Net Gain/Loss

From March 31, 2001 forward includes information from schedule RI Net Gains (Losses) from Sale of Loans and Leases (RIAD5416).

Other Net Gains/Losses

From March 31, 2001 forward includes information from RI Net Gains (Losses) on the Sale of Other Real Estate Owned (RIAD5415) plus Net Gains (Losses) On the Sale of Other Assets (RIADB496).

Other Noninterest Income

From March 31, 2001 forward includes information from schedule RI Other Noninterest Income (RIADB497). For prior quarters includes Other Fee Income (RIAD5407) plus Other Noninterest Income (RIAD5408). Note title no longer includes the description: (Inc Intangibles).

Noninterest Income

Year-to-date total of Noninterest income.

Personnel Expense

Year-to-date Salaries and Employee Benefits, from schedule RI (RIAD4135).

Occupancy Expense

Year-to-date expenses of Premises and Fixed assets (net of rental income), from schedule RI (RIAD4217).

Goodwill Impairment

From March 31, 2002 forward includes information from schedule RI Goodwill Impairment Losses (RIADC216).

Other Intangible Amortization

From March 31, 2002 forward includes information from schedule RI Amortization Expense and Impairment Losses for Other Intangible Assets (RIADC232).

Other Operating Expense

From March 31, 2002 forward includes information from schedule RI Other Noninterest Expense (RIAD4092). From March 31, 2001 to December 31, 2001 includes Amortization of Intangible Assets (RIAD4531) and Other Noninterest Expense (RIAD4092). From December 31, 2001 and prior includes Other Noninterest Expense (RIAD4092). Note that for those quarters Amortization of Intangible Assets was reported as a part of Other Noninterest Expense.

Total Overhead Expense

Sum of personnel, occupancy, goodwill impairment, other intangible amortization and other operating expense.

Domestic Banking Offices (#)

The number of domestic banking

offices (including the "main" office) in operation on the reporting date.

Foreign Branches (#)

NA appears at this caption for banks that do not have foreign offices, International banking facilities (IBFs) are not included in this item.

Assets per Domestic Office

Average domestic assets divided by the number of domestic banking offices, expressed in thousands of dollars per office.

Percent of Average Assets

Noninterest expenses as reported in the Report of Income divided by year-to-date average assets. See previous section for individual Noninterest expense item definitions. Ratios in this section are annualized for interim periods. See Section II, Technical Information for further information.

Personnel Expense

Occupancy Expense

Other Oper Exp
(Including Intangibles)

Total Overhead Expense

Overhead Less Noninterest Income

Other Income/Expense Ratios

These ratios present an additional analysis on a per employee base and the marginal tax rate (RIADB496).

Efficiency Ratio

Total Overhead Expense expressed as a percentage of Net Interest Income (TE) plus Noninterest Income. See definitions on UBPR page 2 for specific components.

Average Personnel Expense per Employee (Thousand$)

The average salary (including benefits) per employee expressed in thousands of dollars ($). For example, 21.35=$21,350 average salary (including benefits) per employee per year.

Average Assets per Employee (Millions$)

Average assets divided by the number of full-time equivalent employee on the payroll at the end of the period. Result is shown in millions of dollars.

Yield On or Cost of:

This section presents yield or cost ratios for various assets and liabilities. Note that all yields and rates are annualized and those averages are year-to-date averages. See Section II for descriptions of annualizing and averaging methods. Yields on individual loan categories are not calculated for banks with assets below $25M because of data limitations. Yields and costs (rates) use averages from Report of Condition, Schedule RC-K whenever the data is reported.

Total Loans & Lease (TE)

Interest and fees on loans and income on direct lease-financing receivables, plus the tax benefit on tax-exempt loan and lease income, divided by average total loans and lease-financing receivables. See Appendix B regarding the calculation of tax benefits.

Total Loans or Loans in Domestic Offices

Interest and fees on loans held in domestic offices divided by average domestic office loans.

Real Estate Loans

Interest and fees on domestic office loans secured primarily by real estate, divided by average domestic real estate loans.

Loans Secured by 1–4 Family Residential Property

Interest and fees on loans secured by 1–4 family real estate divided by average loans secured by 1–4 family real estate.

All Other Loans Secured By Real Estate

Interest and fees on all other loans secured real estate divided by average loans secured by real estate.

Commercial & Industrial Loans

Interest and fees on domestic office commercial and industrial loans, divided by average domestic commercial and industrial loans.

Individual Loans

Interest and fees on domestic office loans to individuals for household, family and other personal expenditures, divided by average domestic loans to individuals for household, family, and other personal expenditures.

Credit Card

Interest and fees on credit card plans divided by average credit card and related plans.

Agricultural Loans

Interest and fees on domestic office loans to finance agricultural production divided by average domestic loans to finance agricultural production.

Loans in Foreign Offices

Interest and fees on loans in foreign offices divided by average loans in foreign offices. Available for banks filing call form 031.

Total Investment Securities (TE)

Income on securities not held in trading accounts, plus the estimated tax benefit on tax-exempt municipal securities income, divided by average U.S. Treasury and U.S. government agency securities, state and political subdivisions, and other debt and equity securities.

Total Investment Securities(Book)

Income on securities not held in trading accounts, divided by average U.S. Treasury and U.S. government agency securities, state and political subdivisions, and other debt and equity securities.

US Treasury & Agency (Excluding MBS)

Income on U.S. Treasury securities and U.S. government agency obligations divided by average U. S. Treasury securities and U.S. government agency obligations. Excludes mortgage backed securities. Available from March 31, 2001 forward.

Mortgage Backed Securities

Income on mortgage backed securities divided by the average for those securities.

All Other Securities

Income on all other securities divided by the average for those securities. Includes taxable and tax-exempt obligations issued by state and local subdivisions.

Interest-Bearing Bank Balances

Interest on balances due from depository institutions divided by the average of interest-bearing balances due from depository institutions carried in domestic and foreign office.

Federal Funds Sold & Resales

Income on federal funds sold and securities purchased under agreements to resell divided by the average of federal funds sold and securities purchased under agreements to resell.

Total Interest-Bearing Deposits

Interest on all interest-bearing time and savings deposits in domestic and foreign offices divided by average interest-bearing time and savings deposits in domestic and foreign offices.

Transaction Accounts

Interest on transaction accounts (NOW accounts, ATS accounts, and telephone and preauthorized transfer accounts) divided by the average balance of such deposits.

Other Savings Deposits

For quarters from March 31 2001 forward includes interest on other savings deposits (all nontransaction accounts and time deposits) divided by the average of such deposits. For quarters prior to March 31, 2001 excludes MMDA's.

Time Dep of $100M or More

Interest on time certificates of deposit of $100 thousand or more issued by domestic offices divided by the average of domestic time certificates of deposit of $100 thousand or more. From March 31, 1997, time deposits open accounts; are included.

All Other Time Deposits

Interest on all domestic time deposits of less than $100,000 and open-account time deposits of $100,000 or more, divided by the average of such deposits. From March 31, 1997 forward, time deposit open accounts not included.

Foreign Office Deposits

Interest on deposits in foreign offices, Edge and Agreement subsidiaries and IBF's divided by the average for such deposits. Available for banks filing call form 031.

Federal Funds Purchased & Repos

The expense of federal funds purchased and securities sold under agreements to repurchase divided by the average of federal funds purchased and securities sold under agreements to repurchase.

Other Borrowed Money

Interest on demand notes (note balances) issued to the U.S. Treasury and on other borrowed money divided by the average of interest-bearing demand notes (note balances) issued to the U.S. Treasury and other liabilities for borrowed money.

Subordinated Notes & Debentures

Interest on notes and debentures subordinated to deposits divided by the average of notes and debentures subordinated to deposits.

All Interest-Bearing Funds

Interest on all interest-bearing deposits in domestic offices, interest-bearing foreign office deposits, demand notes (note balances) issued to the U.S. Treasury, other borrowed money, subordinated notes and debentures, and expense on federal funds purchased and securities sold under agreements to repurchase, interest expense on mortgage and capitalized leases divided by the average of the liabilities or funds that generated those expenses.

	06/30/2008	06/30/2007	12/31/2007	12/31/2006	12/31/2005	PERCENT CHANGE 1 QTR	1 YEAR
ASSETS							
REAL ESTATE LOANS	77,578,050	83,807,911	81,546,155	84,680,338	78,452,819	-3.09	-7.43
COMMERCIAL LOANS	30,093,522	25,696,946	26,211,424	27,108,340	25,473,574	6.29	17.11
INDIVIDUAL LOANS	12,820,677	12,569,323	12,923,881	12,973,537	15,250,527	1.38	2.00
AGRICULTURAL LOANS	91,702	99,283	107,248	118,107	118,338	-13.92	-7.64
OTHER LN&LS IN DOMESTIC OFFICES	9,634,403	9,296,265	11,520,740	8,486,200	9,241,436	-4.06	3.64
LN&LS IN FOREIGN OFFICES	0	0	0	0	0	N/A	N/A
LOANS HELD FOR SALE	5,186,141	12,356,706	8,750,379	11,659,728	13,695,613	-24.39	-58.03
LOANS NOT HELD FOR SALE	125,032,213	119,113,022	123,559,069	121,706,794	114,841,081	0.59	4.97
LN&LS ALLOWANCE	1 668 775	1 049 117	1 281 213	1 043 245	1 026 834	8.07	59.06
NET LOANS & LEASES	128,549,579	130,420,611	131,028,235	132,323,277	127,509,860	-0.82	-1.43
U S TREASURY & AGENCY SECURITIES	9,684,218	9,596,175	9,564,863	15,683,563	16,877,470	1.24	0.92
MUNICIPAL SECURITIES	969,854	971,933	1,006,845	971,882	881,719	-15.86	-0.21
FOREIGN DEBT SECURITIES	4 800	4 800	4 800	4 800	4 800	0.00	0.00
ALL OTHER SECURITIES	2,076,558	1,852,254	3,092,593	6,181,593	6,283,409	-19.86	12.11
INTEREST-BEARING BANK BALANCES	5,410	13,643	9,916	11,658	8,805	-7.49	-60.35
FEDERAL FUNDS SOLD & RESALES	2,810,477	2,098,597	2,567,769	5,303,335	3,552,318		
TRADING ACCOUNT ASSETS	7 586 997	12 012 798	7 199 765	1 735 068	1 660 730	-3.81	-36.84
TOTAL INVESTMENTS	23,138,314	26,550,200	23,446,551	29,891,899	29,269,251		
TOTAL EARNING ASSETS	151,687,893	156,970,811	154,474,786	162,215,176	156,779,111		
NONINT CASH & DUE FROM BANKS	3 527 809	4 256 467	4 272 366	4 486 422	4 977 493	-12.95	-17.12
PREMISES, FIX ASSTS, CAP LEASES	1,291,265	1,716,159	1,379,680	1,760,028	1,617,839	-0.25	-24.76
OTHER REAL ESTATE OWNED	358,453	160,557	242,063	97,892	38,043	12.76	123.26
INV IN UNCONSOLIDATED SUBS	3,627	0	3,666	0	0		
ACCEPTANCES & OTH ASSETS	14,631,806	13,963,152	14,734,965	14,028,638	13,818,804	-7.19	4.79
TOTAL ASSETS	171,500,853	177,067,146	175,107,526	182,588,156	177,231,290	-1.84	-3.14
AVERAGE ASSETS DURING QUARTER	168,682,848	175,010,458	169,674,500	181,124,691	172,962,613	-1.31	-3.62
LIABILITIES							
DEMAND DEPOSITS	9,466,361	9,472,361	9,501,787	10,166,559	10,643,400	-1.04	-0.06
ALL NOW & ATS ACCOUNTS	2,182,323	1,657,925	1,921,197	1,476,750	1,653,918	-2.79	31.63
MONEY MARKET DEPOSIT ACCOUNTS	58,220,524	53,771,242	57,395,718	54,656,968	57,926,598	-1.52	8.27
OTHER SAVINGS DEPOSITS	3,966,450	4,698,516	3,917,099	5,198,980	5,423,878	-0.59	-15.58
TIME DEP UNDER $100M	15 931 309	16 568 240	17 097 331	16 642 446	13 225 322	-4.62	-3.84
CORE DEPOSITS	89,766,967	86,168,284	89,833,132	88,141,703	88,873,116	-2.03	4.18
TIME DEP OF $100M OR MORE	24,509,150	28,411,225	24,239,495	30,412,961	24,756,238	5.92	-13.73
DEPOSITS IN FOREIGN OFFICES	6,604,586	10,546,491	5,675,306	8,016,517	9,995,269	71.30	-37.38
TOTAL DEPOSITS	120 880 703	125 126 000	119 747 933	126 571 181	123 624 623	1.91	-3.39
FEDERAL FUNDS PURCH & RESALE	8,620,190	10,470,385	10,408,376	16,095,806	12,691,947		
FED HOME LOAN BOR MAT < 1 YR	634,874	1,248,770	1,629,769	100,630	825,286	-59.40	-49.16
FED HOME LOAN BOR MAT > 1 YR	7,791,546	6,272,543	8,057,404	7,791,863	8,349,578	-1.60	24.22
OTH BORROWING MAT < 1 YR	405 543	500 690	500 350	0	3 093 039	-18.93	-19.00
OTH BORROWING MAT > 1 YR	6,819,215	6,618,949	6,938,843	5,412,990	2,627,290	-12.07	3.03
ACCEPTANCES & OTHER LIABILITIES	3,711,471	4,103,573	4,858,999	3,838,700	4,057,502	-19.67	-9.56
TOTAL LIABILITIES (INCL MORTG)	148,863,542	154,340,910	152,141,674	159,811,170	155,269,265	-1.55	-3.55
SUBORD NOTES AND DEBENTURES	3 334 741	3 391 247	3 312 078	3 446 917	3 696 687	-6.75	-1.67
ALL COMMON & PREFERRED CAPITAL	19,302,570	19,334,989	19,653,774	19,330,069	18,265,338	-3.17	-0.17
TOTAL LIBILITIES & CAPITAL	171,500,853	177,067,146	175,107,526	182,588,156	177,231,290	-1.84	-3.14
MEMORANDA							
OFFICER, SHAREHOLDER LOANS (#)	10	13	12	14	12		
OFFICER, SHAREHOLDER LOANS ($)	89,161	167,178	170,044	282,038	331,871	-46.72	-46.67
NON-INVESTMENT ORE	308,897	124,388	204,020	75,022	38,043	13.03	148.33
HELD-TO-MATURITY SECURITIES	0	0	0	0	0	N/A	N/A
AVAILABLE-FOR-SALE-SECURITIES	12,735,430	12,425,162	13,669,101	22,841,838	24,047,398	-4.35	2.50
ALL BROKERED DEPOSITS	15,301,426	16,659,978	14,661,667	18,150,059	15,644,932	8.89	-8.15

Balance Sheet—Assets, Liabilities and Capital ($000)

This page presents end-of-period figures to facilitate comparison of asset and liability composition from period to period. The major components of total assets have been aligned into earning and nonearning asset categories to facilitate earning asset analysis.

Annual and one-quarter percentage changes are provided for most of the data presented on this page. The annual changes are the percent change from the prior year comparable quarter to the current quarter. One quarter change is the percent change from the immediate prior quarter to the current quarter.

Data on this page comes from Report of Condition schedules RC, RC-B, RC-C, RC-D and RC-E.

There is a single version of this page for all banks.

Assets

Real Estate Loans

Total of domestic-office loans secured by real estate.

Commercial Loans

Total of domestic-office commercial and industrial loans, loans to depository institutions, acceptances of other banks, and obligations (other than securities) of states and political subdivisions.

Individual Loans

Domestic-office loans to individuals for household, family and other personal expenditures.

Agricultural Loans

Total domestic-office loans to finance agricultural production and other loans to farmers.

Other Loans and Leases in Domestic Offices

All other loans, and all lease-financing receivables, in domestic offices.

Loans and Leases in Foreign Offices

All loans and leases in foreign offices. NA appears for banks without foreign offices.

Loans Held For Sale

Loans and leases held for sale as reported on schedule RC is available from Mach 31, 2001 forward.

Loans Not Held For Sale

Loans and leases not held for sale as reported on schedule RC is available from March 31, 2001 forward. For prior quarters total loans and leases are displayed.

Less: Loan and Lease Allowance

The allowance for loan and lease losses.

Net Loans and Leases

Gross loans and leases, less allowance and reserve and unearned income. Note that this figure includes loans held for sale as reported on schedule RC.

Memo: Unearned Income

Unearned income, and the total of loan and lease loss reserves and transfer risk reserves, are subtracted from Gross Loans and Leases.

U.S. Treasury and Agency Securities

Total of U.S. Treasury securities and U.S. Government agency and corporation obligations.

Municipal Securities

Securities issued by states and political subdivisions in the U.S.

Foreign Securities

All debt and equity foreign securities.

All Other Securities

All other domestic securities, including holdings of private certificates of participation in pools of residential mortgages.

Interest-Bearing Bank Balances

Interest-bearing balances due from depository institutions.

Federal Funds Sold and Resales

Federal funds sold and securities purchased under agreements to resell.

Trading Account Assets

Total assets held in trading accounts.

Total Investments

Sum of all securities, interest-bearing bank balances, federal funds sold, and trading account assets.

Total Earning Assets

Sum of Net Loans and Leases and Total Investments.

Noninterest-Bearing Cash and Due From Banks

Total currency, coin, and non-interest-bearing balances due from depository institutions.

Premises, Fixed Assets and Capitalized Leases

All premises and fixed assets, including capitalized leases.

Other Real Estate Owned

Includes investment and non-investment other real estate owned.

Investment in Unconsolidated Subsidiaries

Bank's investment in unconsolidated subsidiaries and associated companies.

Acceptances and Other Assets

From schedule RC combines Customers Liability to This Bank on Acceptances (RCFD2155) with Other Assets (RCFD2160) and Intangible Assets (RCFD2143) for all quarters.

Total Assets

Average Assets During Quarter

Average assets for one quarter from Schedule RC-K.

Liabilities

Demand Deposits

Total demand deposits from Schedule RC-E.

All NOW & ATS Accounts

Total transaction accounts minus total demand deposits. This consists of all NOW accounts (including Super NOWs), plus other transaction accounts such as ATS accounts and certain accounts (other than MMDAs) that permit third party payments from RC-E.

MoneyMarket Deposit Accounts (MMDAs)

The amount of MMDAs reported from RC-E.

Other Savings Deposits

Reported total savings deposits, less MMDAs. This comprises all savings deposits other than MMDAs, and includes regular passbook accounts and overdraft protection plan accounts from RC-E.

Time Deposits Under $100 Thousand

Total time deposits of less than $100 Thousand from RC-E.

Core Deposits

The sum of demand deposits, all NOW and ATS accounts, MMDA savings, other savings deposits, and time deposits under $100 thousand.

Time Deposits of $100M or More

Time certificates of deposit of $100 thousand or more plus open-account time deposits of $100 thousand or more from RC-E.

Deposits in Foreign Offices

Total deposits in foreign offices and Edge and agreement subsidiaries and IBFs.

Total Deposits

Total of all deposit categories previously detailed.

Federal Funds Purchased & Resales

Federal Funds purchased and securities sold under agreements to repurchase.

Federal Home Loan Bank Borrowing Maturing Under 1 Year

From March 31, 2001 forward includes information from schedule RC-M Federal Home Loan Bank Advances with a Remaining Maturity of One Year or Less (RCFD2651).

Federal Home Loan Bank Borrowing Maturing Over 1 Year

From March 31, 2001 forward includes information from schedule RC-M Federal Home Loan Bank Advances with a Remaining Maturity of One to Three Years (RCFDB565) plus Federal Home Loan Bank Advances with a Remaining Maturity of Over Three Years (RCFDB566).

Other Borrowing Maturing Under 1 Year

From March 31, 2001 forward includes information from schedule RC-M Other Borrowed Money with a Remaining Maturity of One Year or Less (RCFDB571) For prior quarters includes Other Borrowed Money with a Remaining Maturity One Year or Less (RCFD2332).

Other Borrowing Maturing Over 1 Year

From March 31, 2001 forward

includes information from schedule RC-M Other Borrowed Money with a Remaining Maturity of One to Three Years (RCFDB567) plus Other Borrowed Money with Remaining Maturity of Over Three Years (RCFDB568) For prior quarters includes Other Borrowed Money with a Remaining Maturity of One to Three years (RCDA547) plus Other Borrowed Money With Remaining Maturity of Over Three Years (RCFDA548).

Acceptances & Other Liabilities

The sum of the bank's liability on acceptances executed and outstanding, mortgage indebtedness and liability for capitalized leases, and all other liabilities not included above.

Total Liabilities (Including Mortgages)

Total Liabilities (excluding notes and debentures subordinated to deposits).

Subordinated Notes & Debentures

Notes and debentures subordinated to deposits.

All Common & Preferred Capital

All preferred and common stock, surplus, undivided profits and capital reserves, and cumulative foreign currency translation adjustments.

Total Liabilities & Capital

The total of the various liability and capital items listed above.

Memoranda

Officer, Shareholder Loans (#)

The aggregate number officers, directors, principal shareholders and related interests with extensions of credit exceeding $500,000 or 5% of total capital.

Officer, Shareholder Loans ($)

The aggregate amount of loans to officers, directors, principal shareholders and related interests.

Non-Investment ORE

All other real estate owned. Excludes direct and indirect investment in real estate ventures. Reported for savings banks only.

Held-To-Maturity Securities

Held-to-maturity securities reported at cost beginning March 31, 1994. This caption reflects total investment securities excluding trading assets for prior periods.

Available-For-Sale Securities

Securities available-for-sale reported at fair value beginning March 31, 1994.

All Brokered Deposits

Total brokered deposits from schedule RC-E.

OUTSTANDING ($000)	06/30/2008	06/30/2007	12/31/2007	12/31/2006	12/31/2005	PERCENT CHANGE 1 QTR	1 YEAR
HOME EQUITY (1-4 FAMILY)	20,146,280	20,258,308	20,424,891	18,959,843	15,712,324	-1.45	-0.55
CREDIT CARD	1 866 073	1 695 432	1 808 527	1 519 682	1 165 686	1.5	10.06
COMMERCIAL RE SECURED BY RE	4,357,215	6,629,272	5,501,284	6,451,700	6,051,264	-6.23	-34.27
1-4 FAMILY RESIDENTIAL	1,971,152	4,100,054	2,968,814	N/A	N/A	-16.04	-51.92
COMML RE, OTH CONST & LAND	2,386,063	2,529,218	2,532,470	N/A	N/A	3.78	-5.66
COMMERCIAL RE NOT SECURED BY RE	832 821	663 074	726 867	735 254	766 754	3.86	25.6
ALL OTHER	56,497,337	54,358,145	54,936,245	71,131,017	66,031,890	-1.51	3.94
SECURITIES UNDERWRITING	0	0	0	0	0		
MEMO UNUSED COMMIT W/MAT GT 1 YR	36,599,569	38,569,453	36,634,005	38,356,222	37,633,546	2.06	-5.11
STANDBY LETTERS OF CREDIT	17,968,799	15,690,967	15,838,741	13,042,308	13,594,551	11.13	14.52
AMOUNT CONVEYED TO OTHERS	3,960,962	3,474,666	3,268,146	167,731	261,431	18.38	14
COMMERCIAL LETTERS OF CREDIT	131 248	170 457	132 270	123 408	177 260	-9.98	-23
ASSETS SECURITIZED OR SOLD W REC	123,748,341	104,109,136	112,601,626	89,188,715	69,765,105	4.01	18.86
AMOUNT OF RECOURSE EXPOSURE	135,513	138,713	139,473	96,219	53,469	-14.28	-2.31
CREDIT DERIVS BANK AS GTR	1,297,509	302,260	358,012	344,772	664,267	50.76	329.27
CREDIT DERIVS BANK AS BENEF	1,806,222	662,419	819,437	634,419	902,947	39.27	172.67
ALL OTH OFF-BALANCE SHEET ITEMS	0	112 928	0	5 325	6 629	-100	-100
OFF-BALANCE SHEET ITEMS	228,651,845	204,652,398	213,147,900	202,136,443	174,838,677	2.74	11.73

OUTSTANDING (% OF TOTAL)	BANK	PG 1	PCT	BANK	PG 1	PCT	BANK	PG 1	PCT	BANK	PG 1	BANK	PG 1
HOME EQUITY (1-4 FAMILY)	11.75	3.28	94	11.44	3.51	90	11.66	3.32	94	10.38	3.48	8.87	3.46
CREDIT CARD	1.09	1.13	75	0.96	1.12	72	1.03	1.09	72	0.83	1.10	0.66	1.18
COMMERCIAL RE SECURED BY RE	2.54	3.69	38	3.74	4.36	47	3.14	4.13	43	3.53	4.18	3.41	3.93
1-4 FAMILY RESIDENTIAL	1.15	0.91	65	2.32	1.19	79	1.70	1.09	71	N/A	N/A	N/A	N/A
COMML RE, OTH CONST & LAND	1.39	2.60	30	1.43	2.93	30	1.45	2.80	31	N/A	N/A	N/A	N/A
COMMERCIAL RE NOT SECURED BY RE	0.49	0.16	85	0.37	0.19	79	0.42	0.17	81	0.40	0.17	0.43	0.08
ALL OTHER	32.94	11.59	94	30.70	12.61	88	31.37	12.16	92	38.96	12.27	37.26	11.74
TOTAL LN&LS COMMITMENTS	48.80	23.35	92	47.22	25.70	88	47.63	24.16	91	54.11	25.02	50.63	24.62
SECURITIES UNDERWRITING	0 00	N/A	97	0.00	N/A	96	0.00	N/A	96	0.00	N/A	0.00	N/A
STANDBY LETTERS OF CREDIT	10.48	2.18	95	8.86	2.26	93	9.05	2.12	94	7.14	2.27	7.67	2.14
AMOUNT CONVEYED TO OTHERS	2.31	0.14	96	1.96	0.16	94	1.87	0.16	94	0.09	0.16	0.15	0.15
COMMERCIAL LETTERS OF CREDIT	0.08	0.09	68	0.10	0.08	71	0.08	0.07	69	0.07	0.08	0.10	0.09
ASSETS SECURITIZED OR SOLD W REC	72.16	0.85	98	58.80	0.80	98	64.30	0.92	97	48.85	0.84	39.36	1.08
AMOUNT OF RECOURSE EXPOSURE	0.08	0.12	74	0.08	0.12	75	0.08	0.14	73	0.05	0.11	0.03	0.11
CREDIT DERIVS BANK AS GTR	0.76	0.04	93	0.17	0.01	92	0.20	0.03	91	0.19	0.02	0.37	0.01
CREDIT DERIVS BANK AS BENEF	1.05	0.11	92	0.37	0.07	91	0.47	0.10	90	0.35	0.07	0.51	0.07
ALL OTH OFF-BALANCE SHEET ITEMS	0.00	0.56	75	0.06	0.80	80	0.00	0.55	78	0.00	0.69	0.00	0.55
OFF-BALANCE SHEET ITEMS	133.32	35.66	92	115.58	38.44	91	121.72	37.04	91	110.71	37.05	98.65	38.13

UBPR Page 05

Off-Balance Sheet Items

The top part of this page presents the amounts of various selected commitments, contingencies, contracts and other items reported in Report of Condition Schedule RC-L (Commitments and Contingencies) that are not reported as part of the balance sheet of the Report of Condition. Refer to the instructions for the Report of Condition Schedule RC-L for more detailed explanations of the captions appearing on UBPR page 05.

Annual and one-quarter percentage changes are provided for data displayed in dollars presented on this page. The annual changes are the percent change from the prior year comparable quarter to the current quarter. One quarter change is the percent change from the immediate prior quarter to the current quarter.

Page five displays the same captioned items in two different formats. Definitions apply to both sections. The top half displays information in dollar format. The bottom half displays the items as a percent of total assets.

Outstanding

Unused commitments on the following categories of loans and securities.

Home Equity (1-4 Family)

Credit Card

Commercial RE Secured by RE

1–4 Family Residential

Commercial Real Estate, Other Construction & Land

Commercial RE Not Secured by RE

All Other

Securities Underwriting

Memo: Unused Commit W/Mat Gt 1 YR

Unused commitments reported the previous 6 categories with an original maturity beyond one year.

Standby Letters of Credit

The amount of outstanding and used standby letters of credit issued by the bank.

Amount Conveyed to Others

The amount of standby letters of credit conveyed to others.

Commercial Letters of Credit

Assets Securitized or Sold W/ Recourse

Recourse exposure for above mortgage pools.

Amount of Recourse Exposure

Principal balance of FNMA, FHLMC, Private and Farmer Mac mortgage pools transferred with recourse.

Credit Derivs Bank as Guarantor

Credit Derivatives on which the bank is guarantor, available from June 30, 1997 forward.

Credit Derivs Bank as Beneficiary

Credit Derivatives on which the bank is beneficiary, available from June 30, 1997 forward.

All Other Off-Balance Sheet Items

Contracts on other commodities and equities, all other off-balance sheet liabilities, participation in acceptances conveyed and acquired, securities borrowed, securities lent, commitments to purchase and sell when-issued securities.

Off-Balance Sheet Items

Sum of all off-balance sheet items listed above.

OFF-BALANCE SHEET ITEMS & DERIVATIVES ANALYSIS

	06/30/2008	06/30/2007	12/31/2007	12/31/2006	12/31/2005
NOTIONAL AMOUNT ($000)					
DERIVATIVE CONTRACTS	265,717,847	198,258,129	201,860,361	145,738,252	114,768,701
INTEREST RATE CONTRACTS	244,082,644	179,453,027	184,509,853	127,820,337	99,678,730
FOREIGN EXCHANGE CONTRACTS	9,236,749	8,128,363	7,055,862	6,282,242	5,435,343
EQUITY, COMM & OTH CONTRACTS	12,398,454	10,676,739	10,294,646	11,635,673	9,654,628
DERIVATIVES POSITION					
FUTURES AND FORWARDS	69,599,512	65,206,190	52,699,227	30,725,865	21,196,149
WRITTEN OPTIONS	35,265,984	17,531,663	19,186,876	18,228,064	12,772,871
EXCHANGE TRADED	14,731,690	770,485	2,563,844	943,303	206,000
OVER-THE-COUNTER	20 534 294	16 761 178	16 623 032	17 284 761	12 566 871
PURCHASED OPTIONS	30,465,550	17,020,068	13,435,642	15,673,894	8,932,359
EXCHANGE TRADED	15,514,372	1,031,055	3,153,228	1,335,023	391,000
OVER-THE-COUNTER	14,951,178	15,989,013	10,282,414	14,338,871	8,541,359
SWAPS	130 386 801	98 500 208	116 538 616	81 110 429	71 867 322
HELD-FOR-TRADING	218,809,593	114,895,282	146,370,116	100,062,186	79,632,039
INTEREST RATE CONTRACTS	200,321,199	98,288,851	131,312,767	83,504,363	64,728,016
FOREIGN EXCHANGE CONTRACTS	6 822 838	5 929 692	4 762 703	4 922 150	5 249 395
EQUITY, COMM & OTH CONTRACTS	11,665,556	10,676,739	10,294,646	11,635,673	9,654,628
NON-TRADED	46,908,254	83,362,847	55,490,245	45,676,066	35,136,662
INTEREST RATE CONTRACTS	43,761,445	81,164,176	53,197,086	44,315,974	34,950,714
FOREIGN EXCHANGE CONTRACTS	2 413 911	2 198 671	2 293 159	1 360 092	185 948
EQUITY, COMM & OTH CONTRACTS	732,898	0	0	0	0
MEMO MARKED-TO-MARKET	46,908,254	83,362,847	55,490,245	45,676,066	35,136,662
DERIVATIVE CONTRACTS (RBC DEF)	175,837,321	143,389,945	154,720,064	115,572,003	97,598,092
ONE YEAR OR LESS	54,892,018	51,321,439	47,188,078	38,427,006	30,827,893
OVER 1 YEAR TO 5 YEARS	83,967,409	61,135,459	72,271,487	44,939,269	37,083,610
OVER 5 YEARS	36 977 894	30 933 047	35 260 499	32 205 728	29 686 589
GROSS NEGATIVE FAIR VALUE	2,302,025	2,592,586	2,897,797	1,863,111	1,657,778
GROSS POSTIVE FAIR VALUE	3,167,705	2,280,962	3,240,733	1,578,880	1,637,033
HELD-FOR-TRADING	2 433 782	2 044 516	2 638 387	1 454 670	1 535 733
NON-TRADED	733,923	236,446	602,346	124,210	101,300
MEMO MARKED-TO-MARKET	733,923	236,446	602,346	124,210	101,300
CURR CREDIT EXP ON RBC DERIV CONTR	1,528,166	2,280,962	3,240,733	1,578,880	1,637,033
CREDIT LOSSES OFF-BS DERIVS	0	0	0	0	120
PAST DUE DERIV INSTRUMENTS					
FAIR VALUE CARRIED AS ASSETS	0	0	0	0	0
IMPACT NONTRADED DERIV CONTRACTS					
INCREASE (DECR) IN INTEREST INC	N/A	N/A	N/A	N/A	-18,653
INCREASE (DECR) IN INTEREST EXP	N/A	N/A	N/A	N/A	-47,793
INCREADE (DECR) IN NONINT ALLOC	N/A	N/A	N/A	N/A	0
INCREASE (DECR) IN NET INCOME	N/A	N/A	N/A	N/A	-66,446

UBPR Page 05A

Derivative Instruments

This page presents the amounts of derivatives and related information in thousands of dollars. The information comes mostly from call schedule RC-L Off-Balance Sheet Items, but also from schedules RC-M Memoranda, RC-N Past Due and Nonaccrual Loans Leases and Other Assets, RC-R Regulatory Capital and the RI report of income memoranda section. Derivatives are summarized in several ways using the position indicators in the RC-L matrix. Data on this page is available from the March 31, 1995 call report forward unless otherwise noted.

Notional Amount ($000)

Derivative Contracts

From March 31, 2001 forward the sum of RC-L items 12 and 13.a, all columns. From March 31, 2001 and prior the total of all derivative contracts, or the sum of RC-L items 15 and 16.a and 16.b, columns A through D. All interest rate, foreign exchange, equity, commodity and other contracts are combined.

Interest Rate Contracts

For quarters from March 31, 2001 forward the sum of RC-L items 14.a through e, column A. For quarters prior to March 31, 2001 total interest rate contracts, or the sum of RC-L items 14.a through e, column A.

Foreign Exchange Contracts

For quarters from March 31, 2001 forward total foreign exchange contracts, or the sum of RC-L items 11.a through e., column B. For prior quarters total foreign exchange contracts, or the sum of RC-L items 14.a through e, column B.

Equity, Commodity & Other Contracts

For quarters from March 31, 2001 forward total equity, commodity and other contracts, or the sum of RC-L items 11.a through e, columns C. and D. For prior quarter's total equity, commodity and other contracts, or the sum of RC-L items 14.a through e, columns C and D.

Derivatives Position

Futures and Forwards

For quarters from March 31, 2001 forward total futures and forward contracts, or the sum of RC-L items 11.a and 11.b, columns A through D. For prior quarters total futures and forward contracts, or the sum of RC-L items 14.a and 14.b, columns A through D.

Written Options

For quarters from March 31, 2001 forward total written options both exchange traded and over-the-counter, or the sum of RC-L items 11.c.1 and 11.d.1, columns A through D. For prior quarters total written options both exchange traded and over-the-counter, or the sum of RC-L items 14.c.1 and 14.d.1, columns A through D.

Exchange Traded

For quarters from March 31, 2001 forward total written options which are exchange traded, or the sum of RC-L items 11.c.1, columns A through D. For prior quarters total written options which are exchange traded, or the sum of RC-L items 14.c.1, columns A through D.

Over-The-Counter

For quarters from March 31, 2001 forward total written options which are traded over-the-counter, or the sum of RC-L items 11.d.1, columns A through D. For prior quarters total written options which are traded over-the-counter, or the sum of RC-L items 14.d.1, columns A through D.

Purchased Options

For quarters from March 31, 2001

forward total purchased options both exchange traded and over-the-counter, or the sum of RC-L items 11.c.2 and 11.d.2, columns A through D. For quarters prior total purchased options both exchange traded and over-the-counter, or the sum of RC-L items 14.c.2 and 14.d.2, columns A through D.

Exchange Traded

For quarters from March 31, 2001 forward total purchased options which are exchange traded, or the sum of RC-L items 11.c.2 columns A through D. For quarters prior total purchased options which are exchange traded, or the sum of RC-L items 14.c.2 columns A through D.

Over-The-Counter

For quarters from March 31, 2001 forward total purchased options which are traded over-the-counter, or the sum of RC-L items 11.d.2 columns A through D. For prior quarters total purchased options which are traded over-the-counter, or the sum of RC-L items 14.d.2 columns A through D.

Swaps

For quarters from March 31, 2001 forward total swaps, or the sum of RC-L items 11.e, columns A through D. For prior quarters total swaps, or the sum of RC-L items 14.e, columns A through D.

Held-For-Trading

For quarters from March 31, 2001 forward total derivative contracts held for trading, or the sum of RC-L item 12, columns A through D. For prior quarters total derivative contracts held for trading, or the sum of RC-L item 15, columns A through D.

Interest Rate Contracts

For quarters from March 31, 2001 forward total interest rate contracts or RC-L item 12, column A. For prior quarters total interest rate contracts or RC-L item 15, column A.

Foreign Exchange Contracts

For quarters from March 31, 2001 forward total foreign exchange contracts, or RC-L item 12, column B. For prior quarters total foreign exchange contracts, or RC-L item 15, column B.

Equity, Commodity and Other Contracts

For quarters from March 31, 2001 forward total equity, commodity and other contracts or the sum of RC-L items 12, columns C and D. For prior quarter's total equity, commodity and other contracts or the sum of RC-L items 15, columns C and D.

Non-Traded

From March 31, 2001 forward total non-traded derivatives, or the sum of RC-L item 13, columns A through D. For quarter's prior total non-traded derivatives, or the sum of RC-L items 16.a and b, columns A through D.

Interest Rate Contracts

For quarters from March 31, 2001 forward total non-traded interest rate contracts, or the sum of RC-L item 13, column A. For prior quarters total non-traded interest rate contracts, or the sum of RC-L items 16.a and b, column A.

Foreign Exchange Contracts

For quarters from March 31, 2001 forward total non-traded foreign exchange contracts, or the sum of RC-L item 13, column B. For prior quarters total non-traded foreign exchange contracts, or the sum of RC-L items 16.a and b, column B.

Equity, Commodity and Other Contracts

For quarters from March 31, 2001 forward total non-traded equity, commodity and other contracts, or the sum of RC-L item 13, columns A

and B. For prior quarters total non-traded equity, commodity and other contracts, or the sum of RC-L items 16.a and b, columns A and B.

Memo: Marked-to-Market

For quarters from March 31, 2001 forward total non-traded contracts that are marked-to-market, or the sum of RC-L item 13, columns A through D. For prior quarters total non-traded contracts that are marked-to-market, or the sum of RC-L items 16.a, columns A through D.

Derivative Contracts (RBC Def.)

Total derivative contracts as defined for risk-based capital purposes, or the sum of RC-R items 2.a through f, columns A, B and C. For quarters prior to March 31, 2001 this item is available only for banks that answer "yes" to RC-R item 1 or have assets greater then $1 billion or otherwise complete all of RC-R.

One Year or Less

Total derivative contracts maturing one year or less as defined for risk-based capital purposes, or the sum of RC-R memoranda items 2.a through f, column A. For quarters prior to March 31, 2001 this item is available only for banks that answer "yes" to RC-R item 1 or have assets greater then $1 billion or otherwise complete all of RC-R.

Over 1 Year to 5 Years

Total derivative contracts maturing one to five years as defined for risk-based capital purposes, or the sum of RC-R memoranda items 2.a through f, column B. For quarters prior to March 31, 2001 this item is available only for banks that answer "yes" to RC-R item 1 or have assets greater then $1 billion or otherwise complete all of RC-R.

Over 5 Years

Total derivative contracts maturing over five years as defined for risk-based capital purposes, or the sum of RC-R memoranda items 2.a through

f, column C. For Quarters prior to March 31, 2001 this item is available only for banks that answer "yes" to RC-R item 1 or have assets greater then $1 billion or otherwise complete all of RC-R.

Gross Negative Fair Value

For quarters from March 31, 2001 forward total of all derivative contracts with a negative fair value, or the sum of RC-L items 14.a.2, b.2 and c.2, columns A through D. For prior quarters total of all derivative contracts with a negative fair value, or the sum of RC-L items 17.a.2, b.2 and c.2, columns A through D. Not available for banks filing FFIEC 034.

Gross Positive Fair Value

For quarters from March 31, 2001 forward total of all derivative contracts with a positive fair value, or the sum of RC-L items 14.a.1, b.1 and c.1, columns A through D. For prior quarters total of all derivative contracts with a positive fair value, or the sum of RC-L items 17.a.1, b.1 and c.1, columns A through D. Not available for banks filing FFIEC 034.

Held-For-Trading

For quarters from March 31, 2001 forward total of all derivative contracts held-for-trading with a positive fair value, or the sum of RC-L items14. a.1, columns A through D. For prior quarters total of all derivative contracts held-for-trading with a positive fair value, or the sum of RC-L items17. a.1, columns A through D. Not available for banks filing FFIEC 034.

Non-Traded

For quarters from March 31, 2001 forward total of all derivative contracts not held for trading purposes with a positive fair value, or the sum of RC-L items 14.b.1, columns A through D. For prior quarters total of all derivative contracts not held for trading purposes with a positive fair value, or the sum of RC-L items 17. b.1 and c.1, columns A through D. Not available for banks filing FFIEC 034.

Memo: Marked-to-Market

For quarters from March 31, 2001 forward total of all derivative contracts not held for trading purposes that are marked to market and have a positive fair value, or the sum of RC-L items 14.b.1, columns A through D. For prior quarters total of all derivative contracts not held for trading purposes that are marked to market and have a positive fair value, or the sum of RC-L items 17.b.1, columns A through D. Not available for banks filing FFIEC 034.

Current Credit Exposure on RBC Derivative Contracts

Current credit exposure across all off-balance sheet contracts covered by the risk-based capital standards, or RC-R, memoranda item 1. For quarters prior to March 31, 2001 this item is available only for banks that answer "yes" to RC-R item 1 or have assets greater then $1 billion or otherwise complete all of RC-R.

Credit Losses Off-Balance Sheet Derivatives

Credit losses on off-balance sheet derivatives, or RI, memoranda section, item 10. For quarters prior to March 31, 2001 this item is available only for banks filing FFIEC call form 031 and 032 from March 31, 1996 forward.

Past Due Derivative Instruments:

Fair Value Carries as Assets 90 Days PD

For quarters prior to March 31, 2001 book value of amounts carried as assets of interest rate, foreign exchange, commodity and other contracts past due 90 days or more, from RC-N memoranda. From March 31, 2001 forward fair value is used.

Impact of Non-traded Derivative Contracts:

Increase (Decrease) in Interest Income

Impact of off-balance sheet derivatives held for purposes other than trading on interest income, or RI memoranda item 9.a. For quarters prior to March 31, 2001 item not available for banks filing FFIEC 034.

Increase (Decrease) in Interest Expense

Impact of off-balance sheet deriva-tives held for purposes other than trading on interest expense or RI memoranda item 9.b. For quarters prior to March 31, 2001 item not available for banks filing FFIEC 034.

Increase (Decrease) in Other Noninterest Allocations

Impact of off-balance sheet derivatives held purposes other than trading on other noninterest allocations or RI memoranda item 9.b. For quarters prior to March 31, 2001 item not available for banks filing FFIEC 034.

Increase (Decrease) in Net Income

Impact of off-balance sheet derivatives held for purposes other than trading on net income or the sum of RI memoranda items 9.a, b & c. For quarters prior to March 31, 2001 not available for banks filing FFIEC 034.

OFF-BALANCE SHEET ITEMS & DERIVATIVES ANALYSIS　　　　　　　　　　　PAGE 05B

	06/30/2008			06/30/2007			12/31/2007			12/31/2006		12/31/2005	
PERCENT OF NOTIONAL AMOUNT	BANK	PG 1	PCT	BANK	PG 1	PCT	BANK	PG 1	PCT	BANK	PG 1	BANK	PG 1
INTEREST RATE CONTRACTS	91.86	80.59	25	90.51	69.60	28	91.40	70.89	27	87.71	68.67	86.85	73.25
FOREIGN EXCHANGE CONTRACTS	3.48	4.05	73	4.10	6.52	74	3.50	5.93	71	4.31	6.54	4.74	6.34
EQUITY, COMM, & OTHER CONTR	4.67	1.24	88	5.39	1.20	88	5.10	1.48	88	7.98	1.23	8.41	0.78
FUTURES AND FORWARDS	26.19	12.87	77	32.89	18.62	74	26.11	17.65	71	21.08	18.03	18.47	17.54
WRITTEN OPTIONS	13.27	7.37	79	8.84	7.00	68	9.51	7.24	69	12.51	6.37	11.13	7.21
EXCHANGE TRADED	5.54	0.03	97	0.39	0.04	91	1.27	0.04	94	0.65	0.07	0.18	0.01
OVER-THE-COUNTER	7.73	7.01	73	8.45	6.52	71	8.23	6.83	72	11.86	5.60	10.95	6.81
PURCHASED OPTIONS	11.47	4.46	80	8.58	5.29	72	6.66	6.04	68	10.75	5.02	7.78	4.97
EXCHANGE TRADED	5.84	0.05	98	0.52	0.05	90	1.56	0.06	94	0.92	0.09	0.34	0.03
OVER-THE-COUNTER	5.63	4.09	70	8.06	4.84	74	5.09	5.38	67	9.84	4.47	7.44	4.56
SWAPS	49.07	53.44	31	49.68	47.46	39	57.73	50.38	41	55.65	47.97	62.62	51.87
HELD-FOR-TRADING	82.35	34.35	71	57.95	29.70	68	72.51	33.90	70	68.66	28.80	69.38	25.31
INTEREST RATE CONTRACTS	75.39	28.15	78	49.58	20.51	76	65.05	25.34	79	57.30	21.48	56.40	18.29
FOREIGN EXCHANGE CONTRACTS	2.57	1.78	79	2.99	2.72	79	2.36	2.84	75	3.38	3.40	4.57	3.06
EQUITY, COMM & OTH CONTRACTS	4.39	0.26	93	5.39	0.32	93	5.10	0.39	92	7.98	0.30	8.41	0.17
NON-TRADED	17.65	28.35	28	42.05	39.83	31	27.49	32.77	29	31.34	35.34	30.62	38.95
INTEREST RATE CONTRACTS	16.47	33.48	32	40.94	43.17	36	26.35	35.20	35	30.41	38.64	30.45	42.95
FOREIGN EXCHANGE CONTRACTS	0.91	0.24	87	1.11	0.43	86	1.14	0.31	87	0.93	0.43	0.16	0.34
EQUITY, COMM & OTH CONTRACTS	0.28	0.11	89	0.00	0.07	87	0.00	0.11	87	0.00	0.09	0.00	0.14
MEMO MARKED-TO-MARKET	17.65	28.35	28	42.05	39.83	31	27.49	32.77	29	31.34	35.34	30.62	38.95
DERIVATIVE CONTRACTS (RBC DEF)	66.17	76.15	24	72.32	78.56	24	76.65	80.44	26	79.30	80.04	85.04	81.80
ONE YEAR OR LESS	20.66	19.58	59	25.89	23.17	60	23.38	24.27	55	26.37	22.73	26.86	26.23
OVER 1 YEAR TO 5 YEARS	31.60	31.84	50	30.84	29.96	52	35.80	31.20	53	30.84	29.11	32.31	29.54
OVER 5 YEARS	13.92	16.85	51	15.60	16.82	53	17.47	17.20	55	22.10	19.02	25.87	18.04
GROSS NEGATIVE FAIR VALUE	0.87	1.09	40	1.31	0.63	85	1.44	1.05	72	1.28	0.64	1.44	0.80
GROSS POSTIVE FAIR VALUE	1.19	1.21	54	1.15	0.80	76	1.61	1.17	66	1.08	0.75	1.43	0.67
BY TIER ONE CAPITAL													
GROSS NEGATIVE FAIR VALUE (X)	0.18	0.04	89	0.20	0.02	92	0.23	0.03	92	0.15	0.02	0.14	0.02
GROSS POSTIVE FAIR VALUE (X)	0.25	0.04	91	0.18	0.02	92	0.26	0.03	92	0.12	0.02	0.14	0.02
HELD-FOR-TRADING (X)	17.48	1.44	92	8.86	1.27	91	11.86	1.29	92	7.80	1.28	6.80	1.00
NON TRADED (X)	3.75	0.74	92	6.43	0.96	92	4.50	0.77	93	3.56	1.06	3.00	1.11
NON-TRADED MARKED-TO-MKT(X)	3.75	0.74	92	6.43	0.96	92	4.50	0.77	93	3.56	1.06	3.00	1.11
CURR CREDIT EXPOSURE (X)	0.12	0.03	88	0.18	0.02	92	0.26	0.03	92	0.12	0.02	0.14	0.02
CREDIT LOSSES ON DERIVATIVES	0.00	N/A	95	0.00	N/A	97	0.00	N/A	97	0.00	N/A	0.00	N/A
PAST DUE DERIVATIVE INSTRUMENTS													
FAIR VALUE CARRIED AS ASSETS	0.00	N/A	98	0.00	N/A	98	0.00	N/A	97	0.00	N/A	0.00	N/A
OTHER RATIOS													
CUR CREDIT EXPOSURE/ RISK WT AST	0.94	0.32	86	1.43	0.17	92	2.00	0.28	92	0.98	0.19	1.05	0.18
CREDIT LOSSES ON DERIVS /CR ALLOW	0.00	N/A	95	0.00	N/A	97	0.00	0.00	94	0.00	N/A	0.01	N/A
IMPACT OF NONTRADED DERIV CONTRACTS													
INCR(DEC) INTEREST INC/NET INC	N/A	N/A	N/A	N/A	N/A	N/A	N/A	N/A	N/A	N/A	N/A	-0.92	-0.03
INCR(DEC) INTEREST EXP/NET INC	N/A	N/A	N/A	N/A	N/A	N/A	N/A	N/A	N/A	N/A	N/A	-2.35	0.25
INCR(DEC) NONINT ALLOC/NET INC	N/A	N/A	N/A	N/A	N/A	N/A	N/A	N/A	N/A	N/A	N/A	0.00	0.02
INCR(DEC) NET INCOME/NET INC	N/A	N/A	N/A	N/A	N/A	N/A	N/A	N/A	N/A	N/A	N/A	-3.27	0.07

UBPR Page 05B

Derivatives Analysis

This page presents the amounts of derivatives and related information in percentage format, generally in comparison to total derivatives. The information comes mostly from call schedule RC-L Off-Balance Sheet Items, but also from schedules RC-M Memoranda, RC-N Past Due and Nonaccrual Loans Leases and Other Assets, RC-R Regulatory Capital and the RI report of income memoranda section. Derivatives are summarized in several ways using the position indicators in the RC-L matrix. Data on this page is available from the March 31, 1995 call report forward unless otherwise noted. Please refer to page 5a for specific line item definitions.

Percent of Notional Amount

Total Derivative Contracts

The total of all derivative contracts, all interest rate, foreign exchange, equity, commodity and other contracts are combined. **This item does not appear on page 5B, but is used in computations below.**

Interest Rate Contracts

Total interest rate contracts as a percent of total derivative contracts.

Foreign Exchange Contracts

Total foreign exchange contracts as a percent of total derivative contracts.

Equity, Commodity & Other Contracts

Total equity, commodity and other contracts as a percent of total derivative contracts.

Derivatives Position

Futures and Forwards

Total futures and forward contracts as a percent of total derivative contracts.

Written Options

Total written options both exchange traded and over-the-counter as a percent of total derivative contracts.

Exchange Traded

Total written options which are exchange traded as a percent of total derivative contracts.

Over-The-Counter

Total written options which are traded over-the-counter as a percent of total derivative contracts.

Purchased Options

Total purchased options both exchange traded and over-the-counter as a percent of total derivative contracts.

Exchange Traded

Total purchased options which are exchange traded as a percent of total derivative contracts.

Over-The-Counter

Total purchased options which are traded over-the-counter as a percent of total derivative contracts.

Swaps

Total swaps as a percent of total derivative contracts.

Held-For-Trading

Total derivative contracts held for trading as a percent of total derivative contracts.

Interest Rate Contracts

Total interest rate contracts as a percent of total derivative contracts.

Foreign Exchange Contracts

Total foreign exchange contracts as a percent of total derivative contracts.

Equity, Commodity and Other Contracts

Total equity, commodity and other contracts as a percent of total derivative contracts.

Non-Traded

Total non-traded derivatives as a percent of total derivative contracts.

Interest Rate Contracts

Total non-traded interest rate contracts as a percent of total derivative contracts.

Foreign Exchange Contracts

Total non-traded foreign exchange contracts as a percent of total derivative contracts.

Equity, Commodity and Other Contracts

Total non-traded equity, commodity and other contracts as a percent of total derivative contracts.

Memo: Marked-to-Market

Total non-traded contracts that are marked-to-market as a percent of total derivative contracts.

Derivative Contracts (RBC Def.)

Total derivative contracts as defined for risk-based capital purposes as a percent of total derivative contracts. For quarters prior to March 31, 2001 this item is computed only for banks that answer "yes" to RC-R item 1 or have assets greater then $1 billion or otherwise complete all of RC-R.

One Year or Less

Total derivative contracts maturing one year or less as defined for risk-based capital purposes as a percent of total derivative contracts. Prior to March 31, 2001 this item is computed only for banks that answer "yes" to RC-R item 1 or have assets greater then $1 billion or otherwise complete all of RC-R.

Over 1 Year to 5 Years

Total derivative contracts maturing one to five years as defined for risk-based capital purposes as a percent of total derivative contracts. Prior to March 31, 2001 this item is computed only for banks that answer "yes" to RC-R item 1 or have assets greater then $1 billion or otherwise complete all of RC-R.

Over 5 Years

Total derivative contracts maturing over five years as defined for risk-based capital purposes as a percent of total derivative contracts. Prior to March 31, 2001 this item is computed only for banks that answer "yes" to RC-R item 1 or have assets greater then $1 billion or otherwise complete all of RC-R.

Gross Negative Fair Value

Total of all derivative contracts with a negative fair value as a percent of total derivative contracts. Prior to March 31, 2001 not computed for banks filing FFIEC 034.

Gross Positive Fair Value

Total of all derivative contracts with a positive fair value as a percent of total derivative contracts. Prior to March 31, 2001 not computed for banks filing FFIEC 034.

Percent of Tier One Capital:

(note that most computations involving tier one capital (X) are NOT converted to percent format)

Gross Negative Fair Value (X)

Total of all derivative contracts with a negative fair value divided by tier one capital. Prior to March 31, 2001 not computed for banks filing FFIEC 034.

Gross Positive Fair Value (X)

Total of all derivative contracts with a positive fair value divided by tier

one capital. Prior to March 31, 2001 not computed for banks filing FFIEC 034.

Held-For-Trading (X)

Total of all derivative contracts held-for-trading with a positive fair value divided by tier one capital. Prior to March 31, 2001 not computed for banks filing FFIEC 034.

Non-Traded (X)

Total of all derivative contracts not held for trading purposes with a positive fair value divided by tier one capital. Prior to March 31, 2001 not computed for banks filing FFIEC 034.

Non Traded Marked-to-Market (X)

Total of all derivative contracts not held for trading purposes that are marked to market and that have a positive fair value divided by tier one capital. Prior to March 31, 2001 not computed for banks filing FFIEC 034.

Current Credit Exposure on RBC Derivative Contracts (X)

Current credit exposure across all off-balance sheet contracts covered by the risk-based capital standards, or RC-R, memoranda item 1 divided by tier one capital. Prior to March 31, 2001 this item is available only for banks that answer "yes" to RC-R item 1 or have assets greater then $1 billion or otherwise complete all of RC-R.

Credit Losses Off-Balance Sheet Derivatives

Credit losses on off-balance sheet derivatives, or RI, memoranda section, item 10 as a percent of tier one capital. Prior to March 31, 2001 this item is available only for banks filing FFIEC call form 031 and 032 from March 31, 1996 forward.

Past Due Derivative Instruments:

Fair Value Carried as Asset 90 Days PD

Prior to March 31, 2001 book value of amounts carried as assets of interest

rate, foreign exchange, commodity and other contracts past due 90 days or more, or RC-N memoranda item 4.a, column B as a percent of tier one capital. For quarters from March 31, 2001 forward fair value used.

Other Ratios:

Current Credit Exposure/ Risk-Weighted Assets

Current credit exposure across all off-balance sheet contracts covered by the risk-based capital standards, or RC-R, memoranda item 1, as a percent of total risk-weighted assets. This ratio is computed only for banks that answer "yes" to RC-R item 1 or have assets greater then $1 billion or otherwise complete all of RC-R.

Credit Losses on Derivatives/Credit Allowance

Credit losses on off-balance sheet derivatives, or RI, memoranda section, item 10 as a percent of the ending balance in the allowance for credit losses, or item RI-B.II.6. This item is calculated only for banks filing FFIEC call form 031 and 032 from March 31, 1996 forward.

Impact of Non-Traded Derivative Contracts:

Increase (Decrease) in Interest Income/ Net Income

Impact of off-balance sheet derivatives held for purposes other than trading on interest income, or RI memoranda item 9.a as percent of net income. Computed only for banks filing FFIEC call form 031 and 032.

Increase (Decrease) in Interest Expense/ Net Income

Impact of off-balance sheet derivatives held for purposes other than trading on interest expense, or RI memoranda item 9.b as percent of net income. Computed only for banks filing FFIEC call form 031 and 032.

Increase (Decrease) in Other Noninterest Allocations/Net Income

Impact of off-balance sheet derivatives held purposes other than trading on other noninterest allocations, or RI memoranda item 9.b as percent of net income. Computed only for banks filing FFIEC call form 031 and 032.

Increase (Decrease) in Net Income/Net Income

Impact of off-balance sheet derivatives held for purposes other than trading on net income or the sum of RI memoranda items 9.a, b and c as percent of net income. Computed only for banks filing FFIEC call form 031 and 032.

BALANCE SHEET - PERCENTAGE COMPOSITION OF ASSETS AND LIABILITIES

PAGE 06

	06/30/2008			06/30/2007			12/31/2007			12/31/2006		12/31/2005	
ASSETS, PERCENT OF AVG ASSETS	BANK	PG 1	PCT	BANK	PG 1	PCT	BANK	PG 1	PCT	BANK	PG 1	BANK	PG 1
LOANS HELD FOR SALE	3.99	0.67	93	6.97	0.81	93	6.20	0.84	93	6.29	0.85	5.75	0.77
LOANS NOT HELD FOR SALE	71.53	66.53	57	65.75	63.47	43	67.63	64.51	51	66.15	61.79	65.71	60.04
LESS LN&LS ALLOWANCE	0.86	0.88	47	0.57	0.71	28	0.62	0.75	29	0.58	0.71	0.62	0.73
NET LOANS & LEASES	74.66	67.12	73	72.15	64.85	68	73.21	65.79	70	71.86	63.11	70.84	61.45
INTEREST-BEARING BANK BALANCES	0.00	0.52	20	0.01	0.55	29	0.01	0.54	28	0.01	0.52	0.01	0.56
FEDERAL FUNDS SOLD & RESALES	1.50	2.02	64	2.04	2.24	60	1.78	2.13	59	2.61	1.95	3.01	1.93
TRADING ACCOUNT ASSETS	4.35	0.55	92	6.21	0.41	94	5.43	0.51	92	1.10	0.29	0.97	0.28
HELD-TO-MATURITY SECURITIES	0.00	0.81	40	0.00	1.43	40	0.00	1.17	41	0.00	1.55	0.00	1.84
AVAILABLE-FOR-SALE SECURITIES	7.62	13.29	23	8.51	15.89	21	8.16	15.32	20	13.22	16.99	14.83	18.93
TOTAL EARNING ASSETS	88.13	89.48	35	88.92	89.99	34	88.59	89.63	37	88.80	89.87	89.66	89.95
NONINT CASH & DUE FROM BANKS	2.27	2.27	49	2.35	2.28	57	2.38	2.30	56	2.49	2.45	2.77	2.61
PREMISES, FIX ASSTS & CAP LEASES	0.76	1.03	38	0.97	1.03	51	0.93	1.10	47	0.93	0.99	0.98	1.05
OTHER REAL ESTATE OWNED	0.18	0.10	77	0.07	0.05	72	0.09	0.06	73	0.04	0.04	0.02	0.04
ACCEPTANCES & OTHER ASSETS	8.66	6.67	72	7.70	6.23	71	8.00	6.56	68	7.74	6.18	5.96	5.96
SUBTOTAL	11.87	10.52	64	11.08	10.01	65	11.41	10.37	62	11.20	10.13	10.34	9.97
TOTAL ASSETS	100.00	100.00		100.00	100.00		100.00	100.00		100.00	100.00	100.00	100.00
STANDBY LETTERS OF CREDIT	9.59	2.16	94	7.59	2.26	91	8.16	2.17	92	7.39	2.25	7.78	2.10
LIABILITIES, PERCENT OF AVG ASST													
DEMAND DEPOSITS	5.47	4.41	63	5.43	5.03	56	5.37	4.85	57	5.76	5.44	6.20	6.10
ALL NOW & ATS ACCOUNTS	1.22	1.62	44	0.90	1.63	32	0.94	1.61	34	0.89	1.61	0.96	1.81
MONEY MARKET DEPOSIT ACCOUNTS	33.52	22.81	79	29.95	22.82	67	30.94	24.33	68	30.69	22.44	34.91	23.39
OTHER SAVINGS DEPOSITS	2.28	6.85	30	2.75	7.51	35	2.61	7.08	33	3.01	8.10	3.70	8.67
TIME DEP LESS THAN $100M	9.54	13.31	33	9.20	11.77	37	9.43	12.59	35	8.48	9.81	6.65	8.86
CORE DEPOSITS	52.03	53.97	39	48.23	55.80	27	49.30	55.63	27	48.83	54.06	52.43	54.09
TIME DEP OF $100M OR MORE	13.79	10.44	70	16.37	11.83	77	15.69	11.64	77	15.77	12.54	10.98	10.54
DEPOSITS IN FOREIGN OFFICES	3.10	1.92	76	4.83	1.74	80	4.23	1.74	80	5.02	1.71	4.58	1.60
TOTAL DEPOSITS	68.91	70.03	42	69.43	72.39	37	69.21	72.02	37	69.62	71.49	67.99	69.67
FEDERAL FUNDS PURCH & REPOS	5.61	6.45	47	7.77	6.29	65	6.81	6.64	59	8.48	6.19	8.02	7.06
TOTAL FED HOME LOAN BORROWINGS	5.29	5.58	47	4.24	3.97	57	4.76	4.37	57	4.71	4.40	5.64	4.89
TOTAL OTH BORROWINGS	4.40	2.18	76	3.23	1.52	79	3.68	1.59	80	2.57	1.67	4.54	2.25
MEMO SHT TER N CORE FUNDING	24.07	26.67	46	28.25	24.45	69	26.93	24.42	67	28.36	24.63	24.93	23.59
ACCEPTANCES & OTHER LIABILITIES	2.53	1.56	83	2.79	1.62	80	2.77	1.66	81	2.20	1.73	2.24	1.86
TOTAL LIABILITIES (INCL MORTG)	86.74	88.82	23	87.46	89.02	23	87.23	88.83	26	87.58	89.22	88.43	89.41
SUBORDINATED NOTES & DEBENTURES	1.96	0.60	84	1.89	0.58	85	1.90	0.60	84	1.99	0.57	2.01	0.57
ALL COMMON & PREFERRED CAPITAL	11.30	10.39	68	10.65	10.21	63	10.87	10.39	63	10.42	10.01	9.56	9.83
TOTAL LIABILITIES & CAPITAL	100.00	100.00		100.01	100.00		99.99	100.00		99.99	100.00	100.00	100.00
MEMO ALL BROKERED DEPOSITS	8.44	3.74	81	9.74	3.60	85	9.45	3.49	83	9.69	3.55	6.52	3.01
INSURED BROKERED DEP	1.63	3.08	55	0.00	2.76	31	0.59	2.75	47	0.00	2.60	0.00	2.04
DIRECT & INDIRECT INV IN RE	0.00	0.01	79	0.00	0.01	79	0.00	0.01	78	0.00	0.01	0.00	0.01
LOANS HFS AS A % LOANS	5.28	1.04	90	9.59	1.33	92	8.40	1.35	90	8.69	1.38	8.04	1.28

Balance Sheet—Percentage Composition of Assets and Liabilities

This page presents the major components of assets, liabilities, and capital as a percentage of total assets. Averages used on this page are a year-to-date average of end-of-period balances, including the prior year-end. Thus, for December, an average would be composed of the balance at December for the prior year, March, June, September and December of the current year. Please note that the averages used on this page are not used for earnings analysis on pages 1, 3 and 12.

Assets, Percent of Average Assets

Loans Held For Sale

Average loans and leases held for sale as reported on schedule RC-C is divided by average total assets. Avaialble from March 31, 2002 forward.

Loans Not Held For Sale

Average loans and leases not held for sale as reported on schedule RC is divided by average total assets. Loans and leases not held for sale are displayed from March 31, 2001 forward while total loans and leases are displayed for earlier quarters.

Less: Loan & Lease Allowance

Average loan and lease allowance divided by average total assets.

Net Loans & Leases

Average loans and lease-financing receivables net of unearned income and loss allowances/reserves divided by average total assets.

Interest-Bearing Bank Balances

Average of all interest-bearing balances due from depository institutions divided by average total assets.

Federal Funds Sold & Resales

Average federal funds sold and securities purchased under agreements to resell divided by average total assets.

Trading Account Assets

Average trading account assets divided by average total assets.

Held-to-Maturity Securities

For March 31, 1994 and subsequent quarters, held-to-maturity securities are included. For prior periods, total securities excluding trading assets are used.

Available-for-Sale Securities

For March 31, 1994 and subsequent quarters, available-for-sale securities are shown.

Total Earning Assets

The sum of the averages for net loans and lease-financing receivables, held-to-maturity and available-for-sale securities, interest-bearing balances due from depository institutions, federal funds sold and resold, and trading-account securities, divided by average total assets.

Noninterest Cash & Due From Banks

Average Noninterest-bearing balances due from depository institutions, plus average currency and coin, divided by average total assets.

Premises, Fixed Assets & Capital Leases

Average bank premises, furniture and fixtures, equipment, and other assets representing bank premises (including capitalized leases) divided by average total assets.

Other Real Estate Owned

Average real estate owned other than bank premises divided by average total assets.

Acceptance & Other Assets

The sum of the average for customers liability to the bank on acceptances outstanding, investments in unconsolidated subsidiaries and associated companies, and all other assets not included above, divided by average total assets.

Subtotal

The amount of noninterest cash and due from depository institutions, premises, and fixed assets (including capitalized leases), other real estate owned, acceptances and other assets divided by average total assets.

Total Assets

The total of the various percentages listed above. In all instances, the figure should approximate 100 percent.

Standby Letters of Credit

Average standby letters of credit divided by average total assets.

Liabilities, Percent of Average Assets

Demand Deposits

Average demand deposits divided by average total assets.

All NOW and ATS Accounts

Average NOW and ATS accounts divided by average total assets. See the description of these accounts for UBPR Page 04.

Money Market Deposit Accounts

Average MMDAs divided by average total assets.

Other Savings Deposits

The average of all savings deposits other than MMDAs, divided by average total assets.

Time Deposits Under $100 Thousand

Average total time deposits of less

than $100 thousand, divided by average total assets.

Core Deposits

The average of total deposits, less time deposits of $100 thousand or more, less deposits in foreign offices, divided by average total assets.

Time Deposits of $100M or More

The sum of the averages for time certificates of deposit of $100 thousand or more and other time deposits in amounts of $100 thousand or more divided by average total assets.

Deposits in Foreign Offices

The average of total deposits in foreign offices (including both interest-bearing and Noninterest bearing), Edge and agreement subsidiaries, and IBFs, divided by average total assets.

Total Deposits

Sum of all deposit categories above.

Federal Funds Purch & Repos

Average federal funds purchased and securities sold under agreements to repurchase divided by average total assets.

Total Federal Home Loan Bank Borrowings

From March 31, 2001 forward includes information from schedule RC-M Five period average of Federal Home Loan Bank Borrowings with a remaining maturity of under one year

(RCFD2651) plus remaining maturity of one through 3 years (RCFDB565) plus remaining maturity of over three years (RCFDB566) expressed as a percentage of average total assets.

Total Other Borrowings

From March 31, 2001 forward includes information from schedule RC-M Five period average of Other Borrowed Money with a remaining maturity of under one year (RCFDB571) plus remaining maturity of one through 3 years (RCFDB567) plus remaining maturity of over three years (RCFDB568) expressed as a percentage of average total assets. For prior quarters includes Other Borrowed Money with a remaining maturity of under one year (RCFD2332) plus remaining maturity of one through three years (RCFDA547) plus remaining maturity of over three years (RCFDA548).

Memo: Short Term Noncore Funding

See definition on page 4 for this caption.

Acceptances & Other Liabilities

The sum of the averages for the bank's liability on acceptances executed and outstanding, mortgage indebtedness and liability for capitalized leases, and all other liabilities not included above, divided by average total assets.

Total Liabilities (Including Mortgages)

Average total liabilities (excluding notes and debentures subordinated

to deposits) divided by average total assets.

Subordinated Notes & Debentures

Average notes and debentures subordinated to deposits divided by average total assets.

All Common & Preferred Capital

Average of all preferred and common stock, surplus, undivided profits and capital reserves, and cumulative foreign currency translation adjustments, divided by average total assets.

Total Liabilities & Capital

The total of the various percentages listed above. In all instances, this figure should approximate 100 percent.

Memo: All Brokered Deposits

Average total brokered deposits divided by average assets.

Insured Brokered Dep

Average Brokered deposits issued in denominations less than $100,000 or participated out in shares less than $100,000 divided by average assets.

Direct and Indirect Investment in RE

Average direct and indirect investments in real estate ventures divided by average assets.

Loans Held for Sale

Loans held for sale as reported on schedule RC divided by average gross loans.

ANALYSIS OF CREDIT ALLOWANCE AND LOAN MIX

CHANGE CREDIT ALLOWANCE ($000)	06/30/2008	06/30/2007	12/31/2007	12/31/2006	12/31/2005
BEGINNING BALANCE	1,281,213	1,043,245	1,043,245	1,026,834	873,107
GROSS CREDIT LOSSES	677,849	196,422	514,039	355,960	314,130
MEMO LOANS HFS WRITEDOWN	0	2,234	2,234	0	0
RECOVERIES	58 199	45 273	91 185	109 835	115 700
NET CREDIT LOSSES	619,650	151,149	422,854	246,125	198,430
PROVISION FOR CREDIT LOSS	1,007,212	161,121	664,922	262,536	176,886
OTHER ADJUSTMENTS	0	-4 100	-4 100	0	175 271
ENDING BALANCE	1,668,775	1,049,117	1,281,213	1,043,245	1,026,834
AVERAGE TOTAL LOANS & LEASES	130,256,741	132,106,959	130,878,107	130,592,332	113,257,245

ANALYSIS RATIOS	BANK	PG 1	PCT	BANK	PG 1	PCT	BANK	PG 1	PCT	BANK	PG 1	BANK	PG 1
LOSS PROVISION TO AVERAGE ASSETS	1.19	0.79	78	0.18	0.16	64	0.38	0.28	72	0.15	0.13	0.11	0.13
RECOVERIES TO PRIOR CREDIT LOSS	22.64	24.78	52	25.44	37.01	39	25.62	41.22	36	34.96	38.27	39.34	37.73
NET LOSS TO AVERAGE TOTAL LN&LS	0.95	0.57	77	0.23	0.20	68	0.32	0.28	67	0.19	0.16	0.18	0.20
GROSS LOSS TO AVERAGE TOT LN&LS	1.04	0.62	77	0.30	0.26	62	0.39	0.35	64	0.27	0.23	0.28	0.28
RECOVERIES TO AVERAGE TOT LN&LS	0.09	0.07	71	0.07	0.07	59	0.07	0.07	61	0.08	0.07	0.10	0.09
LN&LS ALLOW TO LN&LS NOT HFS	1.33	1.43	51	0.88	1.13	20	1.04	1.22	31	0.86	1.13	0.89	1.17
LN&LS ALLOWANCE TO TOTAL LN&LS	1.28	1.41	48	0.80	1.09	19	0.97	1.20	23	0.78	1.09	0.80	1.13
LN&LS ALLOWANCE TO NET LOSSES (X)	1.35	4.18	19	3.47	11.12	24	3.03	7.24	28	4.24	10.82	5.17	10.50
LN&LS ALL TO NONACCURAL LN&LS (X)	0.67	1.72		1.43	3.56		0.90	2.50		2.08	4.16	3.79	3.68
EARN COVER OF NET LN&LS LOSS (X)	2.75	8.62	28	10.72	36.52	34	7.23	17.37	32	13.62	32.42	15.63	35.22
NET LOSSES BY TYPE OF LN&LS													
REAL ESTATE LOANS	1.22	0.48	85	0.17	0.08	81	0.28	0.13	82	0.06	0.05	0.06	0.05
LOANS TO FINANCE COMML REAL EST	0.02	0.10	79	0.00	0.02	88	0.00	0.07	80	0.00	0.00	0.00	0.00
CONTRUCTION & LAND DEV	0.87	1.07	60	0.02	0.05	61	0.08	0.21	51	0.00	0.03	0.06	0.01
1-4 FAMILY CONSTRUCTION	1.41	1.66	66	0.04	0.06	71	0.11	0.27	55	N/A	N/A	N/A	N/A
OTHER CONST & LAND	0.25	0.66	56	0.00	0.04	66	0.04	0.14	59	N/A	N/A	N/A	N/A
SECURED BY FARMLAND	0.00	0.02	85	0.00	-0.01	90	0.00	0.01	85	0.00	0.02	0.00	0.01
SINGLE & MULTI FAMILY MORTGAGE	1.54	0.34	91	0.23	0.08	86	0.38	0.12	88	0.08	0.05	0.07	0.05
HOME EQUITY LOANS	2.43	0.48	91	0.52	0.13	93	0.75	0.16	94	0.16	0.08	0.16	0.05
1-4 FAMILY NONREVOLVING	1.21	0.29	91	0.14	0.07	80	0.25	0.10	84	0.05	0.04	0.04	0.06
MULTIFAMILY LOANS	0.00	0.12	68	0.00	0.02	79	0.00	0.05	69	0.00	0.02	0.00	0.02
NONFARM NONRESIDENTIAL MTG	0.02	0.09	55	0.02	0.03	66	0.02	0.05	55	0.02	0.03	0.01	0.04
OWNER OCCUPIED NONFARM NONRESI	0.04	0.07	66	0.00	0.03	64	0.01	0.04	62	N/A	N/A	N/A	N/A
OTHER NONFARM NONRESIDENTIAL	-0.01	0.09	5	0.05	0.02	81	0.02	0.04	60	N/A	N/A	N/A	N/A
RE LOANS IN FOREIGN OFFICES	N/A	0.05	N/A	N/A	0.03	N/A	N/A	0.04	N/A	N/A	0.27	N/A	-0 04
AGRICULTURAL LOANS	0.00	0.02	78	0.00	0.03	78	0.00	0.06	68	0.00	0.03	0.00	0.02
COMMERCIAL AND INDUSTRIAL LOANS	0.34	0.62	37	0.25	0.27	58	0.30	0.37	55	0.46	0.30	0.13	0.28
LEASE FINANCING	0.02	0.23	50	0.32	0.16	80	0.15	0.22	65	0.02	-0.02	0.50	0.33
LOANS TO INDIVIDUALS	1.13	1.20	55	0.44	0.73	43	0.60	0.86	47	0.33	0.65	0.58	0.92
CREDIT CARD PLANS	2.81	3.37	44	-11.03	2.79	2	0.16	2.44	23	N/A	1.96	N/A	2.08
ALL OTHER LOANS & LEASES	1.01	0.37	84	0.73	0.23	86	0.89	0.34	84	0.82	0.27	0.85	0.22
LOANS TO FOREIGN GOVERNMENTS	0.00	0.06	86	0.00	-0.24	94	0.00	-0.16	94	0.00	0.00	0.00	0.01

UBPR Page 07

Analysis of Credit Allowance and Loan Mix

The top portion of this page presents data regarding the allowance for loan and lease financing receivables losses. The dollar figures provide a reconcilement of changes to the reserve from schedule RI-B, and the ratios are provided to highlight trends and permit assessment of the adequacy of the reserve.

The bottom portion of page 7 presents net loan losses by type of loan. For each type of loan, the charge off rate is annualized. Negative values for those ratios indicate net recoveries.

Page 7 A presents a detailed analysis of the loan portfolio mix.

Change: Credit Allowance ($000)

Beginning Balance

Balance of the allowance for possible loan and lease losses at the beginning of the year. From March 31, 1998 includes credit transactions. Prior periods include loan and lease activity only.

Gross Credit Losses

Gross amount of loan and lease losses year to date. From March 31, 1998 includes credit transactions. Prior periods include loan and lease activity only. Note that gross credit losses includes the writedown taken on loans held for sale. This item is added back to allow reconcilement with loan loss data by type of loan as reported on schedule RI-B, section a.

Memo: Loans Held For Sale Writedown

Writedown arising from transfer of loans to a held for sale status as reported on schedule RI-B, section b.

Recoveries

Gross amount of recoveries on previ-

ously charged off loans and leases year to date.

From March 31, 1998 includes credit transactions. Prior periods include loan and lease activity only.

Net Credit Losses

Gross loan and lease losses less gross loan and lease recoveries. From March 31, 1998 includes credit transactions. Prior periods include loan and lease activity only.

Provision for Credit Losses

Bank's provision for possible loan and lease losses charged to current operating expenses for the year to date. From March 31, 1998 includes credit transactions. Prior periods include loan and lease activity only.

Other Adjustments

Amount of other increases (decreases) in the reserve, including changes incident to mergers and absorption. From March 31, 1998 includes credit transactions. Prior periods include loan and lease activity only.

Ending Balance

Beginning balance, minus net loan and lease losses, plus the provision for credit losses and other adjustments. From March 31, 1998 includes credit transactions. Prior periods include loan and lease activity only.

Average Total Loans and Leases

Average total loans for the first reporting period of the year and for each subsequent reporting period divided by the number of reporting periods plus lease financing receivables outstanding as of the last reporting period (December 31) of the preceding year and for each reporting period during the year divided by the number of reporting periods. See Section II, Technical Information, for more information concerning the calculation of averages.

Analysis Ratios

Loss Provision to Average Assets

Provisions for possible credit losses divided by average assets. From March 31, 1998 includes credit transactions. Prior periods include loan and lease activity only.

Recoveries to Prior-Period Losses

Gross credit recoveries in the current year divided by gross credit losses of the preceding year. From March 31, 1998 includes credit transactions. Prior periods include loan and lease activity only.

Net Loss to Average Total Loan & Lease

Gross loan and lease charge offs, less gross recoveries, divided by average total loans and leases. If gross recoveries exceed gross losses, NA is shown at this caption.

Gross Loss to Average Total Loans & Leases

Gross loan and lease losses divided by average total loans and leases.

Recoveries to Average Total Loans & Leases

Gross loan and lease recoveries divided by average total loans and leases.

Loan & Lease Allowance to Loans & Leases Not Held For Sale

Ending balance of the allowance for possible loan and lease losses divided by total loans and lease-financing receivables not held for sale. Available from March 31, 2001 forward.

Loan and Lease Allowance to Total Loans & Leases

The ending balance of the allowance for loan and lease losses divided by total loans and leases.

Loan and Lease Allowance to Net Losses (X)

The ending balance of the allowance for loan and lease losses divided by net loan and lease losses. If gross loss recoveries exceed gross losses, NA is shown at this caption.

Loan and Lease Allowance to Nonaccrual Loan & Lease (X)

The ending balance of the allowance for loan and lease losses divided by the aggregate amount of nonaccrual loans and leases.

Earnings Coverage of Net Losses (X)

Net operating income before taxes, securities gains or losses, and extraordinary items, plus the provision for possible loan and lease losses divided by net loan and lease losses. If gross recoveries exceed gross losses, NA is shown at this caption.

Net Losses by Type of Loan and Lease

Each of these ratios consists of the year to date net loss (change offs less recoveries from Schedule RI-B) for that type of loan divided by the year to date average for that type of loan. Charge off rates are annualized. Negative values for these ratios indicate net recoveries. The loan definitions follow those used for RI-B. As a consequence averages used will come from 4 period average of schedule RC-K when available or 5 period average from schedule RC-C. Ratio definitions give source of average loans by category of loans.

Real Estate Loans

Average real estate loans from RC-K used.

Loans to Finance Commercial Real Estate

Average loans to finance commercial real estate from RC-C.

Construction and Land Dev

Construction and land development loans from schedule RC-C.

1–4 Family Construction

Construction loans secured by 1–4 family properties from schedule RC-C.

Other Construction

Construction loans secured by other real estate properties from RC-C.

Secured by Farmland

Real estate loans secured by farmland from RC-C.

Single and Multifamily Mortgage

One to four and five or more family residential mortgages from RC-C.

Home Equity Loans

Home equity loans on 1–4 family residential mortgages from RC-C.

1–4 Family Nonrevolving

All other loans secured by 1–4 family residential properties from RC-C.

Multifamily Loans

Five or more multifamily residential mortgages from RC-C

Nonfarm Nonresidential Mtg

Nonfarm nonresidential mortgages from RC-C.

Owner Occupied Nonfarm Nonresidential

Loans secured by owner occupied nonfarm nonresidential properties from schedule RC-C.

Other Nonfarm Nonresidential

Loans secured by other nonfarm nonresidential mortgages from schedule RC-C.

RE Loans in Foreign Offices

Average real estate loans in foreign offices from RC-C used.

Agricultural Loans

Average agricultural loans from RC-K used.

Commercial and Industrial Loans

Average commercial and industrial loans from RC-K used.

Lease Financing

Average lease financing form RC-K used.

Loans to Individuals

Average loans to individuals from RC-K used.

Credit Card Plans

From March 31, 2001 forward average from RC-K is used for all banks. Prior to March 31, 2001 average credit card loans from RC C for FFIEC 031 and 032 filers and RC K for 033 and 034 filers.

All Other Loans and Leases

From March 31, 2001 forward for banks filing call form 041 derived from RC-K: average total loans less loans secured by real estate, commercial and industrial loans and loans to individuals. For prior quarters available for banks filing call form 031 and 032.

From March 31, 2001 forward for banks filing call form 031 derived from RC-K: average total loans less loans secured by real estate, commercial and industrial loans, loans to individuals and loans to finance agricultural production.

For quarters prior to March 31, 2001 for banks filing call form 031 or 032 derived from RC-K: average total loans less loans secured by real estate, commercial and industrial loans, loans to individuals and loans to finance agricultural production.

Loans to Foreign Governments

Average loans to foreign governments from RC-C for FFIEC 031 and 032 filers.

ANALYSIS OF LOAN AND LEASE ALLOWANCE AND LOAN MIX

	06/30/2008			06/30/2007			12/31/2007			12/31/2006		12/31/2005	
LOAN MIX, % AVERAGE GROSS LN&LS	BANK	PG 1	PCT	BANK	PG 1	PCT	BANK	PG 1	PCT	BANK	PG 1	BANK	PG 1
CONTRUCTION & DEVELOPMENT	10.25	11.98	48	10.73	11.06	55	10.73	11.75	52	9.75	9.66	7.59	7.87
1-4 FAMILY CONSTRUCTION	5.49	3.40	72	6.41	3.42	77	6.32	3.46	74	N/A	N/A	N/A	N/A
OTHER CONST & LAND DEVEL	4.75	8.25	35	4.42	7.37	41	4.46	7.91	39	N/A	N/A	N/A	N/A
1 - 4 FAMILY RESIDENTIAL	40.63	22.59	86	43.52	24.43	85	42.79	23.80	85	43.01	25.45	40.66	27.57
HOME EQUITY LOANS	11.61	4.47	89	10.72	4.44	86	10.94	4.34	88	10.62	4.66	10.49	5.31
OTHER REAL ESTATE LOANS	9.88	23.33	18	9.54	22.73	21	9.58	23.45	17	9.59	22.97	10.10	20.91
FARMLAND	0.11	0.51	40	0.10	0.49	42	0.10	0.51	38	0.11	0.44	0.12	0.44
MULTIFAMILY	0.59	1.88	22	0.56	1.82	23	0.55	1.91	22	0.63	2.02	0.68	1.99
NONFARM NONRESIDENTIAL	9.18	19.93	18	8.88	18.28	22	8.93	19.82	18	8.85	18.15	9.30	17.62
OWNER OCCUPIED NFARM NRESID	6.14	7.38	41	5.85	6.95	42	5.94	7.53	40	N/A	N/A	N/A	N/A
OTHER NONFARM NONRESIDENTIAL	3.04	10.97	14	3.05	10.76	18	3.01	10.82	16	N/A	N/A	N/A	N/A
TOTAL REAL ESTATE	60.75	63.62	37	63.79	64.05	41	63.11	64.51	39	62.35	63.63	58.34	62.91
FINANCIAL INSTITUTION LOANS	0.06	0.22	67	0.06	0.14	73	0.06	0.16	71	0.08	0.17	0.08	0.18
AGRICULTURAL LOANS	0.08	0.33	54	0.08	0.32	54	0.08	0.34	53	0.09	0.31	0.12	0.32
COMMERCIAL & INDUSTRIAL LOANS	19.72	19.84	57	18.02	19.06	54	18.07	19.31	51	18.54	18.63	19.76	18.43
LOANS TO INDIVIDUALS	9.75	6.22	71	9.68	7.06	65	9.74	6.59	68	10.49	7.17	12.58	8.06
CREDIT CARD LOANS	0.28	0.40	73	0.00	0.39	55	0.10	0.39	63	0.00	0.40	0.00	0.41
MUNICIPAL LOANS	1.71	0.48	88	1.81	0.46	90	1.77	0.50	89	1.75	0.44	1.99	0.39
FOREIGN OFFICE LOANS & LEASES	0.00	0.49	81	0.00	0.41	81	0.00	0.44	81	0.00	0.43	0.00	0.42
ALL OTHER LOANS	3.78	1.49	82	3.12	1.38	83	3.54	1.43	84	3.57	1.59	4.02	1.32
LEASE FINANCING RECEIVABLES	4.14	1.13	86	3.45	1.18	82	3.63	1.17	84	3.13	1.25	3.11	1.37
SUPPLEMENTAL													
LOANS TO FOREIGN GOVERNMENTS	0.03	0.00	96	0.02	0.00	94	0.02	0.00	94	0.02	0.00	0.03	0.00
LOANS TO FINANCE COMML REAL EST	1.22	0.56	79	1.05	0.48	78	1.09	0.50	79	0.95	0.39	1.23	0.30
MEMORANDUM (% OF AVG TOT LOANS)													
LOAN & LEASE COMMITMENTS	67.34	38.99	84	65.82	44.42	79	66.73	40.77	82	76.57	43.57	73.53	44.98
OFFICER, SHAREHOLDER LOANS	0.07	0.63	37	0.13	0.62	40	0.14	0.64	41	0.22	0.64	0.27	0.64
OFFICER, SHAREH LOANS TO ASSETS	0.05	0.43	38	0.09	0.40	41	0.10	0.42	45	0.15	0.40	0.19	0.39
OTHER REAL ESTATE OWNED % ASSETS													
CONSTRUCTION & LAND DEVELOPMENT	0.01	0.02	58	0.00	0.00	75	0.01	0.01	78	0.00	0.00	0.00	0.00
FARMLAND	0.00	N/A	97	0.00	N/A	97	0.00	N/A	96	0.00	N/A	0.00	N/A
1-4 FAMILY	0.14	0.03	91	0.04	0.01	86	0.06	0.02	86	0.02	0.01	0.01	0.01
MULTIFAMILY	0.00	0.00	86	0.00	0.00	93	0.00	0.00	89	0.00	0.00	0.00	N/A
NONFARM NONRESID	0.0	0.0	65	0.0	0.0	73	0.0	0.0	7:	0.0	0.01	0.01	0.01
FORECLOSED GNMA	0.03	0.00	96	0.02	0.00	96	0.02	0.00	96	0.01	0.00	N/A	N/A
FOREIGN OFFICES	0.00	N/A	95	0.00	0.00	94	0.00	N/A	95	0.00	0.00	0.00	0.00
SUBTOTAL	0.18	0.09	80	0.07	0.04	79	0.09	0.05	80	0.04	0.03	0.02	0.03
DIRECT AND INDIRECT INV	0.00	0.00	88	0.00	0.00	88	0.00	0.00	88	0.00	0.00	0.00	0.00
TOTAL	0.18	0.10	77	0.07	0.05	72	0.09	0.06	73	0.04	0.04	0.02	0.04
ASSET SERVICING % ASSETS													
MORTG SERV W RECOURSE	0.10	0.03	85	0.12	0.05	84	0.11	0.04	84	0.14	0.09	0.18	0.08
MORTG SERV WO RECOURSE	72.02	6.16	95	63.97	6.16	96	65.33	6.68	95	49.93	6.52	59.38	6.74
OTHER FINANCIAL ASSETS	0.33	1.48	61	0.35	1.09	65	0.34	1.27	62	0.36	1.01	0.01	1.03
TOTAL	72.45	9.56	93	64.44	9.16	93	65.78	9.97	93	50.43	9.50	59.57	10.29

UBPR Page 07A

Analysis of Loan and Lease Allowance and Loan Mix

Loan Mix % Average Gross Loans

Loans are distributed by category as a percent of average gross loans. Loans are averaged using the ending balance for the prior year-end plus the interim quarters for the current year. Data comes from report of condition schedule RC-C. Details on individual categories are provided only where call items are combined, otherwise report of condition definitions apply to individual categories of loans.

If bank has foreign offices (FFIEC 031 filer), then categories represent balances in domestic offices only, with loans booked in foreign offices shown as a separate category. Otherwise balances are consolidated for the bank.

Construction and Land Development

1–4 Family Construction

Construction loans secured by 1–4 family properties.

Other Construction

Construction loans secured by other real estate properties.

1–4 Family Residential

Home Equity

Also included in 1–4 family residential.

Other Real Estate Loans

Includes the following categories of loans.

Farmland

Loans secured by farmland.

Multifamily

Secured by multifamily (5 or more) residential properties.

Nonfarm Nonresidential

Owner Occupied Nonfarm Nonresidential

Loans secured by owner occupied nonfarm nonresidential properties.

Other Nonfarm Nonresidential

Loans secured by other nonfarm nonresidential mortgages.

Total Real Estate

Total of previous real estate loan categories.

Financial Institution Loans

Loans to depository institutions.

Agricultural Loans

Loans to Finance agricultural production and other loans to farmers.

Commercial and Industrial Loans

Loans to Individuals

Other loans including single payment, installment.

Credit Card Loans

Municipal Loans

Obligations other than securities to state and local political subdivisions in the U.S.

Acceptances of Other Banks

Foreign Office Loans

For banks filing FFIEC 031 form. Represents the difference between consolidated bank loans and leases and loans and leases in domestic offices.

All Other Loans

Other loans, loans for purchasing and carrying securities and loans to foreign governments.

Lease Financing Receivables

Supplemental

The following categories of loans are included in previous loan mix captions.

Loans to Foreign Governments

Loans to foreign governments. Available for all banks from March 31, 2001 forward. Available Prior to March 31, 2001 for FFIEC 033, 032, 031 filers. Includes domestic and foreign office loans.

Loans to Finance Commercial Real Estate

Loans to finance commercial real estate, construction and development not secured by real estate.

Memorandum (% of Average Total Loans):

Loan & Lease Commitments

Outstanding commitments to make or purchase loans or to extend credit in the form of lease-financing arrangements divided by average total loans.

Officer, Shareholder Loans

Extension of credit to the bank's executive officers, principal shareholders, and their related interest as of the report date divided by average total loans.

Officer, Shareholder Loans to Assets

Extension of credit to the bank's executive officers, principal shareholders, and their related interest divided by total assets.

Other Real Estate Owned % Assets

Provides a distribution of other real estate owned by type property from report of condition RC-M. Average individual categories are divided by average assets.

Construction & Land Development

Construction and land development in domestic offices.

Farmland

Farmland in domestic offices.

1–4 Family

1–4 Family residential property in domestic offices.

Multifamily

Multifamily (5 or more) in domestic offices.

Nonfarm Nonresidential

Nonfarm nonresidential properties in domestic offices.

Foreign Offices

Other real estate owned booked in foreign offices (031 filers only).

Forclosed GNMA

Property securing GNMA mortgages.

Subtotal

Sum of above other real estate owned.

Direct and Indirect Investments

Direct and indirect investments in other real estate ventures.

Total

Total of other real estate owned and direct and indirect investment in real estate ventures.

Asset Servicing % Assets

Provides a distribution of asset servicing by type as a percent of average assets.

Mortgages Serviced With Recourse

Available from March 31, 2001 forward. Principal balance of mortgages serviced with recourse or other servicer provided enhancements as percent of total assets.

Mortgages Serviced Without Recourse

Available from March 31, 2001 forward. Principal balance of mortgages serviced without recourse or other servicer provided enhancements as percent of total assets.

Other Financial Assets

Available from March 31, 2001 forward. Balance of other financial assets as percent of total assets.

Total

Total of above categories as a percent of total assets.

ANALYSIS OF CONCENTRATIONS OF CREDIT

	06/30/2008			06/30/2007			12/31/2007			12/31/2006		12/31/2005	
LOAN & LSE % TOTAL CAPITAL	BANK	PG 1	PCT	BANK	PG 1	PCT	BANK	PG 1	PCT	BANK	PG 1	BANK	PG 1
CONTRUCTION & DEVELOPMENT	78.84	89.46	50	83.64	82.35	57	81.31	89.25	52	79.60	75.00	67.02	61.46
1-4 FAMILY CONSTRUCTION	37.50	25.07	71	49.47	24.07	80	46.71	24.91	76	N/A	N/A	N/A	N/A
OTHER CONST & LAND DEVEL	41.33	61.43	39	34.17	54.31	42	34.60	60.86	39	N/A	N/A	N/A	N/A
1 - 4 FAMILY RESIDENTIAL	294.33	166.85	86	329.15	173.08	86	325.25	170.77	86	333.57	173.60	333.02	193.26
HOME EQUITY LOANS	90.96	34.07	90	82.97	31.69	88	88.01	32.52	89	80.80	31.62	82.73	37.00
OTHER REAL ESTATE LOANS	77.27	180.88	21	73.37	164.74	23	74.72	176.08	20	72.01	162.80	75.94	155.63
FARMLAND	0.81	3.97	39	0.71	3.68	41	0.80	3.87	39	0.84	3.11	0.88	3.24
MULTIFAMILY	4.86	14.75	26	4.18	13.37	26	4.22	14.33	22	4.41	13.76	5.45	13.69
NONFARM NONRESIDENTIAL	71.59	153.89	22	68.49	133.18	24	69.70	149.28	21	66.77	130.54	69.60	125.83
OWNER OCCUPIED NFARM NRESID	47.19	56.95	45	45.12	50.82	47	46.91	57.01	42	N/A	N/A	N/A	N/A
OTHER NONFARM NONRESIDENTIAL	24.40	85.64	17	23.36	77.30	20	22.78	80.60	18	N/A	N/A	N/A	N/A
TOTAL REAL ESTATE	450.43	479.30	37	486.16	461.45	49	481.28	476.32	43	485.17	449.20	475.98	447.79
FINANCIAL INSTITUTION LOANS	0.61	1.40	71	0.45	0.83	75	0.34	1.09	71	0.49	0.89	0.59	0.88
AGRICULTURAL LOANS	0.53	2.49	55	0.58	2.37	55	0.63	2.49	56	0.68	2.21	0.72	2.28
COMMERCIAL & INDUSTRIAL LOANS	161.00	138.72	65	135.02	128.42	55	141.40	135.87	52	141.01	123.80	140.61	121.28
LOANS TO INDIVIDUALS	74.44	44.09	72	72.91	48.22	70	76.28	46.32	72	74.33	48.54	92.53	54.55
CREDIT CARD LOANS	2.26	2.65	75	0.08	2.61	57	2.07	2.81	73	0.00	2.74	0.00	2.84
MUNICIPAL LOANS	13.12	3.61	88	13.59	3.36	91	12.95	3.80	89	13.81	3.17	13.35	2.85
FOREIGN OFFICE LOANS & LEASES	0.00	2.73	81	0.00	2.37	81	0.00	2.76	81	0.00	2.32	0.00	2.37
ALL OTHER LOANS	22.14	9.79	84	25.46	8.76	85	37.28	9.72	91	23.76	8.74	32.67	7.90
LEASE FINANCING RECEIVABLES	33.79	7.51	89	28.47	7.37	88	30.72	7.93	87	24.86	7.51	23.39	8.51
SUPPLEMENTAL													
LOANS TO FOREIGN GOVERNMENTS	0.20	0.00	96	0.17	0.00	94	0.23	0.00	96	0.16	0.00	0.20	0.01
LOANS TO FINANCE COMM REAL EST	9.70	3.69	82	8.69	3.33	82	9.08	3.68	79	7.63	2.69	7.56	1.92
NONOWNER OCC COMML RE % TOT CAP	117.80	216.98	27	119.87	198.04	30	117.39	210.69	25	N/A	N/A	N/A	N/A
TOTAL COMML REAL ESTATE % TOT CAP	165.00	284.30	26	164.99	259.19	30	164.30	279.17	25	N/A	N/A	N/A	N/A
CONSTRUCTION & DEVEL % TOT LNS	10.43	11.76	48	10.97	11.35	55	10.41	11.77	50	N/A	N/A	N/A	N/A
NONOWNER OCC COMML RE % TOT LNS	15.58	28.67	23	15.72	27.42	28	15.03	28.06	21	N/A	N/A	N/A	N/A
TOTAL COMML REAL ESTATE % TOT LNS	21.82	37.55	26	21.63	35.94	28	21.04	37.24	24	N/A	N/A	N/A	N/A

UBPR Page 07B

Analysis of Concentrations of Credit

Loans and Leases as Percentage of Total Capital

Loans are distributed by category as a percent of tier one capital plus the allowance for loan and lease losses. Data for loans comes from call report schedule RC-C, Total Capital comes from RC-R RCFD 3792.

Construction and Land Development

Construction, land development and other land loans (RCON 1415) as a percent of Total Capital RCFD 3792.

1–4 Family Construction

Construction loans secured by 1–4 family properties as a percent of Total Capital RCFD 3792.

Other Construction

Construction loans secured by other real estate properties as a percent of Total Capital RCFD 3792.

1–4 Family Residential

Closed end loans secured by 1–4 family residential properties First liens (RCON 5367) plus Junior liens (RCON 5368) plus Revolving open end loans (RCON 1797) as a percent of Total Capital RCFD 3792.

Home Equity

Revolving open end loans (RCON 1797) as a percent of Total Capital RCFD 3792.

Other Real Estate Loans

Loans secured by farmland (RCON 1420) plus Secured by multifamily residential properties (RCON 1460) plus Secured by nonfarm nonresidential properties (RCON1480) as a percent of Total Capital RCFD 3792.

Farmland

Loans secured by farmland (RCON 1420) as a percent of Total Capital RCFD 3792.

Multifamily

Secured by multifamily residential properties (RCON 1460) as a percent of Total Capital RCFD 3792.

Nonfarm Nonresidentialial

Secured by nonfarm nonresidential properties (RCON 1480) as a percent of Total Capital RCFD 3792.

Owner Occupied Nonfarm Nonresidential

Loans secured by owner occupied nonfarm nonresidential properties as a percent of Total Capital RCFD 3792.

Other Nonfarm Nonresidential

Loans secured by other nonfarm non-residential mortgages as a percent of Total Capital RCFD 3792.

Total Real Estate

Construction, land development and other land loans (RCON 1415) plus Closed end loans secured by 1–4 family residential properties First liens (RCON 5367) plus Junior liens (RCON 5368) plus Revolving open end loans (RCON1797) plus Loans secured by farmland (RCON 1420) plus Secured by multifamily residential properties (RCON 1460) plus Secured by nonfarm nonresidential properties (RCON 1480) as a percent of Total Capital RCFD 3792.

Financial Institution Loans

For banks filing FFIEC 041 Loans to Commercial Banks in the U.S. (RCON 1288) as a percent of Total Capital RCFD 3792.

For banks filing FFIEC 031 Commercial banks in the U.S. (RCON B531) plus Other depository institutions in the U.S. (RCON B534) plus Banks in foreign countries (RCON B535) as a percent of Total Capital RCFD 3792.

Agricultural Loans

For banks filing FFIEC 031 Loans to finance agricultural production in domestic offices (RCON 1590) as a percent of Total Capital RCFD 3792.

For banks filing FFIEC 041 Loans to finance agricultural production (RCFD 1590) as a percent of Total Capital RCFD 3792.

Commercial and Industrial Loans

For banks filing FFIEC 031 Commercial and Industrial Loans to U.S. addressees in domestic offices (RCON 1763) plus Commercial and industrial loans to non-U.S. addressees in domestic offices (RCON 1764) as a percent of Total Capital RCFD 3792.

For banks filing FFIEC 041 Commercial and industrial loans (RCON 1766) as a percent of Total Capital RCFD 3792.

Loans to Individuals

For banks filing FFIEC 031 Credit card plans in domestic offices (RCON B538) plus Other revolving credit plans in domestic offices (RCON B539) plus Other consumer loans in domestic offices (RCON 2011) as a percent of Total Capital RCFD 3792.

For banks filing FFIEC 041 Credit card plans (RCON B538) plus Other revolving credit plans (RCON B539) plus Other consumer loans (RCON 2011) as a percent of Total Capaital RCFD 3792.

Credit Card Loans

For banks filing FFIEC 031 Credit card plans in domestic offices (RCON B538) as a percent of Total Capital RCFD 3792.

For banks filing FFIEC 041 Credit card plans (RCON B538) as a percent of Total Capital RCFD 3792.

Municipal Loans

For banks filing FFIEC 031 Obligations of states and political subdivisions in the U.S. in domestic offices (RCON 2107) as a percent of Total Capital RCFD 3792.

For banks filing FFIEC 041 Obligations of states and political subdivisions in the U.S (RCON 2107) as a percent of Total Capital RCFD 3792.

Acceptances of Other Banks

For banks filing FFIEC 031 or 032 and report dates prior to March 31, 2001 Acceptances of U.S. banks in domestic offices (RCON 1756) plus Acceptances of foreign banks in U.S. offices (RCON 1757) as a percent of Total Capital RCFD 3792.

For banks filing FFIEC 033 and 034 and report dates prior to March 31, 2001 Acceptances of U.S. banks (RCON 1755) as a percent of Total Capital RCFD 3792.

Foreign Office Loans

For banks filing FFIEC 031 Total loans and leases consolidated bank (RCFD 2122) less Total loans and leases domestic offices (RCFD 2122) as a percent of Total Capital RCFD 3792.

All Other Loans

For banks filing FFIEC 031 Loans to foreign governments in domestic offices (RCON 2081) plus Loans for purchasing and carrying securities in domestic offices (RCON 1545) plus All other loans (RCON 1564) as a percent of Total Capital RCFD 3792.

For banks filing FFIEC 041 Loans to foreign governments in domestic offices (RCON 2081) plus All other loans (RCON 1564) as a percent of Total Capital RCFD 3792.

Lease Financing Receivables

For banks filing FFIEC 031 Lease financing receivables in domestic offices (RCON 2165) as a percent of Total Capital RCFD 3792.

For banks filing FFIEC 041 Lease financing receivables (RCON 2165) as a percent of Total Capital 3792.

Supplemental

The following categories of loans are included in previous concentration captions.

Loans to Foreign Governments

For banks filing FFIEC 031 Loans to foreign governments in domestic offices (RCON 2081) as a percent of Total Capital RCFD 3792.

For banks filing FFIEC 041 Loans to foreign governments (RCON 2081) as a percent of Total Capital RCFD 3792.

Loans to Finance Commercial Real Estate

Loans to finance commercial real estate, construction and development not secured by real estate (RCFD 2746) as a percent of Total Capital RCFD 3792.

Construction and Land Development Loans as % of Total Risk-Based Capital

Construction & Land Development Loans (RCON 1415)/Total Risk-based Capital (RCFD or RCON 3792).

Nonowner Occupied Commercial Real Estate Loans as % of Total Risk-Based Capital

Construction & Land Development Loans (RCON 1415) + Multifamily Property Loans (RCON 1460) + Nonowner Occupied Nonfarm Nonresidential Property Loans (RCON F161) + Loans To Finance CRE not secured by Real Estate. (RCON 2746)/Total Risk-Based Capital (RCFD or RCON 3792).

Nonowner Occupied Commercial Real Estate Loans as % of Total Loans

Construction & Land Development Loans (RCON 1415) + Multifamily Loans (RCON 1460) + Other Loans Secured by Nonfarm Nonresidential Properties (RCON F161) + Loans to Finance CRE not secured by Real Estate. (RCON 2746)/Total Loans (RCFD or RCON 2122).

Total Commercial Real Estate Loans as % of Total Risk-Based Capital

Construction & Land Development Loans (RCON 1415) + Multifamily Property Loans (RCON 1460) + Nonfarm Nonresidential Property Loans (RCON 1480) + Loans to Finance CRE not secured by Real Estate. (RCON 2746)/Total Risk-Based Capital (RCFD or RCON 3792).

	06/30/2008	06/30/2007	12/31/2007	12/31/2006	12/31/2005
NONCURRENT LN&LS ($000)					
90 DAYS AND OVER PAST DUE	753,535	448,981	610,947	351,460	371,318
TOTAL NONACCRUAL LN&LS	2,499,442	735,899	1,429,242	502,600	270,796
TOTAL NONCURRENT LN&LS	3,252,977	1,184,880	2,040,189	854,060	642,114
LN&LS 30-89 DAYS PAST DUE	1,799,657	1,279,247	1,883,651	1,127,784	938,493
RESTRUCTURED LN&LS 90+ DAYS P/D	1,768	0	0	0	0
RESTRUCTURED LN&LS NONACCRL	0	0	0	0	0
RESTRUCTURED LN&LS 30-89 DAYS PD	23,358	0	0	0	0
CURRENT 1-4 FAMILY RESTRUC LN&LS	105,788	N/A	N/A	N/A	N/A
CURRENT OTHER RESTRUCTURED LN&LS	0	0	0	0	139
LOANS SECURED 1-4 RE IN FORECLOSURE	1,034,643	N/A	N/A	N/A	N/A
ALL OTHER REAL ESTATE OWNED	308,897	124,388	204,020	75,022	38,043

% OF NONCURR LN&LS BY LN TYPE	BANK	PG 1	PCT	BANK	PG 1	PCT	BANK	PG 1	PCT	BANK	PG 1	BANK	PG 1
REAL ESTATE LNS-90+ DAYS P/D	0.66	0.17	88	0.35	0.09	88	0.47	0.13	91	0.27	0.08	0.25	0.08
-NONACCRUAL	3.02	1.70	80	0.75	0.56	71	1.61	0.88	81	0.45	0.40	0.22	0.35
-TOTAL	3.68	2.03	82	1.11	0.70	76	2.08	1.08	84	0.71	0.54	0.47	0.48
-30-89 DAYS P/D	1.69	1.00	80	0.98	0.61	79	1.67	1.00	82	0.94	0.67	0.51	0.58
LNS FIN COML RE-90+ DAYS P/D	0.00	0.01	85	0.01	0.02	87	0.00	0.00	89	0.00	0.00	0.01	0.00
-NONACCRUAL	0.04	0.27	70	0.02	0.06	78	0.03	0.13	74	0.04	0.03	0.03	0.05
-TOTAL	0.04	0.32	66	0.03	0.16	75	0.03	0.16	70	0.04	0.06	0.04	0.07
-30-89 DAYS P/D	0.07	0.42	65	1.54	0.21	91	0.02	0.27	64	0.08	0.17	0.25	0.28
CONST & LAND DEV-90+ DAYS P/D	1.58	0.20	93	0.15	0.06	82	0.77	0.10	93	0.15	0.03	0.21	0.03
-NONACCRUAL	5.24	4.35	64	0.56	0.69	56	2.17	1.67	66	0.29	0.35	0.22	0.18
-TOTAL	6.82	4.72	71	0.70	0.80	52	2.95	1.85	72	0.44	0.42	0.43	0.26
-30-89 DAYS P/D	3.25	1.52	84	2.11	0.74	89	3.70	1.41	87	2.17	0.72	0.93	0.52
1-4 FAM CONS & L DEV-90+ DAYS	2.93	0.19	97	0.21	0.11	81	1.09	0.15	91	N/A	N/A	N/A	N/A
-NONACCRUAL	8.97	6.20	70	0.82	0.79	62	3.26	2.36	65	N/A	N/A	N/A	N/A
-TOTAL	11.90	6.62	75	1.03	1.00	60	4.34	2.65	61	N/A	N/A	N/A	N/A
-30-89 DAYS P/D	5.80	1.92	89	3.22	1.04	86	6.01	1.72	91	N/A	N/A	N/A	N/A
OTHER CONST & LAND DEV-90+ DAYS	0.36	0.17	81	0.05	0.71	N/A	0.35	1.34	N/A	N/A	N/A	N/A	N/A
-NONACCRUAL	1.85	3.26	45	0.18	0.57	48	0.71	1.19	48	N/A	N/A	N/A	N/A
-TOTAL	2.21	3.62	47	0.23	N/A	44	1.06	N/A	55	N/A	N/A	N/A	N/A
-30-89 DAYS P/D	0.94	1.31	50	0.50	N/A	61	0.59	N/A	49	N/A	N/A	N/A	N/A
SINGLE & MULTI MTG-90+ DAYS P/D	0.56	0.18	84	0.47	0.11	89	0.47	0.16	84	0.33	0.12	0.29	0.13
-NONACCRUAL	3.04	1.00	88	0.89	0.46	81	1.74	0.63	86	0.49	0.35	0.19	0.29
-TOTAL	3.59	1.29	88	1.36	0.65	85	2.21	0.89	88	0.82	0.52	0.48	0.47
-30-89 DAYS P/D	1.58	0.93	77	0.82	0.67	65	1.44	0.95	74	0.74	0.72	0.45	0.70
NONFARM/RESI MTG-90+ DAYS P/D	0.05	0.06	69	0.04	0.02	78	0.11	0.04	83	0.09	0.02	0.06	0.02
-NONACCRUAL	0.54	0.78	50	0.35	0.47	49	0.36	0.50	48	0.43	0.42	0.37	0.50
-TOTAL	0.59	0.89	48	0.40	0.51	52	0.47	0.57	53	0.52	0.46	0.44	0.54
-30-89 DAYS P/D	0.44	0.58	50	0.37	0.36	56	0.43	0.50	51	0.51	0.39	0.41	0.36
OWN OCC NFARM NONRE-90+ DAYS P/D	0.05	0.05	72	0.05	0.02	80	0.10	0.04	81	N/A	N/A	N/A	N/A
-NONACCRUAL	0.59	0.69	51	0.41	0.47	52	0.36	0.53	48	N/A	N/A	N/A	N/A
-TOTAL	0.64	0.77	49	0.45	0.53	52	0.46	0.59	46	N/A	N/A	N/A	N/A
-30-89 DAYS P/D	0.47	0.53	54	0.41	0.35	63	0.54	0.44	66	N/A	N/A	N/A	N/A
OTH NONFARM NONRES-90+ DAYS P/D	0.06	0.05	78	0.03	0.02	80	0.12	0.02	88	N/A	N/A	N/A	N/A
-NONACCRUAL	0.45	0.78	50	0.26	0.38	53	0.35	0.43	56	N/A	N/A	N/A	N/A
-TOTAL	0.51	0.90	48	0.29	0.43	54	0.47	0.50	60	N/A	N/A	N/A	N/A
-30-89 DAYS P/D	0.38	0.59	50	0.30	0.33	57	0.19	0.50	32	N/A	N/A	N/A	N/A

Analysis of Past-Due, Nonaccrual, and Restructured Loans and Leases

These pages analyze noncurrent debt, consisting of loans and leases in past-due or nonaccrual status, including those that had been restructured; and current restructured debt, consisting of loans and leases that have been restructured and are in compliance with modified terms. Loans are grouped by type of loan, however reporting differences require special treatment of noncurrent loan ratios for banks filing call form 033 and 034 prior to March 31, 2001. **From March 31, 2001 forward all banks file past due loan information using the same set of standards.**

Ratio Calculation For Banks Filing FFIEC 031 and 032 Prior to March 31, 2001

The loan and lease categories used under this heading correspond to the categories used in report of condition RC-N and RC-C. For each category the percentage is determined by dividing the end-of-period noncurrent loan and lease figure by the corresponding loan figure from RC-C.

Ratio Calculation For Banks Filing FFIEC 033 and 034 Prior to March 31, 2001

Prior to March 31, 2001 Banks filing call forms 033 and 034 are permitted to categorize loans using their own internal system for schedules RC-N and RC-K but not for schedule RC-C. For consistency in definition, noncurrent loan and lease ratios use noncurrent loan information from RC-N and outstanding loan data from RC-K. Analysis of these data should be made in conjunction with analysis of other information on loans and leases provided in this report.

Noncurrent LN&LS ($000)

A recap in dollars of noncurrent and restructured loans and leases by past due status.

90 Days and Over

Loans and leases past due over 90 days and still accruing.

Total Nonaccrual LN&LS

Loans and leases on which interest is no longer being accrued.

Total Noncurrent LN&LS

Sum of previous two categories.

LN&LS 30–89 Days Past Due

Loans and leases past due 30 through 80 days and still accruing interest.

Restructured LN&LS 90+ Days P/D

Restructured loans and leases past due 90 or more days and still accruing interest.

Restructured LN&LS Nonaccrual

Restructured loans and leases on which interest is no longer being accrued.

Restructured LN&LS 30–89 Days P/D

Restructured loans and leases past due 30 through 89 days and still accruing interest.

Current 1–4 Family Restructured LN&LS

Loans secured by 1–4 family properties that have been restructured and are current by the revised terms.

Current Other Restructured LN&LS

Other restructured loan and leases still current by their restructured terms.

Loans Secured by 1–4 RE In Foreclosure

Loans secured by 1–4 family properties in forclosure.

All Other Real Estate Owned

All other real estate owned. Excludes direct and indirect investments in real estate.

% of Noncurr LN&LS by Type

This section presents a distribution of past due loans by type of loan and status of delinquency. In each category of past due loans, e.g. Real Estate Loans 90+ Days Past Due that category is divided by the total for that type of loan, e.g. Real Estate Loans.

The gross loans and leases category reflects all categories of loans and leases by delinquency to gross loans. See previous description in this section of calculations for specific report form types. Details are provided only where specific loan categories are grouped together or where a call report exception applies. The call report definition applies otherwise.

Each category of loans displays four types of loan delinquency:

Loans 90+ Days Past Due

Loans on Nonaccrual

Total (of the first two categories)

Loans 30–89 Days Past Due

(Note that loans 30-89 days are NOT a part of the previous total.)

Real Estate Loans

From March 31, 2001 forward includes loans secured by real estate.

For quarters prior to March 31, 2001 for banks filing 033 and 034 includes real estate loans. For banks filing 031 and 032 forms includes loans secured by real estate.

Loans Finance Commercial RE

Loans for the purpose of financing commercial real estate from RC-C.

Construction & Land Development

Loans secured by real estate for the purpose of construction and lend development from RC-C.

1–4 Family Construction

Construction loans secured by 1–4 family properties.

Other Construction

Construction loans secured by other real estate properties.

Single & Multi Mortgage

Includes loans secured by mortgages secured by 1–4 and multifamily (5 or more) properties from RC-C.

Nonfarm/Residential Mortgage

Loans secured by mortgages on non-farm, nonresidential property from RC-C.

Owner Occupied Nonfarm Nonresidential

Loans secured by owner occupied nonfarm nonresidential properties.

Other Nonfarm Nonresidential

Loans secured by other nonfarm nonresidential mortgages.

ANALYSIS OF PAST DUE, NONACCRUAL & RESTRUCTURED LOANS & LEASES   PAGE 08A

	06/30/2008			06/30/2007			12/31/2007			12/31/2006		12/31/2005	
% OF NONCURR LN&LS BY LN TYPE	BANK	PG 1	PCT	BANK	PG 1	PCT	BANK	PG 1	PCT	BANK	PG 1	BANK	PG 1
COML & INDUST LNS-90+ DAYS P/D	0.04	0.07	59	0.04	0.05	62	0.07	0.05	70	0.05	0.05	0.06	0.06
-NONACCRUAL	0.37	0.78	34	0.39	0.48	51	0.28	0.50	41	0.39	0.48	0.24	0.58
-TOTAL	0.41	0.89	31	0.42	0.56	46	0.35	0.59	38	0.44	0.56	0.30	0.67
-30-89 DAYS P/D	0.41	0.70	38	0.64	0.47	66	0.39	0.62	36	0.23	0.48	0.66	0.52
LOANS TO INDIVDLS-90+ DAYS P/D	1.79	0.11	97	1.14	0.09	97	1.62	0.11	97	0.87	0.09	1.06	0.14
-NONACCRUAL	0.28	0.19	72	0.08	0.12	54	0.29	0.16	78	0.12	0.11	0.19	0.15
-TOTAL	2.07	0.36	95	1.22	0.25	94	1.91	0.33	94	0.99	0.23	1.24	0.34
-30-89 DAYS P/D	2.59	1.13	88	1.87	1.02	82	2.41	1.26	83	1.74	1.15	2.45	1.16
CREDIT CARD PLANS-90+ DAYS P/D	1.37	0.76	71	0.00	0.53	38	0.00	0.59	38	100.00	0.76	100.00	0.61
-NONACCRUAL	0.00	0.32	69	0.00	0.13	73	0.00	0.24	71	0.00	0.12	0.00	0.12
-TOTAL	1.37	1.27	57	0.00	0.80	26	0.00	0.97	27	100.00	1.06	100.00	0.86
-30-89 DAYS P/D	1.63	1.65	47	0.00	1.61	16	0.00	1.51	21	0.00	1.50	0.00	1.46
LEASE FINANCING-90+ DAYS P/D	0.03	0.02	78	0.00	0.01	74	0.09	0.02	85	0.03	0.02	0.00	0.02
-NONACCRUAL	0.24	0.40	61	0.02	0.17	57	0.15	0.23	68	0.22	0.21	0.00	0.29
-TOTAL	0.00	0.44	57	0.00	0.20	50	0.00	0.30	65	0.00	0.27	0.00	0.37
-30-89 DAYS P/D	0.76	0.68	68	0.58	0.47	66	2.28	0.69	85	1.06	0.47	0.00	0.45
AGRICULTURAL LNS-90+ DAYS P/D	0.00	0.00	85	0.95	0.02	97	0.00	0.02	80	0.38	0.01	0.00	0.00
-NONACCRUAL	0.22	0.34	70	0.20	0.37	62	0.19	0.31	68	0.15	0.28	0.04	0.26
-TOTAL	0.22	0.36	68	1.15	0.48	82	0.19	0.36	63	0.53	0.30	0.04	0.34
-30-89 DAYS P/D	0.01	0.42	55	0.01	0.30	54	0.20	0.23	71	1.04	0.27	1.37	0.31
OTHER LN&LS-90+ DAYS P/D	0.07	0.02	90	0.00	0.02	70	0.04	0.02	80	0.00	0.02	0.00	0.02
-NONACCRUAL	0.03	0.14	60	0.02	0.11	58	0.02	0.08	62	0.03	0.06	0.20	0.09
-TOTAL	0.10	0.21	63	0.03	0.18	53	0.07	0.15	63	0.03	0.12	0.20	0.16
-30-89 DAYS P/D	0.09	0.33	53	0.69	0.33	80	0.02	0.28	44	0.04	0.28	0.14	0.37
GROSS LN&LS-90+ DAYS P/D	0.58	0.16	88	0.34	0.09	87	0.46	0.13	88	0.26	0.09	0.29	0.10
-NONACCRUAL	1.92	1.34	72	0.56	0.49	65	1.08	0.72	74	0.38	0.37	0.21	0.39
-TOTAL	2.50	1.60	77	0.90	0.62	75	1.54	0.91	80	0.64	0.51	0.50	0.52
-30-89 DAYS P/D	1.38	1.02	73	0.97	0.63	79	1.42	0.96	79	0.85	0.72	0.73	0.69

OTHER PERTINENT RATIOS

NONCUR LN&LS TO-LN&LS ALLOWANCE	194.93	110.71	84	112.94	57.62	85	159.24	83.77	85	81.87	47.35	62.53	51.16
-EQUITY CAPITAL	16.85	11.48	74	6.13	4.19	72	10.38	6.20	78	4.42	3.37	3.52	3.54
%TOTAL P/D LN&LS-INCL NONACCRUAL	3.88	2.67	75	1.87	1.34	75	2.97	1.94	81	1.49	1.30	1.23	1.26
IENC-LOANS TO TOTAL LOANS	N/A	N/A	N/A	N/A	N/A	N/A	N/A	N/A	N/A	N/A	N/A	N/A	N/A
NONCURR LNS+OREO TO LNS+OREO	2.73	1.77	77	0.99	0.69	74	1.69	1.01	81	0.70	0.56	0.53	0.57
NONCURR RESTRUCT DEBT/GR LN&LS	0.00	0.01	76	0.00	0.00	82	0.00	0.00	78	0.00	0.00	0.00	0.00
CURR+NONCURR RESTRUCT/GR LN&LS	0.09	0.04	81	0.00	0.01	71	0.00	0.02	63	0.00	0.01	0.00	0.02
CURRENT RESTRUCT LN&LS	0.08	0.04	81	0.00	0.00	81	0.00	0.01	77	0.00	0.00	0.00	0.01
LOANS SEC 1-4 FAM RE IN FORCLOSURE													
AS % TOTAL LOANS SEC 1-4 FAM RE	2.04	0.44	91	N/A	0.03	80	N/A	0.08	87	N/A	N/A	N/A	N/A

Analysis of Past Due, Nonaccrual & Restructured Loans & Leases Memoranda Information

This section presents additional information for past due real estate loans as well as information on current restructured loans by type.

The additional information on past due real estate loans comes from schedule RC-N memoranda section and applies to all banks. Ratios are calculated by dividing the individual past due loan category by the corresponding balance from RC-C. Two sub-sections provide both dollar and ratio information using the same loan captions. Details are provided only where items are combined, otherwise call report definitions apply. Each category displays loans 90 plus days past due, loans on nonaccrual, total noncurrent and loans 30–89 days past due.

An additional section displays other pertinent ratios including other analyses of past due and restructured loans by type that are current by their revised terms.

% of Noncurr LN&LS by LN Type

Commercial & Industrial Loans

From March 31, 2001 forward includes commercial and industrial loans for all banks. Prior to March 31, 2001 for banks filing FFIEC form 031 and 032 includes commercial and industrial loans. Prior to March 31, 2001 for banks filing FFIEC form 033 and 034 includes commercial, time and demand and all other loans.

Loans to Individuals

From March 31, 2001 forward includes loans to individuals other than credit card plans, for all banks. For banks filing FFIEC form 031 and 032 in quarters prior to March 31, 2001 includes credit cards and other loans to individuals. For banks filing 033 and 034 in quarters prior to March 31, 2001 includes installment loans.

Credit Card Plans

Credit card and related plans from RC-C.

Foreign Government Loans

For banks filing FFIEC 031 and 032.

Lease Financing

Lease financing receivables from RC-C.

Agricultural Loans

Loans to finance agricultural production. Note that banks with less than $300 million assets report this item subject to a reporting threshold and as a supplement.

Other Loans & Leases

From March 31, 2001 forward for 031 filers includes loans to commercial banks in the US, to other depository institutions in the US, to banks in foreign countries, state and local political subdivisions, for purchasing or carrying securities and all other loans.

From March 31, 2001 forward for 041 filers includes loans to depository institutions, state and local political subdivisions, for purchasing and carrying securities, all other loans and to finance agricultural production.

Prior to March 31, 2001 for banks filing FFIEC Form 033 or 034 includes lease-financing receivables. Prior to March 31, 2001 for banks filing 031 or 032 includes all other loans, lease financing and loans to foreign governments and institutions.

Gross LN&LS

Summation of all categories of due loans by past due status, divided by gross loans.

Other Pertinent Ratios:

Noncurrent LN&LS to LN&LS Allowance

Total 90+ days past due and nonaccrual loans and leases divided by the allowance for loan and lease losses.

Noncurr LN&LS to Equity Capital

Total 90+ days past due and nonaccrual loans and leases divided by total equity capital.

% Total P/D LN&LS—Incl Nonaccrual

Total 90+ days past due, nonaccrual and 30–89 days past due loans and leases divided by gross loans and leases.

IENC—Loans to Total Loans

Income earned or accrued on loans but not collected divided by gross loans.

Noncurr Lns + OREO to Lns + OREO

Loans and leases 90 days and over past due and still accruing

+ Loans and leases on nonaccrual

+ All other real estate owned (non-investment)

/ total loans and leases plus all other real estate owned (noninvestment).

Noncurr Restruc Debt/Gr LN&LS

Total restructured debt that is 90+ days past due or on nonaccrual by its revised terms divided by gross loans and leases.

Curr+Noncurr Restruct/Gr LN&LS

Total of restructured loans and leases that are current 90+ days past due, on nonaccrual divided by gross loans and leases.

The following ratios are not made available to the public, since they involve the confidential items on noncurrent restructured debt from

Schedule RC-N of the Report of Condition.

Current Restructured Loans and Leases

Total loans and leases restructured and in compliance with modified terms as a percentage of total loans and leases.

Loans Secured by 1–4 Family Real Estate in Foreclosure as % of Total Loans Secured by 1–4 Family RE

Loans secured by 1–4 family real estate in foreclosure as a percent of total loans secured by 1–4 family real estate.

	06/30/2008			06/30/2007			12/31/2007			12/31/2006		12/31/2005	
LONG ASSETS INSTS W/ OPTIONS	BANK	PG 1	PCT	BANK	PG 1	PCT	BANK	PG 1	PCT	BANK	PG 1	BANK	PG 1
MORTGAGE LOANS & PASS THRUS	20.75	15.00	73	25.14	15.66	81	23.47	14.99	81	26.95	15.93	27.37	18.10
LOANS & SECURITIES OVER 15 YRS	6.32	4.09	73	7.84	4.24	79	7.64	3.82	82	4.38	3.91	4.70	4.02
LOANS & SECURITIES 5-15 YRS	4.49	3.84	66	6.08	3.75	76	4.85	3.79	68	6.47	4.16	6.66	4.70
OTHER LOANS AND SECURITIES	59.87	62.44	37	54.74	61.94	27	57.43	62.19	31	54.46	61.16	54.76	58.83
LOANS & SECURITIES OVER 15 YRS	2.78	1.92	68	7.81	1.69	94	2.62	1.71	74	7.00	1.75	6.94	1.75
LOANS & SECURITIES 5-15 YRS	5.31	7.06	37	5.12	7.38	34	5.23	7.06	37	5.13	7.03	4.77	6.37
TOTAL LOANS & SECURITIES OVR 15	9.10	6.41	73	15.66	6.36	85	10.26	5.89	79	11.38	5.96	11.64	6.13
CMO'S TOTAL	0.58	3.41	30	0.19	3.92	25	0.54	3.51	31	2.88	4.05	2.98	4.59
AVG LIFE OVER 3 YEARS	0.50	2.22	36	0.12	2.47	27	0.51	2.13	35	2.04	2.40	1.99	2.72
STRUCTURED NOTES	0.00	0.03	78	0.00	0.05	76	0.00	0.06	76	0.00	0.06	0.00	0.08
MORTGAGE SERVICING	0.88	0.08	95	0.79	0.08	95	0.80	0.08	95	0.61	0.08	0.56	0.09
TOTAL	0.88	0.15	92	0.79	0.19	90	0.80	0.20	88	0.61	0.20	0.56	0.26
OVERALL RISK INDICATORS													
AVAILABLE-FOR-SALE	7.43	12.93	23	7.02	15.58	18	7.81	13.93	22	12.51	16.27	13.57	17.95
HELD-TO-MATURITY	0.00	0.80	42	0.00	1.30	43	0.00	1.05	45	0.00	1.38	0.00	1.69
OFF-BALANCE SHEET	133.32	35.66	92	115.58	38.44	91	121.72	37.04	91	110.71	37.05	98.65	38.13
UNREALIZED APPN/DEPN	0.00	-0.01	88	0.00	-0.02	93	0.00	0.00	81	0.00	-0.01	0.00	-0.02
UNREAL APP/DEP % TIER ONE CAP	0.00	-0.09	78	0.00	-0.30	86	0.00	0.01	71	0.00	-0.13	0.00	-0.23
CONTRACTUAL MAT/REPRICE DATA													
LOANS/SECURITIES OVER 3 YEARS	29.98	32.01	45	39.42	33.35	68	32.62	31.39	58	40.23	32.52	40.83	33.71
LIABILITIES OVER 3 YEARS	2.74	2.35	64	4.70	2.11	80	3.48	2.12	74	4.23	2.23	5.35	3.24
NET 3 YEAR POSITION	27.25	29.29	47	34.72	30.69	65	29.14	28.86	53	35.99	29.83	35.47	29.74
LOANS/SECURITIES OVER 1 YEAR	38.80	44.67	33	47.36	46.91	52	41.07	44.85	38	51.61	46.55	52.25	47.48
LIABILITIES OVER 1 YEAR	5.78	7.44	48	6.98	6.35	61	5.06	6.39	49	7.03	6.40	10.47	9.54
NET OVER 1 YEAR POSITION	33.03	36.59	39	40.38	39.54	53	36.01	37.71	45	44.58	39.17	41.79	37.00
NONMATURITY DEPOSITS	43.05	38.53	61	39.31	41.12	42	41.54	39.56	54	39.16	41.81	42.68	43.15
NONMATURITY DEPS % LONG ASSETS	143.59	139.40	60	99.70	142.83	32	127.34	144.13	46	97.35	144.36	104.55	150.30
NET OVER 3 YEAR POSITION	-13.07	-6.36	37	0.12	-8.08	67	-8.92	-8.37	53	1.07	-9.16	-1.86	-9.71
AS % TIER 1 CAPITAL													
STRUCTURED NOTES	0.00	0.36	76	0.00	0.66	74	0.00	0.75	74	0.00	0.75	0.00	1.04
MORTGAGE SERVICING (FV)	12.00	1.18	94	10.84	1.18	94	11.40	1.23	95	8.66	1.12	8.50	1.30
TOTAL	12.00	2.14	90	10.84	2.68	88	11.40	2.88	88	8.66	2.64	8.50	3.52

UBPR Page 09

Interest Rate Risk Analysis

This page presents information that may be used to assess the interest rate risk inherent in a bank's balance sheet. Most of the underlying repricing data is reported in the memoranda sections of RC-B, RC-C, RC-E as well as on RC. The analysis emphasizes the long side of the balance sheet and also takes into account the impact of nonmaturity deposits. Most ratios are presented as a percent of total assets. Information on this page is available from June 30, 1997 forward.

Long Assets Instruments with Options

Mortgage Loans & Pass Thrus

Sum of all repricings for mortgage pass-through securities backed by closed-end first lien residential mortgages and closed end loans secured by liens on 1–4 family residential properties divided by total assets.

Loans and Securities Over 15 Years

Sum of repricings over 15 years for above divided by total assets.

Loans and Securities 5 to 15 Years

Sum of repricings from 5 to 15 years for above divided by total assets.

Other Loans and Securities

Sum of all repricings for securities issued by U.S. Treasury, agencies, state and political subdivisions and all loans and leases other than closed-end loans secured by first liens on 1–4 family residential properties divided by total assets.

Loans and Securities Over 15 Years

Sum of repricings over 15 years for above divided by total assets.

Loans and Securities 5 to 15 Years

Sum of repricings from 5 to 15 years for above divided by total assets.

Total Loans and Securities Over 15

Sum of repricings over 15 years for Mortgage Loans and Pass Throughs and Other Loans and Securities divided by assets.

CMO's Total

Sum of all repricings for other mortgage backed securities (including CMO's, REMIC's and stripped MBS) divided by assets.

Avg Life Over 3 Years

Repricings over three years for above divided by assets.

Structured Notes

Structured notes (included in held-to-maturity and available-for-sale accounts) divided by assets.

Mortgage Servicing

Fair value of mortgage servicing assets divided by assets.

Total

Sum of structured notes, high risk securities, and mortgage servicing divided by assets.

Overall Risk Indicators

Available-For-Sale

Fair value of available-for-sale securities divided by assets.

Held-To-Maturity

Amortized cost of held-to-maturity securities divided by assets.

Off-Balance Sheet

Total of all off-balance sheet accounts, divided by assets.

Unrealized Appn/Depn

Unrealized appreciation/depreciation on held-to-maturity securities divided by assets.

Unrealized App/Dep % Tier One Capital

Unrealized appreciation/depreciation on held-to-maturity securities divided by tier one capital.

Contractual Maturity/ Reprice Data

Loans/Securities Over 3 Years

Sum of repricings over 3 years for mortgage loans and pass-throughs, other loans and securities and CMO's divided by assets.

Liabilities Over 3 Years

Sum of repricings over 3 years for other borrowed money, time deposits less than $100,000 and time deposits of $100,000 or greater divided by assets.

Net 3 Year Position

Loans/Securities over 3 years less liabilities over 3 years divided by assets.

Loans/Securities Over 1 Year

Sum of repricings over 1 year for mortgage loans and pass throughs, other loans and securities and all CMO's.

Liabilities Over 1 Year

Sum of repricings over 1 year for other borrowed money, time deposits less than $100,000 and time deposits of $100,000 or greater divided by assets.

Net Over 1 Year Position

Loans/Securities over 1 year less liabilities over 1 year divided by assets.

Nonmaturity Deposits

Demand deposits, NOW and ATS accounts, money market accounts and all other savings divided by assets.

Nonmaturity Deposits by Long Assets

Nonmaturity deposits divided by repricings over 3 years for loans and securities.

Net Over 3 Year Position

Repricings over 3 years for loans and securities less nonmaturity deposits divided by assets.

As % Tier 1 Capital

Structured Notes

Structured notes (included in held-to-maturity and available-for-sale accounts) divided by tier one capital.

Mortgage Servicing

Fair value of mortgage servicing assets divided by tier one capital.

Total

Sum of structured notes, high risk securities, OBS exposed to rising rates and mortgage servicing divided by tier one capital.

	06/30/2008	06/30/2007	12/31/2007	12/31/2006	12/31/2005
SHORT TERM INVESTMENTS	2,851,833	2,145,112	2,614,497	5,500,233	3,948,269
SHORT TERM ASSETS	26,066,378	26,791,105	26,779,773	28,857,058	24,830,095
SHORT TERM NONCORE FUNDING	41,080,147	49,038,577	43,683,279	52,566,009	47,556,959
NONCORE LIABLILITIES	55,906,853	62,648,560	58,562,927	66,506,224	61,274,059
FED HOME LOAN BOR MAT < 1 YR	634,874	1,248,770	1,629,769	100,630	825,286
FED HOME LOAN BOR MAT > 1 YR	7,791,546	6,272,543	8,057,404	7,791,863	8,349,578
OTH BORROWING MAT < 1 YR	405,543	500,690	500,350	0	3,093,039
OTH BORROWING MAT > 1 YR	6,819,215	6,618,949	6,938,843	5,412,990	2,627,290
DEBT SECURITIES 90+ DAYS P/D	0	0	0	0	0
TOTAL NONCURRENT DEBT SEC	0	0	0	0	0
FAIR VALUE STRUCTURED NOTES	0	0	0	0	0
	0	0	0	0	0

	06/30/2008			06/30/2007			12/31/2007			12/31/2006		12/31/2005	
PERCENT OF TOTAL ASSETS	BANK	PG 1	PCT	BANK	PG 1	PCT	BANK	PG 1	PCT	BANK	PG 1	BANK	PG 1
SHORT TERM INVESTMENTS	1 66	5 07	47	1 21	5 33	23	1 49	5 41	37	3 01	5 55	2 23	5 06
MARKETABLE EQUITY SEC (MES)	0 70	0 09	94	0 77	0 09	95	1 10	0 11	95	0 99	0 09	0 83	0 10
CORE DEPOSITS	52 34	54 23	41	48 66	56 09	27	51 30	54 36	35	48 27	54 18	50 15	54 04
S T NONCORE FUNDING	23 95	26 99	47	27 69	24 56	68	24 95	25 72	52	28 79	24 54	26 83	24 16
LIQUIDITY RATIOS													
NET S T NONCORE FUND DEPENDENCE	27 01	25 33	57	32 81	22 20	77	28 35	23 56	62	30 35	22 23	28 84	22 30
NET NONCORE FUND DEPENDENCE	37 48	38 13	50	42 33	32 73	71	38 62	34 74	5S	39 34	33 66	37 91	33 16
BROKERED DEPOSITS TO DEPOSITS	12 66	5 90	78	13 31	5 29	82	12 24	4 92	81	14 34	5 33	12 66	5 07
BROKER DEP MAT < 1YR TO BKR DEPS	96 78	59 21	64	96 01	57 44	65	95 58	61 37	64	96 42	59 53	96 47	54 21
SHORT TRM INV TO S T NCORE FUND	6 94	19 09	47	4 37	23 73	20	5 99	24 33	35	10 46	25 60	8 30	24 07
SHORT TERM ASSET TO S T LIABS	49 72	75 10	27	42 21	76 82	21	47 32	76 89	25	42 89	78 64	44 38	77 74
NET S T LIAB TO ASSETS	15 37	9 71	64	20 71	9 20	77	17 03	9 87	67	21 05	8 60	17 56	9 65
NET LOANS & LEASES TO DEPOSITS	106 34	97 35	70	104 23	91 46	73	109 42	94 26	77	104 54	90 72	103 14	89 61
NET LN&LS TO CORE DEPOSITS	143 20	127 12	71	151 36	122 47	81	145 86	125 24	77	150 13	125 57	143 47	123 57
NET LN&LS & SBLC TO ASSETS	85 43	70 13	89	82 52	68 30	86	83 87	68 71	87	79 61	66 64	79 62	64 87
SECURITIES MIX													
HELD-TO-MATURITY % TOTAL SECS													
US TREAS & GOVT AGENCIES	0 00	0 35	82	0 00	0 83	76	0 00	0 64	8C	0 00	1 07	0 00	1 23
MUNICIPAL SECURITIES	0 00	1 62	53	0 00	1 61	53	0 00	1 46	55	0 00	1 65	0 00	1 53
PASS-THROUGH MTG BACKED SECS	0 00	0 61	62	0 00	0 91	63	0 00	0 66	63	0 00	0 93	0 00	1 10
CMO & REMIC MTG BACKED SECS	0 00	0 41	82	0 00	0 58	80	0 00	0 52	81	0 00	0 59	0 00	0 86
ASSET BACKED SECURITIES	0 00	N/A	96	0 00	N/A	97	0 00	N/A	97	0 00	N/A	0 00	N/A
OTHER DOMESTIC DEBT SECS	0 00	0 13	80	0 00	0 01	87	0 00	0 02	84	0 00	0 02	0 00	0 04
FOREIGN DEBT SECURITIES	0 00	0 00	87	0 00	0 00	87	0 00	0 00	87	0 00	0 00	0 00	0 00
TOTAL HELD-TO-MATURITY	0 00	6 90	35	0 00	7 70	38	0 00	6 44	3S	0 00	8 39	0 00	8 28
AVAILABLE-FOR-SALE % TOTAL SECS													
US TREASURY & GOVT AGENCIES	4 66	12 87	44	1 97	18 08	23	2 81	15 73	32	6 11	18 89	9 17	19 20
MUNICIPAL SECURITIES	7 62	7 85	59	7 82	6 34	64	7 37	6 60	6C	4 25	5 27	3 67	4 43
PASS-THROUGH MTG BACKED SECS	68 15	28 55	92	73 89	24 68	92	65 73	25 03	91	52 01	24 23	48 82	25 63
CMO & REMIC MTG BACKED SECS	7 82	19 88	37	2 76	19 85	31	6 95	19 55	35	22 99	19 76	21 97	20 84
ASSET BACKED SECURITIES	0 40	1 55	74	2 32	1 02	83	1 54	1 42	75	4 87	1 02	6 29	0 97
OTHER DOMESTIC DEBT SECS	1 87	1 58	69	0 21	1 85	53	1 44	1 84	65	1 82	1 86	3 94	1 45
FOREIGN DEBT SECURITIES	0 04	0 13	81	0 04	0 09	79	0 04	0 17	78	0 02	0 11	0 02	0 12
INV MUT FND & OTH MKTBL	9 46	0 81	94	10 98	0 65	98	14 13	0 97	94	7 93	0 78	6 12	0 62
OTHER EQUITY SECURITIES	N/A	N/A	N/A	N/A	N/A	N/A	N/A	N/A	N/A	N/A	N/A	N/A	N/A
TOTAL AVAILABLE-FOR-SALE	100 00	89 01	99	100 00	87 09	99	100 00	88 92	9S	100 00	85 34	100 00	86 15
OTHER SECURITIES RATIOS:													
APP (DEP) HI RISK & STRUC/T1CAP	0 00	-0 03	96	0 00	-0 07	98	0 00	0 00	93	0 00	-0 04	0 00	-0 08
APP (DEP) IN HTM SEC TO HTM SEC	N/A	-0 35	N/A	N/A	-0 92	N/A	N/A	0 44	N/A	N/A	0 00	N/A	-0 03
APP (DEP) IN HTM SEC TO EQY CAP	0 00	-0 07	80	0 00	-0 24	86	0 00	0 01	72	0 00	-0 12	0 00	-0 19
PLEDGED SECURITIES TO TOT SEC	38 31	67 36	14	42 88	63 20	22	38 61	64 67	17	67 71	61 36	69 96	62 29

UBPR Page 10

Liquidity and Investment Portfolio

The top portion of this page presents dollar information and ratios that can be used to assess the bank's liquidity position. The bottom portion of the page presents the principal components of the investment portfolio expressed as a percentage of total investment securities. End-of-period calculations that may be used to analyze the maturity distribution and the degree of appreciation or depreciation in the investment portfolio are also shown.

Short Term Investments ($000)

The sum of:

Interest-bearing bank balances

+ Federal funds sold and securities purchased under agreements to resell

+ Debt securities with a remaining maturity of one year or less

+ Acceptances of other banks (loans) prior to March 31, 2001.

Short Term Assets ($000)

The sum of:

Short term investments (defined above)

+ Loans and leases with a remaining maturity of one year or less

- Acceptances of other banks prior to March 31, 2001.

Short Term Noncore Funding ($000)

The sum of:

+ Time deposits of $100M or more with a remaining maturity of one year or less

+ Brokered deposits issued in denominations of less than $100M with a remaining maturity or one year or less

+ Other borrowed money with a remaining maturity one year or less

+ Time deposits with a remaining maturity of one year or less in foreign offices

+ Securities sold under agreements to repurchase and federal funds purchased

+ Demand notes issued to the U.S. Treasury (Not available from March 31, 2001 forward).

Noncore Liabilities ($000)

The sum of:

Total time deposits of $100M or more

+ Other borrowed money (all maturities)

+ Foreign office deposits

+ Securities sold under agreements to repurchase and federal funds purchased

+ Insured brokered deposits issued in denominations of less than $100,000

+ Demand notes issued to the U.S. Treasury (Not available from March 31, 2001 forward).

Federal Home Loan Bank Borrowing Maturity Under 1 Year

From March 31, 2001 forward includes information from schedule RC-M Federal Home Loan Bank Advances with a Remaining Maturity of One Year or Less (RCFD2651).

Federal Home Loan Bank Borrowing Maturing Over 1 Year

From March 31, 2001 forward that includes information from schedule RC-M Federal Home Loan Bank Advances with a Remaining Maturity of One to Three Years (RCFDB565) plus Federal Home Loan Bank Advances with a Remaining Maturity of Over Three Years (RCFDB566).

Other Borrowing Maturing Under 1 Year

From March 31, 2001 forward includes information from schedule

RC-M Other Borrowed Money with a Remaining Maturity of One Year or Less (RCFDB571). For prior quarters includes Other Borrowed Money with a Remaining Maturity One Year or Less (RCFD2332).

Other Borrowing Maturing Over 1 Year

From March 31, 2001 forward includes information from schedule RC-M Other Borrowed Money with a Remaining Maturity of One to Three Years (RCFDB567) plus Other Borrowed Money With Remaining Maturity of Over Three Years (RCFDB568). For prior quarters includes Other Borrowed Money with a Remaining Maturity of One to Three Years (RCFDA547) plus Other Borrowed Money With a Remaining Maturity of Over Three Years (RCFDA548).

Long Term Assets ($000)

Is used in ratio calculations below but does not appear on the page. It is calculated as follows:

Net loans and leases

- Acceptances of other banks (loans) prior to March 31, 2001

+ Held-to-maturity securities

+ Available-for-sale securities

- Debt securities with a remaining maturity of one year or less

+ Other real estate owned (non–investment).

Core Deposits ($000)

Is used in ratio calculations but does not appear on the page. See page 4, balance sheet.

All demand and savings deposits including money market deposit accounts and NOW and ATS accounts, savings deposits, plus time deposits in amounts of less than $100 thousand.

Short Term Liabilities ($000)

Is used in ratio calculations but does not appear on the page.

The sum of:

Time deposits less than $100,000 with a remaining maturity of one year or less

+ Time deposits of $100M or more with a remaining maturity of one year or less

+ Other borrowed money with remaining maturity 1 year or less

+ Deposits in foreign offices with remaining maturity 1 year or less

+ Securities sold under agreements to repurchase and federal funds purchased

+ Demand notes issued to the U.S. Treasury (Not available from March 31, 2001 forward).

Not available prior to March 1996.

Debt Securities 90+ Days P/D

Displays dollar data for 90+ days past due debt securities from schedule RC-N and RC-B.

Total Noncurrent Debt Sec

Displays dollar data for noncurrent debt securities from schedule RC-N and RC-B.

Fair Value Structured Notes

Percent of Total Assets

Each category is divided by total assets at the end of the period.

Short Term Investments

Temporary investments divided by total assets.

Marketable Equity Securities (MES)

Investments in mutual funds and other equity securities with readily determinable values divided by total assets.

Core Deposits

Core deposits divided by total assets.

S.T. Noncore Funding

Short term noncore funding divided by total assets.

Liquidity Ratios

Net S. T. Noncore Funding Dependence

Short term noncore funding less short term investments divided by long term assets. Available from March 1996 forward.

Net Noncore Funding Dependence

Noncore liabilities less short term investments divided by long term assets. Available for all periods.

Brokered Deposits to Deposits

Deposits acquired from brokers and dealers for the account of others divided by total deposits.

Brokered Deposits Maturing < 1 year to Brokered Deposits

Brokered deposits issued in amounts of less than $100M and maturing in less than one year plus brokered deposits issued in amounts of $100M or greater divided by total brokered deposits. Not available prior to March 1996.

Short Term Investments to Short Term Noncore Funding

Short Term investments divided by short term noncore funding.

Short Term Assets to Short Term Liabilities

Short term assets divided by short term liabilities.

Net Short Term Liabilities to Assets

Short term liabilities less short term assets divided by total assets.

Net Loans & Leases to Deposits

Net loans, plus lease-financing receivables, divided by total deposits.

Net Loans & Leases to Core Deposits

Net loans, plus lease-financing receivables, divided by total core deposits.

Net Loans, Leases & Standby Letters of Credit to Assets

Net loans, plus lease-financing receivables and standby letters of credit, divided by total assets.

Securities Mix
(Percent of Total Securities)

Securities are displayed in two groups based on whether they are classified as held-to-maturity or available-for-sale. Held-to-maturity securities are shown at cost, while available-for-sale securities are shown at fair value.

Within each group, a distribution by type of security is displayed. Individual outstanding balances for each security is divided by the end-of-period total of held-to-maturity and available-for-sale securities.

U.S. Treasury & Government Agencies

Securities issued by U.S. Treasury and U.S. Agencies and U.S. government sponsored agencies are displayed.

Municipal Securities

General obligation, revenue and industrial development bonds are shown. Available prior to March 31, 2001.

Pass-Through Mtg. Backed Secs

Pass through GNMA, FNMA and privately issued mortgage-backed securities are displayed.

CMO & Remic Mtg Backed ecs

CMO's and REMIC's issued by FNMA and FHLMC, collateralized by MBS guaranteed by FNMA, FHLMC, GNMA and other private issues are displayed.

Asset Backed Securities

Available from March 31, 2001 forward. Asset backed securities include those backed by credit card receivables, home equity lines, automobile loans, other consumer loans, commercial loans and other assets.

Other Domestic Debt Securities

Foreign Debt Securities

Inv Mut F. & Oth MKTBL

Investments in mutual funds and other marketable securities. Shown in available-for-sale only.

Other Equity Securities

Includes other equity securities. Displayed as available-for-sale securities only.

Total Held-To-Maturity

Sum of all securities classified as held-to-maturity as a percent of total securities.

Total Available-For-Sale

Sum of all securities classified as available-for-sale as a percent of total securities.

Other Securities Ratios:

App (Dep) Hi Risk & Struc/TlCap

Fair value of high risk mortgage securities plus structured notes less amortized cost divided by tier one capital.

App (Dep) in HTM sec to HTM Sec

Prior to March 31, 1994, the total market value of all investment securities, less the total book value of all investment securities divided by the total book value of all investment securities.

From March 31, 1994 and subsequent, calculated for held-to-maturity securities.

App (Dep) in HTM Sec to Eqy Cap

Prior to March 31, 1994, the total market value of all investment securities, less the total book value of all investment securities divided by total equity capital.

From March 31 and subsequent, calculated for just held-to-maturity securities.

Pledged Securities to Total Securities

The book value of all securities as defined above that are pledged to secure deposits, repurchase transactions, or other borrowing (regardless of the balance of the deposits or other liabilities against which the securities are pledged), as performance bonds under futures or forward contracts, or for any other purpose, divided by total securities.

	06/30/2008	06/30/2007	12/31/2007	12/31/2006	12/31/2005
END OF PERIOD CAPITAL ($000)					
PERPETUAL PREFERRED	0	0	0	0	0
+ COMMON STOCK	21,600	21,600	21,600	21,600	21,600
+ SURPLUS	11,669,925	11,318,880	11,669,878	11,318,879	11,306,611
+ UNDIVIDED PROFITS	7,374,753	7,718,866	7,153,856	7,626,425	6,568,063
+ ACCUM OTHER COMP INCOME	236 292	275 643	808 440	363 165	369 064
+ OTHER EQUITY CAPITAL COMP	0	0	0	0	0
TOTAL EQUITY CAPITAL	19,302,570	19,334,989	19,653,774	19,330,069	18,265,338
SUBORD NOTES & DEBENTURES	3 334 741	3 391 247	3 312 078	3 446 917	3 696 687
CHANGES IN TOTAL EQUITY ($000)					
BALANCE AT BEGINNING OF PERIOD	19,653,774	19,330,069	19,330,069	18,265,338	9,873,582
+ NET INCOME	860 897	1 171 705	1 871 083	2 125 292	2 032 286
+ SALE OR PURCHASE OF CAPITAL	0	0	0	0	0
+ MERGER & ABSORPTIONS	0	0	0	0	0
+ RESTATE DUE TO ACCTG ERROR&CHG	0	-222,224	-222,224	0	0
+ TRANS WITH PARENT	47	-68 453	158 158	5 338	7 979 993
- DIVIDENDS	640,000	640,000	1,780,000	1,060,000	1,324,000
+ OTHER COMPREHENSIVE INCOME	-572,148	-236,108	296,688	-5,899	-296,523
BALANCE AT END OF PERIOD	19,302,570	19,334,989	19,653,774	19,330,069	18,265,338
INTANGIBLE ASSETS					
MORTGAGE SERVICING RIGHTS	1,193,450	942,012	1,049,425	810,509	657,604
+ PURCH CRED CARD RELATION	0	0	0	0	0
+ OTHER INTANGIBLES	155 030	223 595	186 938	263 373	353 980
+ GOODWILL	6,433,012	6,433,589	6,433,125	6,425,876	6,392,746
TOTAL INTANGIBLES	7,781,492	7,599,196	7,669,488	7,499,758	7,404,330
MEMO GRANDFATHERED INTANG	0	0	0	0	0

CAPITAL RATIOS	BANK	PG 1	PCT	BANK	PG 1	PCT	BANK	PG 1	PCT	BANK	PG 1	BANK	PG 1
PERCENT OF TOTAL EQUITY													
NET LOANS & LEASES (X)	6.66	6.83	43	6.75	6.66	50	6.67	6.62	47	6.85	6.47	6.98	6.59
SUBORD NOTES & DEBENTURES	17.28	6.50	79	17.54	6.30	80	16.85	6.43	78	17.83	6.25	20.24	6.84
LONG TERM DEBT	17.28	6.50	79	17.54	6.30	80	16.85	6.43	78	17.83	6.25	20.24	6.84
COM RE & RELATED VENTURES	144.74	243.73	29	144.21	224.13	32	139.24	230.88	28	139.56	211.83	130.32	196.87
PERCENT OF AVERAGE TOTAL EQUITY													
NET INCOME	8.77	5.95	57	12.12	11.47	56	9.66	9.61	49	11.30	12.89	13.59	13.91
DIVIDENDS	6.52	3.95	74	6.62	6.93	51	9.19	6.63	68	5.64	6.26	8.85	6.85
RETAINED EARNINGS	2.25	0.98	51	5.50	3.67	59	0.47	2.12	36	5.66	5.65	4.74	6.21
OTHER CAPITAL RATIOS													
DIVIDENDS TO NET OPER INCOME	74.34	50.74	67	54.62	59.92	47	95.13	65.99	66	49.88	47.35	65.15	47.57
EQUITY CAPITAL TO ASSETS	11.26	10.29	69	10.92	10.18	66	11.22	10.45	68	10.59	10.16	10.31	9.84
GROWTH RATES													
TOTAL EQUITY CAPITAL	-0.17	19.32	24	3.71	15.34	31	1.67	19.48	27	5.83	17.86	84.99	15.06
EQUITY GROWTH LESS ASST GROWTH	2.97	1.12	62	6.12	4.57	61	5.77	3.94	63	2.81	3.61	49.47	3.07
INTANG ASSETS % TOTAL EQUITY													
MORTGAGE SERVICING RIGHTS	6.18	0.82	92	4.87	0.79	90	5.34	0.82	90	4.19	0.77	3.60	0.88
GOODWILL	33.33	18.38	75	33.27	16.62	77	32.73	18.73	73	33.24	16.12	35.00	15.53
PURCH CREDIT CARD RELATION	0.00	0.01	84	0.00	0.01	87	0.00	0.01	85	0.00	0.01	0.00	0.01
ALL OTHER INTANGIBLES	0.80	1.55	37	1.16	1.40	50	0.95	1.63	41	1.36	1.42	1.94	1.45
TOTAL INTANGIBLES	40.31	22.13	76	39.30	20.14	77	39.02	22.65	73	38.80	19.63	40.54	19.74

Capital Analysis

This page presents end-of-period capital by call report definition, a reconcilement of total equity capital from period to period, an analysis of intangible assets and a series of capital ratios. Ratios using after tax income and dividends have been adjusted for assumed tax rates. See Section II Technical Information.

End-of-Period Capital ($000)

The dollar figures for each category are brought directly forward from the end-of-period Report of Condition schedule RC.

Perpetual Preferred Stock

Common Stock

Surplus

Undivided Profits

Accumulated Other Comprehensive Income

From March 31, 2001 forward includes accumulated other comprehensive income. For prior quarters includes accumulated G/L cash flow hedges, unrealized G/L available-for-sale securities, cumulative foreign current adjustment.

Other Equity Capital Components

Available from March 31, 2001 forward and includes other equity capital components.

Total Equity Capital

Sum of all capital components above.

Subordinated Notes & Debentures

Subordinated notes and debentures as reported on schedule RC.

Changes in Total Equity ($000)

Displays the reconcilement of changes

in equity capital from schedule RI-A. The source of a change in capital may be identified in this section.

Balance at Beginning of Period

Net Income

Sale or Purchase Of Capital

Merger & Absorptions

Restatements due to Accounting Errors and Changes

From March 31, 2001 forward includes restatements due to corrections of material accounting errors and changes in accounting. For prior quarters includes cumulative accounting changes as well as restatements due to accounting errors and changes.

Transactions With Parent

Less: Dividends

Other Comprehensive Income

From March 31, 2001 forward includes other comprehensive income. For prior quarters includes net other increases or decreases which is defined as net change in holding gains (losses) on available-for-sale securities and foreign currency translation adjustments.

Balance At End Of Period

Intangible Assets

Displays categories of intangible assets as reported in schedule RC-M.

Mortgage Servicing Rights

Purchased Credit Card Relation

Other Intangibles

Goodwill

Total Intangibles

Memo: Grand fathered Intangibles

Intangible assets that have been grandfathered for regulatory capital purposes.

Capital Ratios

Ratios are calculated by dividing by total equity capital as shown on schedule RC.

Percent of Total Equity:

Net Loans & Leases (X)

Unlike the other ratios displayed under this heading, this ratio is *multiple*, e.g., shows the number of times net loans and lease-financing receivables *exceed* equity capital.

Subordinated Notes and Debentures—Percent of Total Equity

Subordinated notes and debentures divided by total equity capital.

Long-Term Debt—Percent of Total Equity

Subordinated notes and debentures, plus mortgage indebtedness and liability for capitalized leases, divided by total equity capital.

Com Re & Related Ventures

The sum of construction and land development loans, nonfarm nonresidential mortgages, unsecured loans to finance commercial real estate, construction and land development, other real estate owned, investments in unconsolidated subsidiaries and associated companies divided by total equity.

Percent of Average Total Equity:

The following ratios use average equity derived from end-of-period balance for the prior year end and current year's end-of-period balances.

Net Income—Percent of Average Total Equity

Net income divided by average total equity capital.

Dividends—Percent of Average Total Equity

Cash dividends declared on common & preferred stock.

Retained Earnings—Percent of Average Total Equity

Net income, less cash dividends declared, divided by average total equity.

Other Capital Ratios:

Dividends to Net Operating Income

Cash dividends declared, as a percent of Net Operating Income as defined for UBPR Page 02.

Equity Capital to Assets

All common stock plus perpetual preferred stock, plus surplus, plus undivided profits and reserve for contingencies and other capital reserves, divided by assets.

Growth Rates:

For each of the captions in this grouping, the growth rate is determined by subtracting the account balance at the end of the corresponding period in the prior year from the current account balance and dividing the result by the account balance at the end of the corresponding period in the prior year. The "equity growth less asset growth" ratio is included in this grouping for analysis purposes even though it is not technically a growth rate.

Total Equity Capital

Equity Growth Less Asset Growth

The difference between equity capital and asset growth rates.

Intangibles Assets % Total Equity

Individual categories of intangible assets are shown as a percent of total equity.

Mortgage Servicing Rights

Goodwill

Purchased Credit Card Relation

Other Intangibles

Total Intangibles

RISK-BASED CAPITAL ($000)	06/30/2008	06/30/2007	12/31/2007	12/31/2006	12/31/2005
TIER ONE CAPITAL					
TOTAL EQUITY CAPITAL ADJUSTED	19 186 745	19 541 327	18 966 354	19 450 491	18 372 947
- INELIGIBLE DEF TAX ASSETS	0	0	0	0	0
- INELIGIBLE INTANGIBLES	6,540,927	6,595,025	6,565,686	6,618,789	6,658,104
- CUMUL CHANGE F.V. FINANCIAL LIAB	128,393	-21,687	62,329	0	0
NET TIER ONE	12 517 425	12 967 989	12 338 339	12 831 702	11 714 843
TIER TWO CAPITAL					
+ QUALIF DEBT AND REDEEM PFD	2,778,057	2,730,580	2,745,224	3,026,832	3,276,819
+ CUMULATIVE PREFERRED STOCK	0	0	0	0	0
+ ALLOWABLE LN&LS LOSS ALLOW	1,677,416	1,050,935	1,288,914	1,045,791	1,030,471
+ UNRL GAIN MKTBL EQY SEC (45%)	250,076	489,224	571,290	549,290	460,410
+ OTHER TIER 2 CAPITAL COMP	0	0	0	0	0
NET ELIGIBLE TIER TWO	4,705,549	4,270,739	4,605,428	4,621,913	4,767,700
TOTAL RBC BEFORE DEDUCTIONS					
TIER ONE & TIER TWO	17,222,974	17,238,728	16,943,767	17,453,615	16,482,543
TIER THREE & FIN SUB ADJ	0	0	0	0	0
- RECIPROCAL CAPITAL HOLDINGS	0	0	0	0	0
- DEDUCTIONS FOR TOTAL RBC	0	0	0	0	0
TOTAL RISK-BASED CAPITAL	17,222,974	17,238,728	16,943,767	17,453,615	16,482,543
RISK-WEIGHTED ASSETS					
ON-BALANCE SHEET					
CATEGORY TWO - 20%	4,001,214	3,925,774	4,146,709	6,519,354	6,845,044
CATEGORY THREE - 50%	16,591,814	20,766,713	19,149,453	21,624,062	20,569,806
CATEGORY FOUR - 100%	103,499,131	96,405,334	100,898,699	97,136,896	92,486,405
TOTAL ON-BALANCE SHEET	124,092,159	121,097,821	124,194,861	125,280,312	119,901,255
MEMO CATEGORY ONE - 0%	2 094 378	1 519 608	1 887 750	1 771 501	1 858 908
OFF- BALANCE SHEET					
CATEGORY TWO - 20%	825,576	757,792	742,136	110,172	69,766
CATEGORY THREE - 50%	1,520,912	1,769,870	2,323,658	1,362,282	1,305,765
CATEGORY FOUR - 100%	33,161,612	32,647,744	31,791,402	32,597,724	33,357,927
TOTAL OFF-BALANCE SHEET	35,508,100	35,175,406	34,857,196	34,070,179	34,733,458
MEMO CATEGORY ONE - 0%	0	8,099	5,626	2,510	0
ADJUSTMENTS TO RISK-WGT ASSETS					
RISK-WEIGHTED ASSET BEFORE DED	159,600,260	156,273,228	159,052,057	159,350,491	154,634,713
- INELIGIBLE DEF TAX ASSETS	0	0	0	0	0
- INELIGIBLE INTANGIBLES	0	0	0	0	0
- RECIPROCAL CAPITAL HOLDINGS	0	0	0	0	0
- EXCESS ALLOWABLE LN&LS LOSS AL	0	0	0	0	0
- ALLOCATED TRANSFER RISK RESERV	0	0	0	0	0
+ MKT RISK ASSETS & FIN SUB ADJ	2,870,367	2,890,742	3,310,415	1,549,083	1,677,626
TOTAL RISK-WEIGHTED ASSETS	162,470,627	159,163,971	162,362,472	160,899,575	156,312,340

RISK-BASED CAPITAL	BANK	PG 1	PCT	BANK	PG 1	PCT	BANK	PG 1	PCT	BANK	PG 1	BANK	PG 1
TIER ONE RBC TO RISK-WGT ASSETS	7.70	10.00	10	8.15	10.51	12	7.60	10.10	10	7.97	10.61	7.49	10.77
TOTAL RBC TO RISK-WEIGHT ASSETS	10.60	11.85	19	10.83	12.15	23	10.44	11.82	16	10.85	12.22	10.54	12.46
TIER ONE LEVERAGE CAPITAL	7.72	8.04	46	7.70	8.17	44	7.56	8.02	39	7.35	8.15	7.04	7.87
OTHER CAPITAL RATIO													
DEF TAX ASSET TO T1 CAP	0.00	3.98	23	0.00	2.67	28	0.00	2.53	33	0.00	2.46	0.00	2.44

NOTE FROM MARCH 31, 2001 FORWARD RISK-BASED CAPITAL RATIOS AND DATA DO INCLUDE ADJUSTMENT FOR FINANCIAL SUBSIDIARIES.
  FOR BANKS WITH FINANCIAL SUBSIDIARIES PLEASE REFER TO CALL REPORT FOR INFORMATION ON THE ADJUSTMENT.

UBPR Page 11A

Risk-Based Capital ($000)

Risk-based capital is the standard for federal banking agency regulatory capital. It relates eligible capital to on and off-balance sheet assets that have been assigned an appropriate conversion factor and risk weight. Assets, both on and off-balance sheet are assigned to one of four broad risk weight categories which are based the obligor, nature of collateral, guarantor or nature of the instrument.

The source for on and off-balance sheet risk weighting information is schedule RC-R, where banks report assets by major risk category. From March 31, 2001 forward all risk-based capital information on page 11a is derived solely from data as reported on the call form. This includes capital; risk-weighted asset details as well as individual ratios displayed on this page. Note that data reported for tier 1 capital, tier 2 capital, total capital and risk-weighted assets are revised to include the adjustment for financial subsidiaries. Those adjustments are needed for correct calculation of risk-based capital ratios.

For quarters prior to March 31, 2001 not all banks are required to file complete RC-R information. For those banks that do not file a complete schedule RC-R, the agencies have developed an estimation module that uses information from the report of condition to estimate risk-weighted assets. Approximately 80% of banks were not required to file details for risk-weighted assets. The module follows that used by the FDIC risk-based insurance premium assessments.

Capital is separated into three major groups—tier one and tier two and tier three capital. Tier one is an adjusted equity capital, while tier two considers certain preferred stock and debt instruments for eligibility. Tier three capital includes an allocation for market risk. All components are combined to form total capital.

Estimated and actual calculations of risk-based capital are available to the general public.

Risk-Based Capital ($000)

Details the components of tier one and tier two capital.

Tier One Capital

Total Equity Capital Adjusted

From March 31, 2001 forward includes data from RC-R: total equity capital, the following adjustments: for net unrealized gains (losses) on available-for-sale securities, for unrealized loss on available-for-sale equity securities, for accumulated gains (losses) on cash flow hedges, for nonqualifying perpetual preferred stock, qualifying minority interest in consolidated subsidiaries, and other additions (deletions) to equity capital. Also the adjustment for financial subsidiaries from schedule RC-R reported in tier 1 capital on schedule RC-R is deducted.

For prior quarters includes the sum of common stock, surplus, undivided profits, net worth certificates, cumulative foreign currency adjustments less unrealized loss on marketable equity securities, noncumulative perpetual preferred stock, minority interest in consolidated subsidiaries.

Minus Ineligible Def. Tax Assets

From March 31, 2001 forward from RC-R. For prior quarters from schedule RC-F.

Minus Ineligible Intangibles

From March 31, 2001 forward from RC-R.

For prior quarters ineligible intangible assets is calculated by subtracting eligible intangible assets from total intangible assets on schedule RC-M. Eligible intangible assets are

composed of purchased credit card relationships and mortgage servicing rights subject to an overall limit of 100% of tier one capital.

Minus Cumulative Change in Fair Value of Financial Liabilities

From schedule RC-R.

Net Tier One

From March 31, 2001 forward tier 1 capital from RC-R less the adjustment for financial subsidiaries. For prior quarters it is the sum of the above capital components.

Tier Two Capital

Qualifying Debt and Redeemable Preferred

From March P31, 2001 forward includes qualifying subordinated debt and redeemable preferred stock from RC-R.

For prior quarters includes:

Allowable subordinated debt and intermediate term preferred stock and other limited life instruments from schedule RC-R. The components are discounted by maturity as follows:

    1 to 2 years = 20%
    2 to 3 years = 40%
    3 to 4 years = 60%
    4 to 5 years = 80%
    over 5 years = 100%

Subordinated debt is also limited to 50% of tier one capital.

Plus mandatory convertible debt from RC-M.

Plus Cumulative Preferred Stock

From March 31, 2001 forward includes cumulative perpetual preferred stock includible in tier w from RC-R. For prior quarters preferred stock minus non cumulative perpetual preferred stock from schedules RC and RC-M.

Plus Allowable Loans & Lease Loss Allowance

From March 31, 2001 forward includes allowance for loan and lease losses includible in tier 2 from RC-R. For prior quarters the allowance for loan and lease losses is limited to 1.25% of gross risk-weighted assets, which is defined as risk-weighted assets minus ineligible intangible assets, and if applicable minus ineligible deferred tax assets. From March 31, 1997 forward for banks filing FFIEC 031, 032 AND 033 based on the Balance end of Current Period from RI B.II. For banks filing FFIEC 034 and for all banks for prior quarters based on Schedule RC Allowance for Loan and Lease Losses.

Plus-Unrealized Gain Marketable Equity Securities (45%)

From March 31, 2001 forward includes unrealized gains on available-for-sale equity securities inbcludible in tier 2 from RC-R. For prior quarters from September 30, 1998 forward 45% of the unrealized gain in marketable equity securities is included in tier two capital.

Other Tier Two Capital Components

Other Tier 2 Capital Components as reported on schedule RC-R item 16.

Net Eligible Tier Two*

From March 31, 2001 forward allowable tier 2 capital from RC-R including other tier two capital components. For prior quarters the sum of all tier two capital components. Tier two capital cannot exceed 100% of tier one capital.

Total RBC Before Deductions

Tier One & Tier Two

Sum of net tier one and net eligible tier two capital.

Tier Three and Financial Subsidiary Adjustment

From March 31, 2001 forward includes tier 3 capital allocated for market risk from RC-R. Also includes

50% of the adjustment for financial subsidiaries reported as reported on schedule RC-R in total capital. For prior quarters includes reported tier three capital from call schedule RC-R for banks filing 031 and 032 call forms, from March 31, 1998 forward.

Minus Reciprocal Capital Holdings

Available for quarters prior to March 31, 2001 includes interbank holdings of capital instruments from schedule RC-M. Reported only in December, so for interim quarters, the prior year end figure is used.

Deductions for Total RBC

Total deductions for risk-based capital as reported on schedule RC-R.

Total Risk-Based Capital

From March 31, 2001 forward total risk-based capital from RC-R less the adjustment for financial subsidiaries. For prior quarters include tier one plus tier two capital plus tier three capital less reciprocal holdings.

Risk-Weighted Assets

On Balance Sheet

From March 31, 2001 forward risk-weighted asset information for all banks is retrieved from RC-R. For prior quarters on balance sheet assets are derived either from schedule RC-R for banks that file complete RC-R data, or from a variety of report of condition schedules for those banks that do not file complete RC-R data. Note that available-for-sale securities are counted at cost for risk-based capital purposes.

Category Two—20%

From March 31, 2001 forward the total of components in the 20% balance sheet asset categories on RC-R is multiplied by 20%.

For prior quarters components listed below are multiplied by 20% risk weight. For banks filing RC-R, it is composed of assets assigned to the 20% risk weight category.

For banks not filing RC-R, federal funds sold, securities purchased under resell agreements, assets held in trading accounts, passthrough securities issued by FNMA and FHLMC, CMOs issued by FNMA and FHLMC, private issue CMOs collateralized or guaranteed by guaranteed by FNMA, FHLMC or GNMA, US government sponsored agencies, general obligation securities of state and political subdivisions in the US, acceptances of other banks.

Additionally, for banks filing FFIEC form 034, add interest bearing bank balances and Noninterest bearing bank balances less currency and coin. For other banks, add cash items in process of collection.

Category Three—50%

From March 31, 2001 forward the total of components in the 50% balance sheet asset category on RC-R is multiplied by 50%. For prior quarters components listed below are multiplied by 50% risk weight.

For banks filing RC-R, it is composed of assets assigned to the 50% risk weight category.

For banks not filing RC-R completely, the sum of loans secured by first liens on 1–4 family residential properties, state and local subdivision revenue obligations, privately issued pass through securities, all other privately issued CMO & REMICs.

Category Four—100%

From March 31, 2001 forward the total of all components in the 100% balance sheet asset category is risk-weighted at 100%. For prior quarters components listed below are multiplied by 100% risk weight.

For banks filing RC-R, it is composed of assets assigned to the 100% risk weight category. For banks filing RC-R items 4 through 9 the estimate of unrealized loss on marketable equity securities is not deducted from March 31, 1997 forward.

For banks not filing RC-R, total assets are adjusted to place available-for-sale securities on a cost basis except for losses on marketable equity securities, plus allowance for loan losses and allocated transfer risk reserve, less assets assigned to 0%, 20%, 50% risk weight categories, less participation in acceptances conveyed to others (banks filing FFIEC 031, 032, 033). From September 30, 1998 forward 45% of the unrealized gain on marketable equity securities is added to risk-weighted assets.

Total On Balance Sheet

Sum of all risk-weighted on balance sheet assets.

Memo: Category One—0%

From March 31, 2001 forward the total of components in the 0% balance sheet category is displayed. For prior quarters components listed below are multiplied by 0% risk weight. (For display no weighting is done).

For banks filing RC-R, it is composed of assets assigned to the 0% risk weight category.

For banks not filing complete RC-R data, U.S. Treasury securities, securities issued by U.S. Treasury agencies, pass through securities guaranteed by GNMA, currency and coin.

Additionally, for banks filing FFIEC 031, 032 and 033, balances due from Federal Reserve.

Off-Balance Sheet

From March 31, 2001 forward risk-weighted asset information for all banks is retrieved from RC-R. For prior quarters off-balance sheet assets are derived from schedule RC-R for banks that file all RC-R data. For banks that do not file all data, information from schedule RC-L is used. For banks not filing RC-R data, the off-balance sheet amounts are first converted to an on balance sheet equivalent using a conversion factor then the appropriate risk weight is applied.

Category Two—20%

From March 31, 2001 forward all

components in the RC-R off-balance sheet 20% category are summed and multiplied by 20%. For prior quarters components listed below are multiplied by 20% risk weight.

For banks filing RC-R, credit equivalents of off-balance sheet items assigned to the 20% risk weight category are used. For banks not filing all RC-R data, the following items are converted at the appropriate rate.

Financial standby letters of credit conveyed to others and securities lent are converted at 100%, and performance standby letters of credit conveyed to others are converted at 50%.

Additionally, for banks filing FFIEC 031, 032 and 033, participation in acceptances conveyed to others are converted at 100% and participation in commitments with an original maturity over 1 year conveyed to others are converted at 50%.

Category Three—50%

From March 31, 2001 forward all components in the RC-R off-balance sheet 50% category are summed and multiplied by 50%. For prior quarters components listed below are multiplied by 50% risk weight.

For banks filing RC-R, credit equivalents of off-balance sheet items assigned to the 50% risk weight category are used.

For banks not filing all RC-R data, the following items are converted at the 100% rate; Principal balance of FNMA and FHLMC pools transferred and principal balance of private mortgage pools transferred. From March 31, 1997 forward includes from RC-L, Outstanding principal balance of first lien 1 to 4 family residential mortgage loans.

Category Four—100%

From March 31, 2001 forward all components in the RC-R off-balance sheet 100% category are summed and risk-weighted at 100%. For prior quarters components listed below are multiplied by 100% risk weight.

For banks filing RC-R, credit equivalents of off-balance sheet items assigned to the 100% risk weight category are used.

For banks not filing all RC-R data, the following items are converted at the appropriate rate.

Financial standby letters of credit less financial letters of credit conveyed to others, participation in acceptances acquired by the reporting bank, outstanding balance of Farmer Mac pools transferred, all other off-balance sheet items are converted at 100%.

Performance standby letters of credit less performance standby letters of credit conveyed to others, unused commitments with an original maturity over 1 year, less that conveyed to others (FFIEC 031, 032 and 033) is converted at 50%.

Total Off-Balance Sheet

Sum of the above risk-weighted credit equivalents of off-balance sheet items.

Memo: Category One—0%

From March 31, 2001 forward all components in the RC-R off-balance sheet 0% category are summed and displayed.

For prior quarters components listed below are multiplied by 0% risk weight. For display purposes no weighting is done.

For banks filing RC-R, credit equivalents of off-balance sheet items assigned to the 0% risk weight category are used.

For banks not filing all RC-R data no estimation is made.

Adjustments to Risk-Weighted Assets

Risk-Weighted Asset Before Deductions

The sum of total on and off-balance sheet risk-weighted assets.

Minus Ineligible Deferred Tax Assets

Not available from March 31, 2001

forward. See tier one capital for definition.

Minus Ineligible Intangibles

Not available from March 31, 2001 forward. See tier one capital for definition.

Minus Reciprocal Capital Holdings

Not available from March 31, 2001 forward. See tier two capital for definition.

Minus Excess Allowable Loans & Lease Allowance

From March 31, 2001 forward excess allowance for loan and lease losses from RC-R. For prior quarters allowance for loan and lease losses less allowable loan and lease loss included in tier two capital.

Minus Allocated Transfer Risk Reserve

Allocated transfer risk reserve.

Market Risk Equivalent Assets & Financial Subsidiary Adjustment

From March 31, 2001 forward includes market risk equivalent assets from RC-R. Also includes the adjustment to risk-weighted assets for financial subsidiaries as reported on schedule RC-R. For prior quarters includes reported market risk equivalent assets from schedule RC-R for banks filing 031 and 032 call forms from March 31, 1998 forward.

Total Risk-Weighted Assets

From March 31, 2001 forward total risk-weighted assets from RC-R less the adjustment for financial subsidiaries. For prior quarters this item is the total of the risk-weighted assets calculated above including adjustments.

Risk-Based Capital

Tier One RBC to Risk-Weighted Assets

From March 31, 2001 forward if the bank reports financial subsidiaries then the tier 1 risk-based capital ratio adjusted for financial subsidiaries is displayed from RC-R. Otherwise the unadjusted tier 1 risk-based capital ratio is displayed from RC-R. For prior quarters tier one capital divided by risk-weighted assets.

Total RBC to Risk Weigh Assets

From March 31, 2001 forward if the bank reports financial subsidiaries then the adjusted total risk-based capital ratio is displayed. Otherwise the unadjusted total risk-based capital ratio is displayed. For prior quarters it is calculated by dividing total risk-based capital by risk-weighted assets.

Tier One Leverage Capital

From March 31, 2001 forward if the bank reports financial subsidiaries then the tier 1 leverage ratio adjusted for financial subsidiaries is displayed from RC-R. Otherwise the unadjusted tier leverage ratio is displayed from RC-R.

For prior quarters tier one capital is divided by adjusted average assets. Average assets from schedule RC-K is adjusted for ineligible intangible assets and deferred tax assets as used in tier one capital.

Other Capital Ratio:

Deferred Tax Asset to Tier One Capital

Deferred tax assets from RC-F divided by tier one capital.

ONE QUARTER ANNUALIZED INCOME ANALYSIS

	06/30/2008			3/31/2008			12/31/2007			9/30/2007		6/30/2007	
EARNINGS AND PROFITABILITY	BANK	PG 1	PCT	BANK	PG 1	PCT	BANK	PG 1	PCT	BANK	PG 1	BANK	PG 1
PERCENT OF AVERAGE ASSETS													
INTEREST INCOME (TE)	4.85	5.20	24	5.30	5.61	26	5.78	6.08	31	5.96	6.34	5.85	6.20
- INTEREST EXPENSE	1.95	2.03	44	2.44	2.51	45	2.87	2.95	47	2.99	3.12	2.97	3.04
NET INTEREST INCOME (TE)	2.89	3.15	33	2.86	3.07	31	2.91	3.13	32	2.97	3.24	2.88	3.17
+ NONINTEREST INCOME	1.58	1.22	72	2.24	1.23	85	1.89	1.15	80	1.64	1.31	1.69	1.31
- NONINTEREST EXPENSE	2.83	2.66	60	2.61	2.59	52	2.98	2.73	63	2.88	2.63	2.61	2.56
- PROVISION LOAN&LEASE LOSSES	1.06	0.87	68	1.31	0.62	84	0.84	0.49	76	0.35	0.25	0.24	0.19
PRETAX OPERATING INCOME (TE)	0.58	0.86	30	1.18	1.16	46	0.98	1.06	39	1.39	1.69	1.72	1.77
+ REALIZED GAINS/LOSSES SECS	1.30	-0.02	99	-0.14	0.03	5	0.01	-0.03	81	0.00	0.01	0.54	0.00
PRETAX NET OPERATING INC (TE)	1.89	0.77	78	1.04	1.16	42	0.99	0.94	42	1.39	1.69	2.26	1.75
NET OPERATING INCOME	1.28	0.50	81	0.75	0.77	42	0.69	0.63	44	0.95	1.11	1.49	1.13
ADJUSTED NET OPERATING INCOME	1.58	0.96	83	1.36	1.03	70	1.14	0.90	61	1.05	1.20	1.52	1.18
NET INCOME ADJUSTED SUB S		0.49	N/A		0.77	N/A		0.64	N/A		1.09		1.12
NET INCOME	1.28	0.49	81	0.75	0.77	42	0.69	0.64	44	0.95	1.09	1.49	1.13
MARGIN ANALYSIS													
INT INC (TE) TO AVG EARN ASSETS	5.37	5.67	28	5.89	6.12	31	6.46	6.66	33	6.63	6.92	6.49	6.76
INT EXPENSE TO AVG EARN ASSETS	2.17	2.22	47	2.71	2.74	46	3.21	3.24	49	3.33	3.41	3.30	3.32
NET INT INC-TE TO AVG EARN ASST	3.21	3.44	36	3.18	3.36	36	3.26	3.45	35	3.31	3.55	3.19	3.47
LOAN & LEASE ANALYSIS													
NET LOSS TO AVERAGE TOTAL LN&LS	0.99	0.66	72	0.91	0.49	79	0.52	0.40	70	0.32	0.26	0.27	0.21
EARNINGS COVERAGE OF NET LOSS(X)	2.09	7.98	28	3.45	9.65	33	4.37	8.83	37	6.75	18.83	9.32	33.47
LN&LS ALLOWANCE TO NET LOSSES(X)	1.29	3.50	28	1.30	4.42	20	1.91	3.61	31	2.63	7.55	2.97	10.00
CAPITALIZATION													
CASH DIVIDENDS TO NET INCOME	59.17	35.28	71	99.97	35.70	85	108.75	60.52	76	202.41	53.55	49.18	61.44
RETAIN EARNS TO AVG TOT EQUITY	4.50	-0.02	63	0.00	2.98	31	-0.53	-1.16	41	-8.62	3.47	6.84	3.12
YIELD ON OR COST OF													
TOTAL LOANS & LEASES (TE)	5.53	6.05	20	6.09	6.59	18	6.66	7.22	17	6.82	7.53	6.72	7.37
LOANS IN DOMESTIC OFFICES	5.54	6.04	20	6.04	6.58	16	6.62	7.22	15	6.79	7.52	6.68	7.37
REAL ESTATE	5.72	6.05	28	6.24	6.51	25	6.77	7.12	30	6.95	7.45	6.82	7.27
SECURED BY 1-4 FAM. RESI PROP	5.85	6.01	42	6.27	6.35	46	N/A	N/A	N/A	N/A	N/A	N/A	N/A
ALL OTHER LOANS SEC. REAL EST	5.43	6.08	20	6.16	6.61	22	N/A	N/A	N/A	N/A	N/A	N/A	N/A
COMMERCIAL & INDUSTRIAL	4.46	5.98	9	4.64	6.61	4	4.84	7.53	3	5.02	8.03	5.01	7.94
INDIVIDUAL	5.83	6.08	20	5.99	7.69	14	6.52	8.14	17	6.56	8.30	6.42	8.16
CREDIT CARD PLANS	10.27	9.96	53	6.44	10.94	14	3.21	10.32	13	2.73	11.88	5.85	11.77
AGRICULTURAL	4.44	6.04	13	5.39	6.16	15	6.90	7.03	28	7.29	7.52	7.36	7.39
LOANS IN FOREIGN OFFICES	N/A	1.29	N/A	N/A	1.55	N/A	N/A	1.92	N/A	N/A	3.27	N/A	2.47
TOTAL INVESTMENT SECURITIES(TE)	6.04	4.94	93	5.79	5.05	89	5.83	5.24	87	5.89	5.26	5.69	5.11
TOTAL INVESTMENT SECURITES(BOOK)	5.90	4.75	94	5.63	4.85	92	5.68	5.03	92	5.74	5.05	5.53	4.91
U S TREAS & AGENCY (EXCL MBS)	4.55	4.27	59	4.63	4.59	48	4.92	4.77	54	5.00	4.91	4.99	4.78
MORTGAGE BACKED SECURITIES	5.80	5.03	90	5.75	5.04	91	5.68	5.13	86	5.71	5.09	5.47	5.00
ALL OTHER SECURITIES	6.95	4.51	95	5.21	4.68	76	5.87	4.90	81	6.08	5.06	5.94	4.92
INTEREST-BEARING BANK BALANCES	3.27	2.33	76	4.77	3.32	85	7.61	4.18	91	5.68	5.05	5.61	4.94
FEDERAL FUNDS SOLD & RESALES	2.06	2.20	36	2.59	3.21	9	4.39	4.68	17	5.04	5.24	5.33	5.33
TOTAL INT-BEARING DEPOSITS	2.30	2.34	48	2.97	2.86	57	3.50	3.36	59	3.65	3.56	3.61	3.48
TRANSACTION ACCOUNTS	1.16	1.02	61	1.85	1.39	69	2.34	1.75	68	2.41	1.98	2.37	1.90
OTHER SAVINGS DEPOSITS	1.30	1.25	57	1.88	1.68	64	2.30	2.20	57	2.27	2.46	2.13	2.39
TIME DEPS OVER $100M	3.68	3.68	48	4.50	4.38	59	5.09	4.76	79	5.22	4.95	5.14	4.85
ALL OTHER TIME DEPOSITS	4.00	3.74	62	4.45	4.26	64	4.64	4.64	51	4.54	4.66	4.54	4.60
DEPOSITS IN FOREIGN OFFICES	1.97	2.17	36	3.12	3.05	56	4.46	4.10	71	5.13	4.54	5.27	4.57
FEDERAL FUNDS PURCHASED & REPOS	1.72	2.33	19	2.55	3.21	14	4.06	4.32	27	4.67	4.72	4.95	4.77
OTHER BORROWED MONEY	4.63	4.13	84	4.79	4.13	81	5.10	4.82	69	5.10	5.13	4.92	5.06
SUBORD NOTES & DEBENTURES	0.42	4.94	4	0.71	5.71	3	1.12	6.12	4	1.12	6.29	1.84	6.14
ALL INTEREST-BEARING FUNDS	2.52	2.48	55	3.13	3.07	53	3.70	3.62	54	3.84	3.83	3.82	3.77

UBPR Page 12

One Quarter Annualized Income Analysis

This page presents a quarter-by-quarter analysis of income and expense. Five consecutive single quarters of historical financial information are shown.

The analysis differs from the year-to-date presentation in the remainder of the UBPR in that the income or expense attributed to one quarter is annualized (multiplied by 4) and compared to average asset or liability balances for that quarter. The resulting information permits the user to associate changes in earnings with a specific quarter and is a useful supplement to year-to-date earnings analysis.

The following rules apply to income, expense, asset and liability balances in **One Quarter Annualized Income Analysis**:

For the second, third and fourth quarters the current income/expense item is subtracted from the prior quarter item then multiplied by 4.

For the first quarter, no subtraction is done, but the income/expense item is multiplied by 4.

For the second, third and fourth quarters when push-down accounting is indicated for the first time that year, no subtraction is performed. The reported value is multiplied by 4.

The appropriate asset or liability, i.e. loans will generally come from schedule RC-K averages for the current quarter. In the few instances where banks do not report sufficient detail on RC-K, end-of-period balances are used.

The presentation of information on page twelve follows that of the analysis on pages one and three. An overall analysis of earnings and profitability is followed by details on loan and lease, capitalization, yield and cost information. The report of condition and report of income com-ponents used in calculations follow those used on pages one and three. Refer to those pages for definition of components used in ratios. Ratios using after tax income and dividends have been adjusted for assumed tax rates. See Section II Technical Information.

Earnings and Profitability

Interest Income (TE)

All income from earning assets plus the tax benefit on tax-exempt loans, leases, and municipal securities, divided by average assets.

Interest Expense

Total interest expense divided by average assets.

Net Interest Income (TE)

Total interest income, plus the tax benefit on tax-exempt income, less total interest expense, divided by average assets.

Noninterest Income

Income derived from bank services and sources other than interest-bearing assets, divided by average assets.

Noninterest Expense

Salaries and employee benefits, expenses of premises and fixed assets and other noninterest expense divided by average assets.

Provision-Loan/Lease Losses

Provision for loan and lease-financing receivables losses divided by average assets.

Pretax Operating Income (TE)

Net interest income on a tax-equivalent basis plus noninterest income, less noninterest expenses, the provision for loan and lease-financing receivables losses and the provision for allocated transfer risk, divided by average assets.

Realized Gain/Loss Secs

Pretax net gains or losses from the sale, exchange, retirement, or redemption of securities not held in trading accounts. After December 31, 1993 includes available-for-sale and held-to-maturity transactions divided by average assets.

Pretax Net Operating Income (TE)

Pretax operating income, plus securities gains or losses, divided by average assets.

Net Operating Income

After tax net operating income, including securities gains or losses, (which does not include extraordinary gains or losses), divided by average assets.

Adjusted Net Oper Income

Net operating income after taxes and securities gains or losses, plus the provision for possible loan and lease losses, less net loan and lease losses, divided by average assets.

Net Income Adjusted Sub S

Net income after securities gains or losses, extraordinary gains or losses, and applicable taxes, divided by average assets adjusted for sub chapter S status. Estimated income taxes are substituted for any reported applicable income taxes for banks that indicate sub chapter S status. Estimated income taxes: Federal income tax rates are applied to net income before extraordinary items and taxes plus non-deductible interest expense to carry tax-exempt securities less tax-exempt income from securities issued by states and political subdivisions, less tax-exempt income from leases, less tax-exempt income from other obligations of states and political subdivisions. (See appendix A-3 for tax table)

Please note that this ratio will be displayed only for banks that elect subchapter S status.

Net Income

Net income after securities gains or losses, extraordinary gains or losses, and applicable taxes divided by average assets.

Margin Analysis:

Interest Income (TE)/Average Earning Assets

Total interest income on a tax-equivalent basis divided by the average of the respective asset accounts involved in generating that income.

Interest Expense/Average Earning Assets

Total interest expense divided by the average of the respective asset accounts involved in generating interest income.

Net Interest Income (TE)/Average Earning Assets

Total interest income on a tax-equivalent basis, less total interest expense, divided by the average of the respective asset accounts involved in generating interest income.

Interest Income (TE) To Average Earned Assets

Loan & Lease Analysis

Net Loss to Average Total Loan & Lease

Gross loan and lease charge-offs, less gross recoveries (includes allocated transfer risk reserve charge-offs and recoveries), divided by average total loans and leases.

Earnings Coverage of Net Loss (X)

Net operating income before taxes, securities gains or losses, and extraordinary items, plus the provision for possible loan and lease-financing receivable losses divided by net loan and lease losses.

Loan & Lease Allowance Net Losses (X)

Ending balance of the allowance for possible loan and lease-financing receivable losses divided by net loan and lease losses. If gross recoveries exceed gross losses, NA is shown at this caption.

Capitalization

Cash Dividends to Net Income

Total of all cash dividends declared year-to-date divided by net income year-to-date. If net income is less than or equal to zero, NA is shown at this caption.

Retain Earns to Average Total Equity

Net income, less cash dividends declared, divided by average equity capital.

Yield on or cost of:

Total Loans & Lease (TE)

Interest and fees on loans and income on direct lease-financing receivables, plus the tax benefit on tax-exempt loan and lease income, divided by average total loans and lease-financing receivables. See Appendix B regarding the calculation of tax benefits.

Loans in Domestic Offices

Interest and fees on loans held in domestic offices divided by average domestic office loans.

Real Estate Loans

Interest and fees on domestic office loans secured primarily by real estate, divided by average domestic real estate loans.

Loans Secured By 1-4 Family Residential Property

Interest and Fees on Loans Secured by 1–4 Family Real Estate Divided by Average Loans Secured by 1–4 Family Real Estate.

All Other Loans Secured By Real Estate

Interest and Fees on All Other Loans Secured Real Estate Divided by Average Loans Secured by Real Estate.

Commercial & Industrial Loans

Interest and fees on domestic office commercial and industrial loans, divided by average domestic commercial and industrial loans.

Individual Loans

Interest and fees on domestic office loans to individuals for household, family and other personal expenditures divided by average domestic loans to individuals for household, family, and other personal expenditures.

Credit Card Plans

Interest and fees on credit card plans divided by the average for credit card and related plans.

Agricultural Loans

Interest and fees on domestic office loans to finance agricultural production divided by average domestic loans to finance agricultural production.

Loans in Foreign Offices

Interest and fees on loans in foreign offices divided by average loans in foreign offices. Available for banks filing call form 031.

Total Investment Securities (TE)

Income on securities not held in trading accounts, plus the estimated tax benefit on tax-exempt municipal securities income, divided by average U.S. Treasury and U.S. government agency securities, state and political subdivisions, and other debt and equity securities.

Total Investment Securities (Book)

Income on securities not held in trading accounts, divided by average U.S. Treasury and U.S. government agency securities, state and political subdivisions, and other debt and equity securities.

US Treasury & Agency (Excluding MBS)

Income on U.S. Treasury securities and U.S. government agency obligations divided by average U. S. Treasury securities and U.S. government agency obligations. Excludes mortgage backed securities. Available from March 31, 2001 forward.

Mortgage Backed Securities

Income on mortgage backed securities divided by the average for those securities.

All Other Securities

Income on all other securities divided by the average for those securities. Includes taxable and tax-exempt obligations issued by state and local subdivisions.

Interest-Bearing Bank Balances

Interest on balances due from depository institutions divided by the average of interest-bearing balances due from depository institutions carried in domestic and foreign office.

Federal Funds Sold & Resales

Income on federal funds sold and securities purchased under agreements to resell divided by the average of federal funds sold and securities purchased under agreements to resell.

Total Interest-Bearing Deposits

Interest on all interest-bearing time and savings deposits in domestic and foreign offices divided by average interest-bearing time and savings deposits in domestic and foreign offices.

Transaction Accounts

Interest on transaction accounts (NOW accounts, ATS accounts, and telephone and preauthorized transfer accounts) divided by the average balance of such deposits.

Other Savings Deposits

For quarters from March 31 2001 forward includes interest on other savings deposits (all savings accounts and money market deposits accounts) divided by the average of such deposits. For quarters prior to March 31, 2001 excludes MMDA's.

Time Deps over $100M or More

Interest on time certificates of deposit of $100 thousand or more issued by domestic offices divided by the average of domestic time certificates of deposit of $100 thousand or more. From March 31, 1997, time deposits open accounts; are included.

All Other Time Deposits

Interest on all domestic time deposits of less than $100,000 and open-account time deposits of $100,000 or more, divided by the average of such deposits. From March 31, 1997 forward, time deposit open accounts not included.

Deposits in Foreign Offices

Interest on deposits in foreign offices, Edge and Agreement subsidiaries and IBF's divided by the average for such deposits. Available for banks filing call form 031.

Federal Funds Purchased & Repos

The expense of federal funds purchased and securities sold under agreements to repurchase divided by the average of federal funds purchased and securities sold under agreements to repurchase.

Other Borrowed Money

Interest on demand notes (note balances) issued to the U.S. Treasury and on other borrowed money divided by the average of interest-bearing demand notes (note balances) issued to the U.S. Treasury and other liabilities for borrowed money.

Subordinated Notes & Debentures

Interest on notes and debentures subordinated to deposits divided by the average of notes and debentures subordinated to deposits.

All Interest-Bearing Funds

Interest on all interest-bearing deposits in domestic offices, interest-bearing foreign office deposits, demand notes (note balances) issued to the U.S. Treasury, other borrowed money, subordinated notes and debentures, and expense on federal funds purchased and securities sold under agreements to repurchase, interest expense on mortgage and capitalized leases divided by the average of the liabilities or funds that generated those expenses.

	06/30/2008	06/30/2007	12/31/2007	12/31/2006	12/31/2005	PERCENT CHANGE 1 QTR	PERCENT CHANGE 1 YEAR
SECURITIZATION ACTIVITIES	122,587,920	102,440,271	111,283,532	89,188,715	69,765,105	4.12	19.67
1-4 FAMILY RESIDENTIAL LOANS	122,013,578	101,818,576	110,689,709	88,535,977	69,741,269	4.15	19.83
HOME EQUITY LINES	0	0	0	0	0	N/A	N/A
CREDIT CARD RECEIVABLES	0	0	0	0	0	N/A	N/A
AUTO LOANS	0	0	0	0	0	N/A	N/A
COMMERCIAL & INDUSTRIAL LOANS	0	0	0	0	0	N/A	N/A
ALL OTHER LOANS AND LEASES	574 342	621 695	593 823	652 738	23 836	-1.49	-7.62
RETAINED INTEREST-ONLY STRIPS	20,653	20,875	23,447	25,664	196	-7.35	-1.06
1-4 FAMILY RESIDENTIAL LOANS	159	1,113	165	1,271	196	-1.24	-85.71
HOME EQUITY LOANS	0	0	0	0	0	N/A	N/A
CREDIT CARD RECEIVABLES	0	0	0	0	0	N/A	N/A
AUTO LOANS	0	0	0	0	0	N/A	N/A
COMMERCIAL & INDUSTRIAL LOANS	0	0	0	0	0	N/A	N/A
ALL OTHER LOANS AND LEASES	20 494	19 762	23 282	24 393	0	-7.39	3.70
RETAINED CREDIT ENHANCEMENTS	82,703	60,577	70,328	70,555	53,273	-14.51	36.53
1-4 FAMILY RESIDENTIAL LOANS	82,703	60,577	70,328	70,555	53,273	-14.51	36.53
HOME EQUITY LOANS	0	0	0	0	0	N/A	N/A
CREDIT CARD RECEIVABLES	0	0	0	0	0	N/A	N/A
AUTO LOANS	0	0	0	0	0	N/A	N/A
COMMERCIAL & INDUSTRIAL LOANS	0	0	0	0	0	N/A	N/A
ALL OTHER LOANS AND LEASES	0	0	0	0	0	N/A	N/A
UNUSED LIQUIDITY COMMITTMENTS	0	0	0	0	0	N/A	N/A
SELLERS INTEREST IN SECS & LOANS	0	0	0	0	0	N/A	N/A
HOME EQUITY LINES	0	0	0	0	0	N/A	N/A
CREDIT CARD RECEIVABLES	0	0	0	0	0	N/A	N/A
COMMERCIAL & INDUSTRIAL LOANS	0	0	0	0	0	N/A	N/A
TOTAL RETAINED CREDIT EXPOSURE	103,356	81,452	93,775	96,219	53,469	-13.17	26.89
ASSET BACKED COMML PAPER COND	8,345,342	9,194,384	9,267,444	8,720,077	7,897,415	-8.51	-9.23
CR EXP SPONS BY BANK & OTHER	738,863	721,210	763,436	697,782	707.084	-4.60	2.45
LIQUID COMM BY BANK & OTHER	7,606,479	8,473,174	8,504,008	8,022,295	7,190,331	-8.87	-10.23
ACTIVITY % TOTAL ASSETS							
SECURITIZATION ACTIVITIES	71.48	57.85	63.55	48.85	39.36		
1-4 FAMILY RESIDENTIAL LOANS	71.14	57.50	63.21	48.49	39.35		
HOME EQUITY LINES	0.00	0.00	0.00	0.00	0.00		
CREDIT CARD RECEIVABLES	0.00	0.00	0.00	0.00	0.00		
AUTO LOANS	0.00	0.00	0.00	0.00	0.00		
COMMERCIAL & INDUSTRIAL LOANS	0.00	0.00	0.00	0.00	0.00		
ALL OTHER LOANS AND LEASES	0.33	0.35	0.34	0.36	0.01		
ASSET BACKED COMML PAPER COND	4.87	5.19	5.29	4.78	4.46		
CR EXP SPONS BY BANK & OTHER	0.43	0.41	0.44	0.38	0.40		
LIQUID COMM BY BANK & OTHER	4.44	4.79	4.86	4.39	4.06		
PERCENT OF TOT MANAGED ASSETS ON							
BALANCE SHEET & SEC ASSETS							
1-4 FAMILY RESIDENTIAL LOANS	62.12	61.67	61.94	59.60	55.97		
HOME EQUITY LINES	6.20	6.11	6.12	6.34	6.88		
CREDIT CARD RECEIVABLES	0.15	0.01	0.14	0.00	0.00		
AUTO LOANS	4.46	4.91	4.73	5.39	7.22		
COMMERCIAL & INDUSTRIAL LOANS	10.97	9.95	9.84	11.06	11 69		
ALL OTHER LOANS AND LEASES	16.10	17.35	17.23	17.61	18.25		

UBPR Page 13

Securitziation and Asset Sale Activities

Data on bank securitization activities comes principally from call report schedule RC-S. This information is available for all banks and was first reported on the June 30, 2001 call report. Bank information is presented in dollar and percentage formats and no peer group information is calculated. One year and annualized quarterly growth rates are calculated for dollar items on page 13.

Securitization Activities

The total of all securitized assets from call schedule RC-S item 1, columns a:g.

1–4 Family Residential Loans

Dollar amount of securitized1–4 Family Residential loans reported on RC-S item 1, column a.

Home Equity Lines

Dollar amount of securitized home equity lines reported on RC-S item 1, column b.

Credit Card Receivables

Dollar amount of securitized credit card receivables reported on RC-S item 1, column c.

Auto Loans

Dollar amount of securitized auto loans reported on RC-S item 1, column d.

Commercial and Industrial Loans

Dollar amount of securitized commercial and industrial loans reported on RC-S item 1, column f.

All Other Loans and Leases

Dollar amount of securitized other consumer loans plus all other loans

reported on RC-S item 1, columns e and g.

Retained Interest Only Strips

The total of all retained interest only strips from call schedule RC-S item 2.a, columns a:g.

1–4 Family Residential Loans

Dollar amount of credit exposure from retained interest only strips on 1–4 Family Residential loans reported on RC-S item 2.a, column a.

Home Equity Lines

Dollar amount of credit exposure from retained interest only strips on home equity lines reported on RC-S item 2.a, column b.

Credit Card Receivables

Dollar amount of credit exposure from retained interest only strips on credit card receivables reported on RC-S item 2.a, column c.

Auto Loans

Dollar amount of credit exposure from retained interest only strips on auto loans reported on RC-S item 2.a, column d.

Comercial and Industrial Loans

Dollar amount of credit exposure from retained interest only strips on commercial and industrial loans reported on RC-S item 2.a, column f.

All Other Loans and Leases

Dollar amount of credit exposure from retained interest only strips on other consumer loans plus all other loans reported on RC-S item 2.a, columns e and g.

Retained Credit Enhancements

From March 31, 2001 through December 31, 2002 includes the total of All Other Credit Enhance-

ments from call schedule RC-S items (RCFDB719) through RCFDB725). From March 31, 2003 forward includes the total of Subordinated Securities, Stand By Letters of Credit and All Other Credit Enhancements from call schedule RC-S items (RCFDC393) through (RCFDC406).

1–4 Family Residential Loans

From March 31, 2001 through December 31, 2002 includes All Other Credit Enhancements on 1–4 Family Residential Loans reported on RC-S item (CFDB719). From March 31, 2003 forward includes Subordinated Securities, Stank by Letters of Credit and All Other Credit Enhancements from call schedule RC-S items (RCFDC393) plus (RCFDC400).

Home Equity Lines

From March 31, 2001 through December 31, 2002 includes RC-S All Other Credit Enhancements on Home Equity Lines reported on RC-S item (RCFDB720). From March 31, 2003 forward includes Subordinated Securities, Stand by Letters of Credit and All Other Credit Enhancements from call schedule RC-S items (RCFDC394) plus (RCDDC401).

Credit Card Receivables

From March 31, 2001 through December 31, 2002 includes All Other Credit Enhancements on Credit Card Receivables reported on RC-S item (RCFDB721). From March 31, 2003 forward includes Subordinated Securities, Stand By Letters of Credit and All Other Credit Enhancements from call schedule RC-S items (RCFDC395) plus (RCFDC402).

Auto Loans

From March 31, 2001 through December 31, 2002 includes All Other Credit Enhancements on Auto Loans reported on RC-S items (RCFDB722). From March 31, 2003 forward includes Subordinated Securities,

Stand By Letters of Credit and All Other Credit Enhancements from call schedule RC-S items (RCFDC396) plus (RCFDC403).

Commercial and Industrial Loans

From March 31, 2001 through December 31, 2002 includes All Other Credit Enhancements on Commerial and Industrial Loans reported on RC-S item (RCFDB724). From March 31, 2003 forward includes Subordinated Securities, Stand By Letters of Credit and All Other Credit Enhancements from call schedule RC-S items (RCFDC398) plus (RCFDC405).

All Other Loans and Leases

From March 31, 2001 through December 31, 2002 includes All Other Credit Enhancements on Other Consumer Loans plus All Other Loans reported on RC-S item (RCFDB723) plus (RCFDB725). From March 31, 2003 forward includes Subordinated Securities, Stand by Letters of Credit and All Other Credit Enhancements from call schedule RC-S or the sum of items (RCFDC397), (RCFDC399), (RCFDC404) and (RCFDC406).

Unused Liquidity Commitments

Dollar amount of unused commitments to provide liquidity to asset sold and securitized as reported on call item 3, columns a:g.

Sellers Interest in Securities and Loans

Dollar amount of ownership (or sellers) interests carried as securities (RC-B) or loans (RC-C). Reported in RC-S items 6.a and 6.b, columns b, c and f.

Home Equity Lines

Dollar amount of ownership (or sellers) interests carried as securities (RC-B) or loans (RC-C). Reported in RC-S items 6.a and 6.b, columns b.

Credit Card Receivables

Dollar amount of ownership (or

sellers) interests carried as securities (RC-B) or loans (RC-C). Reported in RC-S items 6.a and 6.b, columns c.

Commercial and Industrial Loans

Dollar amount of ownership (or sellers) interests carried as securities (RC-B) or loans (RC-C). Reported in RC-S items 6.a and 6.b, columns f.

Total Retained Credit Exposure

The total of all retained interest only strips from call schedule RC-S item 2.a, columns a:g plus total of all other credit enhancements from call schedule RC-S item 2.b, columns a:g.

Asset Backed by Commercial Paper Conduits

Dollar amount of credit enhancements arising from conduit structures and commitments to provide liquidity to conduit structures as reported in RC-S items 3.a, 1 & 2 and 3.b, 1 & 2.

Credit Exposure Sponsored by Bank and Others

Dollar amount of credit enhancements arising from conduit structures as reported in RC-S items 3.a, 1 & 2.

Liquidity Commitments by Bank and Others

Dollar amount of commitments to provide liquidity to conduit structures as reported in RC-S items 3.b, 1 & 2.

Activity % of Total Assets

Each component of securitization activity is expressed as a percentage of total assets.

Securitization Activities

The total of all securitized assets from call schedule RC-S item 1, columns a:g, as a percent of total assets from RC item 12.

1–4 Family Residential Loans

Dollar amount of securitized 1–4 Family Residential loans reported on RC-S item 1, column a, as a percent of total assets from RC item 12.

Home Equity Lines

Dollar amount of securitized home equity lines reported on RC-S item 1, column b, as a percent of total assets from RC item 12.

Credit Card Receivables

Dollar amount of securitized credit card receivables reported on RC-S item 1, column c, as a percent of total assets from RC item 12.

Auto Loans

Dollar amount of securitized auto loans reported on RC-S item 1, column d as a percent of total assets from RC item 12.

Commercial and Industrial Loans

Dollar amount of securitized commercial and industrial loans reported on RC-S item 1, column f as a percent of total assets from RC item 12.

All Other Loans and Leases

Dollar amount of securitized other consumer loans plus all other loans reported on RC-S item 1, columns e and g as a percent of total assets from RC item 12.

Asset Backed by Commercial Paper Conduits

Dollar amount of credit enhancements arising from conduit structures and commitments to provide liquidity to conduit structures as reported in RC-S items 3.a, 1 & 2 and 3.b, 1 & 2 as a percent of total assets from RC item 12.

Credit Exposure Sponsored by Bank and Others

Dollar amount of credit enhancements arising from conduit structures as reported in RC-S items 3.a, 1 & 2 as a percent of total assets from RC item 12.

Liquidity Commitments by Bank and Others

Dollar amount of commitments to provide liquidity to conduit structures as reported in RC-S items 3.b, 1 & 2 as a percent of total assets from RC item 12.

Percent of Total Managed Assets on Balance Sheet & Securitized Assets

The total of managed assets as reported on the balance sheet plus related securitized assets are expressed as a percentage of total assets plus total securitized assets.

1–4 Family Residential Loans

Dollar amount of securitized 1–4 Family Residential loans reported on RC-S item 1, column a. plus loans secured by 1–4 family residential real estate as reported on RC-C items 1.c.2 a & b as a percentage of total assets from RC item 12 plus the total of all securitized assets from call schedule RC-S item 1, columns a:g.

Home Equity Lines

Dollar amount of securitized home equity lines reported on RC-S item 1, column b plus home equity lines of credit from RC-C item 1.2.1 as a percentage of total assets from RC item 12 plus the total of all securitized assets from call schedule RC-S item 1, columns a:g.

Credit Card Receivables

Dollar amount of securitized credit card receivables reported on RC-S item 1, column c. plus loans to individuals on cards on RC-C item 6.a as a percent of total assets from schedule RC item 12 plus the total of all securitized assets from call schedule RC-S item 1, column a:g.

Auto Loans

Dollar amount of securitized auto loans reported on RC-S item 1, column d. plus other consumer loans from RC item 6.c as a percentage of total assets from RC item 12 plus the total of all securitized assets from call schedule RC-S item 1, columns a:g.

Commercial and Industrial Loans

Dollar amount of securitized commercial and industrial loans reported on RC-S item 1, column f plus commercial and industrial loans from RC item 4 as a percentage of total assets from RC item 12 plus the total of all securitized assets from call schedule RC-S item 1, columns a:g.

All Other Loans and Leases

Dollar amount of securitized other consumer loans plus all other loans reported on call schedule RC-S item 1, columns e and g plus total loans and leases RC-C item 12, less revolving lines secured by 1–4 family properties1.c.1, less closed end loans secured by 1–4 family properties item1.c.2, less loans to individuals on credit cards 6.a, less other consumer loans item RC-C 6.c, less commercial and industrial loans from RC-C item 4 as a percentage of total assets from RC item 12 plus the total of all securitized assets from call schedule RC-S item 1, columns a:g.

SECURITIZATION AND ASSET SALE ACTIVITIES

	06/30/2008	06/30/2007	12/31/2007	12/31/2006	12/31/2005
% TOT SECURITIZATION ACT BY TYPE					
RETAINED INT ONLY STRIPS	0.02	0.02	0.02	0.03	0.00
1-4 FAMILY RESIDENTIAL LOANS	0.00	0.00	0.00	0.00	0.00
HOME EQUITY LINES	N/A	N/A	N/A	N/A	N/A
CREDIT CARD RECEIVABLES	N/A	N/A	N/A	N/A	N/A
AUTO LOANS	N/A	N/A	N/A	N/A	N/A
COMMERCIAL & INDUSTRIAL LOANS	N/A	N/A	N/A	N/A	N/A
ALL OTHER LOANS AND LEASES	3.57	3.18	3.92	3.74	0.00
RETAINED CREDIT ENHANCEMENT	0.07	0.06	0.06	0.08	0.08
1-4 FAMILY RESIDENTIAL LOANS	0.07	0.06	0.06	0.08	0.08
HOME EQUITY LINES	N/A	N/A	N/A	N/A	N/A
CREDIT CARD RECEIVABLES	N/A	N/A	N/A	N/A	N/A
AUTO LOANS	N/A	N/A	N/A	N/A	N/A
COMMERCIAL & INDUSTRIAL LOANS	N/A	N/A	N/A	N/A	N/A
ALL OTHER LOANS AND LEASES	0.00	0.00	0.00	0.00	0.00
UNUSED COMM TO PROVIDE LIQUIDITY	0.00	0.00	0.00	0.00	0.00
SELLERS INT IN SECS & LNS % TRUST	0.00	0.00	0.00	0.00	0.00
HOME EQUITY LINES	N/A	N/A	N/A	N/A	N/A
CREDIT CARD RECEIVABLES	N/A	N/A	N/A	N/A	N/A
COMMERCIAL AND INDUSTRIAL LOANS	N/A	N/A	N/A	N/A	N/A
PERCENT OF TIER 1 CAPITAL					
TOTAL RETAINED CREDIT EXPOSURE	0.83	0.63	0.76	0.75	0.46
RETAINED INTEREST-ONLY STRIPS	0.16	0.16	0.19	0.20	0.00
RETAINED CREDIT ENHANCEMENTS	0.66	0.47	0.57	0.55	0.45
30-89 DAY PD SECURITIZED ASSETS					
1-4 FAMILY RESIDENTIAL LOANS	3 420 678	2 316 017	2 973 250	2 093 742	1 568 887
HOME EQUITY LINES	0	0	0	0	0
CREDIT CARD RECEIVABLES	0	0	0	0	0
AUTO LOANS	0	0	0	0	0
COMMERCIAL & INDUSTRIAL LOANS	0	0	0	0	0
ALL OTHER LOANS AND LEASES	29,087	30,896	32,461	33,707	1,698
TOTAL 30-89 DAY PD SECUR ASSET	3,449,765	2,346,913	3,005,711	2,127,449	1,570,585
90+ DAYS PD SECURITIZED ASSETS					
1-4 FAMILY RESIDENTIAL LOANS	2,743,932	899,420	1,774,480	525,497	307,300
HOME EQUITY LINES	0	0	0	0	0
CREDIT CARD RECEIVABLES	0	0	0	0	0
AUTO LOANS	0	0	0	0	0
COMMERCIAL & INDUSTRIAL LOANS	0	0	0	0	0
ALL OTHER LOANS AND LEASES	23,250	23,084	27,954	27,006	2,330
TOTAL 90 + DAY PD SECUR ASSET	2,767,182	922,504	1,802,434	552,503	309,630
TOTAL PAST DUE SECURITIZED ASSETS	6,216,947	3,269,417	4,808,145	2,679,952	1,880,215
NET LOSSES SECURITIZED ASSETS					
1-4 FAMILY RESIDENTIAL LOANS	89	10	37	116	82
HOME EQUITY LINES	0	0	0	0	0
CREDIT CARD RECEIVABLES	0	0	0	0	0
AUTO LOANS	0	0	0	0	0
COMMERCIAL & INDUSTRIAL LOANS	0	0	0	0	0
ALL OTHER LOANS AND LEASES	0	0	4	20	0
TOTAL NET CHARGE OFF SECUR ASSET	N/A	N/A	N/A	N/A	N/A

UBPR Page 13A

% Total Securitization by Type

The type of securitization is expressed as a percentage of total securitized and sold assets by type.

Retained Interest Only Strips

The total of all retained interest only strips from call schedule RC-S item 2.a, columns a:g as a percentage of total of all securitized assets from call schedule RC-S item 1, columns a:g.

1–4 Family Residential Loans

Dollar amount of credit exposure from retained interest only strips on 1–4 Family Residential loans reported on RC-S item 2.a, column a as a percentage of securitized 1–4 family residential loans reported on RC-S item 1, column a.

Home Equity Lines

Dollar amount of credit exposure from retained interest only strips on home equity lines reported on RC-S item 2.a, column b as a percentage of securitized home equity lines reported on RC-S item 1, column b.

Credit Card Receivables

Dollar amount of credit exposure from retained interest only strips on credit card receivables reported on RC-S item 2.a, column c as a percentage of securitized credit card receivables reported on RC-S item 1, column c.

Auto Loans

Dollar amount of credit exposure from retained interest only strips on auto loans reported on RC-S item 2.a, column d as a percentage of securitized auto loans reported on RC-S item 1, column d.

Commercial and Industrial Loans

Dollar amount of credit exposure from retained interest only strips on commercial and industrial loans reported on RC-S item 2.a, column f as a percentage of securitized commercial and industrial loans reported on RC-S item 1, column f.

All Other Loans and Leases

Dollar amount of credit exposure from retained interest only strips on other consumer loans plus all other loans reported on RC-S item 2.a, columns e and g as a percentage of securitized other consumer loans plus all other loans reported on RC-S item 1, columns e and g.

Retained Credit Enhancement

The total of all other credit enhancements from call schedule RC-S item 2, columns a:g as a percentage of total of all securitized assets from call schedule RC-S item 1, columns a:g.

1–4 Family Residential Loans

Dollar amount of all other credit enhancements on 1–4 Family Residential loans reported on RC-S item 2.b, column a as a percentage of securitized 1–4 family residential loans reported on RC-S item 1, column a.

Home Equity Lines

Dollar amount of all other credit enhancements on home equity lines reported on RC-S item 2.b, column b, as a percentage of home equity lines reported on RC-S item 1, column b.

Credit Card Receivables

Dollar amount of all other credit enhancements on credit card receivables reported on RC-S item 2.b, column c as a percentage of securitized credit card receivables reported on RC-S item 1, column c.

Auto Loans

Dollar amount of all other credit enhancements on auto loans reported on RC-S item 2.b, column d as a percentage of securitized auto loans reported on RC-S item 1, column d.

Commercial and Industrial Loans

Dollar amount of all other credit enhancements on commercial and industrial loans reported on RC-S item 2.b, column f as a percentage of securitized commercial and industrial loans reported on RC-S item 1, column f.

All Other Loans and Leases

Dollar amount of all other credit enhancements on other consumer loans plus all other loans reported on RC-S item 2.a, columns e and g as a percentage of securitized other consumer loans plus all other loans reported on RC-S item 1, columns e and g.

Unused Commitments to Provide Liquidity

Dollar amount of unused commitments to provide liquidity to asset sold and securitized as reported on call schedule RC-S item 3, columns a:g as a percentage of all securitized assets from call schedule RC-S item 1, columns a:g.

Sellers Interest in Securities and Loans

Dollar amount of ownership (or sellers) interests carried as securities (RC-B) or loans (RC-C). Reported in RC-S items 6.a and 6.b, columns b, c and f. as a percentage of all securitized assets from call schedule RC-S item 1, columns a:g.

Home Equity Lines

Dollar amount of ownership (or sellers) interests carried as securities (RC-B) or loans (RC-C). Reported in RC-S items 6.a and 6.b, column b, as a percentage of home equity lines reported on RC-S item 1, column b.

Credit Card Receivables

Dollar amount of ownership (or sellers) interests carried as securities (RC-B) or loans (RC-C). Reported in RC-S items 6.a and 6.b, columns c as a percentage of securitized credit card receivables reported on RC-S item 1, column c.

Commercial and Industrial Loans

Dollar amount of ownership (or sellers) interests carried as securities (RC-B) or loans (RC-C). Reported in RC-S items 6.a and 6.b, columns f as a percentage of securitized commercial and industrial loans reported on RC-S item 1, column f.

Percent of Tier 1 Capital

Total Retained Credit Exposure

The total of all retained interest only strips from call schedule RC-S item 2.a, columns a:g plus the total of all other credit enhancements from call schedule RC-S item 2.b, columns a:g as a percentage of tier 1 capital. See definitions on UBPR page 11a for details on tier 1 capital.

Retained Interest Only Strips

The total of all retained interest only strips from call schedule RC-S item 2.a, columns a:g as a percentage of tier 1 capital. See definitions on UBPR page 11a for details on tier 1 capital.

Retainend Credit Enhancements

The total of all other credit enhancements from call schedule RC-S item 2.b as a percentage of tier 1 capital. See definitions on UBPR page 11a for details on tier 1 capital.

30–89 Day Past Due Securitized Assets

1–4 Family Residential Loans

Dollar amount of securitized 1–4 family residential loans 30 to 89 days past due as reported in RC-S item 4.a, column a.

Home Equity Lines

Dollar amount of securitized home equity lines 30 to 89 days past due as reported in RC-S item 4.a, column b.

Credit Card Receivables

Dollar amount of securitized credit card receivables 30 to 89 days past due as reported in RC-S item 4.a, column c.

Auto Loans

Dollar amount of securitized auto loans 30 to 89 days past due as reported in RC-S item 4.a, column d.

Commercial and Industrial

Dollar amount of securitized commercial and industrial loans 30 to 89 days past due as reported in RC-S item 4.a, column f.

All Other Loans and Leases

Dollar amount of securitized all other loans and leases 30 to 89 days past due as reported in RC-S item 4.a, column e & g.

Total 30–89 Day Past Due Securitized Assets

Dollar amount of all securitized loans and leases 30 to 89 days past due as reported in RC-S, item 4.a, columns a:g.

90+ Days Past Due Securitized Assets

1–4 Family Residential Loans

Dollar amount of securitized 1–4 family residential loans 90 days and over past due as reported in RC-S item 4.b, column a.

Home Equity Lines

Dollar amount of securitized home equity lines 90 days and over past due as reported in RC-S item 4.b, column b.

Credit Card Receivables

Dollar amount of securitized credit

card receivables 90 days and over past due as reported in RC-S item 4.b, column c.

Auto Loans

Dollar amount of securitized auto loans 90 days and over as reported in RC-S item 4.b, column d.

Commercial and Industrial

Dollar amount of securitized commercial and industrial loans 90 days and over due as reported in RC-S item 4.b, column f.

All Other Loans and Leases

Dollar amount of securitized all other loans and leases 90 days and over past due as reported in RC-S item 4.b, column e & g.

Total 90 Plus Days Past Due Securitized Assets

Dollar amount of all securitized loans and leases 90 plus days past due as reported in RC-S, item 4.b, columns a:g.

Total Past Due Securitized Assets

Dollar amount of all securitized loans and leases past due as reported in RC-S items 4.a and 4.b, columns a:g.

Net Losses Securitized Assets

Net losses are defined as chargeoffs less recoveries by each securitization category.

1–4 Family Residential Loans

Dollar amount of net chargeoffs for securitized 1–4 family residential loans as reported in RC-S column a, items 5.a less 5.b.

Home Equity Lines

Dollar amount of net chargeoffs for securitized home equity lines as reported in RC-S column b, items 5.a less 5.b.

Credit Card Receivables

Dollar amount of net chargeoffs for securitized credit card receivables as reported in RC-S column c, items 5.a and 5.b.

Auto Loans

Dollar amount of net chargeoffs for securitized auto loans as reported in RC-S column d, items 5.a less 5.b.

Commercial and Industrial

Dollar amount of net chargeoffs for securitized commercial and industrial loans as reported in RC-S column f, items 5.a less 5.b.

All Other Loans and Leases

Dollar amount of net chargeoffs for securitized all other loans and leases as reported in RC-S columns e & g, items 5.a less 5.b.

Total New Chargeoffs Securitized Assets

Dollar amount of all net chargeoffs for securitized loan and leases as reported in RC-S columns a:g, items 5.a less 5.b.

	06/30/2008	06/30/2007	12/31/2007	12/31/2006	12/31/2005
30-89 DAY PD SECURITIZED ASSETS %					
1-4 FAMILY RESIDENTIAL LOANS	2.80	2.27	2.69	2.36	2.25
HOME EQUITY LINES	N/A	N/A	N/A	N/A	N/A
CREDIT CARD RECEIVABLES	N/A	N/A	N/A	N/A	N/A
AUTO LOANS	N/A	N/A	N/A	N/A	N/A
COMMERCIAL & INDUSTRIAL LOANS	N/A	N/A	N/A	N/A	N/A
ALL OTHER LOANS AND LEASES	5.06	4.97	5.47	5.16	7.12
TOTAL 30-89 DAY PD SECUR ASSET	2.81	2.29	2.70	2.39	2.25
90+ DAY PD SECURITIZED ASSETS					
1-4 FAMILY RESIDENTIAL LOANS	2.25	0.88	1.60	0.59	0.44
HOME EQUITY LINES	N/A	N/A	N/A	N/A	N/A
CREDIT CARD RECEIVABLES	N/A	N/A	N/A	N/A	N/A
AUTO LOANS	N/A	N/A	N/A	N/A	N/A
COMMERCIAL & INDUSTRIAL LOANS	N/A	N/A	N/A	N/A	N/A
ALL OTHER LOANS AND LEASES	4.05	3.71	4.71	4.14	9.78
TOTAL 90 + DAY PD SECUR ASSET	2.26	0.90	1.62	0.62	0.44
TOTAL PD SECURITIZED ASSETS %	5.07	3.19	4.32	3.00	2.70
NET LOSSES ON SECURITIZED ASSETS%					
1-4 FAMILY RESIDENTIAL LOANS	0.00	0.00	0.00	0.00	0.00
HOME EQUITY LINES	N/A	N/A	N/A	N/A	N/A
CREDIT CARD RECEIVABLES	N/A	N/A	N/A	N/A	N/A
AUTO LOANS	N/A	N/A	N/A	N/A	N/A
COMMERCIAL & INDUSTRIAL LOANS	N/A	N/A	N/A	N/A	N/A
ALL OTHER LOANS AND LEASES	0.00	0.00	0.00	0.00	0.00
NET LOSSES ON SECUR ASSETS	0.00	0.00	0.00	0.00	0.00
30-89 DAY PD MANAGED ASSETS %					
1-4 FAMILY RESIDENTIAL LOANS	N/A	N/A	N/A	N/A	N/A
HOME EQUITY LINES	1.20	0.73	1.35	0.60	0.39
CREDIT CARD RECEIVABLES	1.63	0.00	0.00	0.00	0.00
COMMERCIAL & INDUSTRIAL LOANS	0.41	0.64	0.39	0.23	0.66
ALL OTHER LOANS AND LEASES	1.42	1.13	1.71	1.14	0.45
TOTAL 30-89 DAY PD MANAGE ASSET	2.08	1.55	2.01	1.46	1.27
90+ DAY PD MANAGED ASSETS %					
1-4 FAMILY RESIDENTIAL LOANS	N/A	N/A	N/A	N/A	N/A
HOME EQUITY LINES	0.02	0.00	0.01	0.00	0.01
CREDIT CARD RECEIVABLES	1.37	0.00	0.00	100.00	100.00
COMMERCIAL & INDUSTRIAL LOANS	0.04	0.04	0.07	0.05	0.06
ALL OTHER LOANS AND LEASES	0.61	0.13	0.37	0.16	0.10
TOTAL 90 + DAY PD MANAGE ASSET	1.39	0.59	0.99	0.41	0.34
TOTAL PAST DUE MANAGED ASSETS %	3.47	2.14	3.00	1.87	1.61
NET LOSSES ON MANAGED ASSETS %					
1-4 FAMILY RESIDENTIAL LOANS	0.30	0.04	0.07	0.02	0.01
HOME EQUITY LINES	2.43	0.52	0.75	0.16	0.16
CREDIT CARD RECEIVABLES	2.60	-4.02	0.12	0.00	20.39
COMMERCIAL & INDUSTRIAL LOANS	0.40	0.29	0.35	0.53	0.15
ALL OTHER LOANS AND LEASES	0.37	0.10	0.11	0.07	0.15
NET LOSSES ON MANAGE ASSETS	0.37	0.10	0.11	0.07	0.15
	0.00	0.00	0.00	0.00	0.00

UBPR Page 13B

30–89 Day Past Due Securitized Assets %

Delinquencies are expressed as a percentage of securitized assets by category.

1–4 Family Residential Loans

Dollar amount of securitized 1–4 family residential loans 30 to 89 days past due as reported in RC-S item 4.a column a as a percentage of securitized 1–4 Family Residential loans reported on RC-S item 1, column a.

Home Equity Lines

Dollar amount of securitized home equity lines 30 to 89 days past due as reported in RC-S item 4.a, column b as a percentage of home equity lines reported on RC-S item 1, column b.

Credit Card Receivables

Dollar amount of securitized credit card receivables 30 to 89 days past due as reported in RC-S item 4.a, column c as a percentage of securitized credit card receivables reported on RC-S item 1, column c.

Auto Loans

Dollar amount of securitized auto loans 30 to 89 days past due as reported in RC-S item 4.a, column d as a percentage of securitized auto loans reported on RC-S item 1, column d.

Commercial and Industrial

Dollar amount of securitized commercial and industrial loans 30 to 89 days past due as reported in RC-S item 4.a, column f as a percentage of securitized commercial and industrial loans reported on RC-S item 1, column f.

All Other Loans and Leases

Dollar amount of securitized all other loans and leases 30 to 89 days past due as reported in RC-S item 4.a, column e & g as a percentage of securitized other consumer loans plus all other loans reported on RC-S item 1, columns e and g.

Total 30–89 Day Past Due Securitized Assets

Dollar amount of all securitized loans and leases 30 to 89 days past due as reported in RC-S, item 4.a, columns a:g as a percentage of the total of all securitized assets from call schedule RC-S item 1, columns a:g.

90+ Day Past Due Securitized Assets %

Delinquencies are expressed as a percentage of securitized assets by category.

1–4 Family Residential Loans

Dollar amount of securitized 1–4 family residential loans 90 plus days past due as reported in RC-S item 4.b, column a as a percentage of securitized 1–4 Family Residential loans reported on RC-S item 1, column a.

Home Equity Lines

Dollar amount of securitized home equity lines 90 plus days past due as reported in RC-S item 4.b, column b as a percentage of home equity lines reported on RC-S item 1, column b.

Credit Card Receivables

Dollar amount of securitized credit card receivables 90 plus days past due as reported in RC-S item 4.b, column c as a percentage of securitized credit card receivables reported on RC-S item 1, column c.

Auto Loans

Dollar amount of securitized auto loans 90 plus days past due as reported in RC-S item 4.b, column d as a percentage of securitized auto loans reported on RC-S item 1, column d.

Commercial and Industrial

Dollar amount of securitized commercial and industrial loans 90 plus days past due as reported in RC-S item 4.b, column f as a percentage of securitized commercial and industrial loans reported on RC-S item 1, column f.

All Other Loans and Leases

Dollar amount of securitized all other loans and leases 90 plus days past due as reported in RC-S item 4.b, column e & g as a percentage of securitized other consumer loans plus all other loans reported on RC-S item 1, columns e and g.

Total 90 + Days Past Due Securitized Assets

Dollar amount of all securitized loans and leases 90 plus days past due as reported in RC-S, item 4.b, columns a:g as a percentage of the total of all securitized assets from call schedule RC-S item 1, columns a:g.

Total Past Due Securitized Assets %

Dollar amount of all past due securitized loans and leases in RC-S, items 4.a and 4.b, columns a:g as a percentage of the total of all securitized assets from call schedule RC-S item 1, columns a:g.

Net Losses Securitized Assets %

Net losses each securitization category are annualized then expressed as a percentage of a 5 quarter annual average of the related securitized assets.

1–4 Family Residential Loans

Annualized net chargeoffs for securitized 1–4 family residential loans as reported in RC-S column a, items 5.a less 5.b as a percentage of securitized 1–4 Family Residential loans reported on RC-S item 1, column a. Securitized assets are averaged for 5 quarters.

Home Equity Lines

Annualized net chargeoffs for securitized home equity lines as reported in RC-S column b, items 5.a less 5.b as a percentage of home equity lines reported on RC-S item 1, column b. Securitized assets are averaged for 5 quarters.

Credit Card Receivables

Annualized net chargeoffs for securitized credit card receivables as reported in RC-S column c, items, 5.a less 5.b as a percentage of securitized credit card receivables reported on RC-S item 1, column c. Securitized assets are averaged for 5 quarters.

Auto Loans

Annualized net chargeoffs for securitized auto loans as reported in RC-S column d, items 5.a less 5.b, as a percentage of securitized auto loans reported on RC-S item 1, column d. Securitized assets are averaged for 5 quarters.

Commercial and Industrial

Annualized net chargeoffs for securitized commercial and industrial loans as reported in RC-S column f, items 5.a less 5.b as a percentage of securitized commercial and industrial loans reported on RC-S item 1, column f. Securitized assets are averaged for 5 quarters.

All Other Loans and Leases

Annualized net chargeoffs for securitized all other loans and leases as reported in RC-S columns e & g, items 5.a less 5.b expressed as a percentage of securitized other consumer loans plus all other loans reported on RC-S item 1, columns e and g. Securitized assets are averaged for 5 quarters.

Net Charge Losses Securitized Assets

Dollar amount of all net chargeoffs for securitized loan and leases as reported in RC-S columns a:g, items 5.a less 5.b as a percentage of the total of all securitized assets from call schedule RC-S, item 1, columns a:g. Securitized assets are averaged for 5 quarters.

30–89 Day Past Due Managed Assets %

Delinquencies are combined for on-balance sheet and securitized assets.

1–4 Family Residential Loans

Dollar amount of securitized 1–4 family residential loans 30 to 89 days past due as reported in RC-S item 4.a, column a plus 1–4 family residential loans 30–89 days past due as reported on RC-N item 1.c.2, column a as a percent of securitized 1–4 Family Residential loans reported on RC-S item 1, column a. plus loans secured by 1–4 family residential real estate as reported on RC-C items 1.c.2 a & b.

Home Equity Lines

Dollar amount of securitized home equity lines 30 to 89 days past due as reported in RC-S item 4.a, column b plus revolving loans 30-89 days past due as reported on RC-N 1.c.1, column a as a percentage of securitized home equity lines reported on RC-S item 1, column b plus home equity lines of credit from RC-C item 1.2.1.

Credit Card Receivables

Dollar amount of securitized credit card receivables 30 to 89 days past due as reported in RC-S item 4.a, column c plus credit cards 30–89 days past due as reported in RC-N item 5.a, column a as a percentage of securitized credit card receivables reported on RC-S item 1, column c. plus loans to individuals on cards on RC-C item 6.a.

Commercial and Industrial

Dollar amount of securitized commercial and industrial loans 30 to 89 days past due as reported in RC-S item 4.a, column f plus commercial and industrial loans 30-89 days past due as reported in RC-N item 4, col-

umn a as a percentage of securitized commercial and industrial loans reported on RC-S item 1, column f plus commercial and industrial loans from RC item 4.

All Other Loans and Leases

Dollar amount of securitized all other loans and leases 30 to 89 days past due as reported in RC-S item 4.a, column e & g plus loans and leases 30 to 89 days past due as reported on RC-N column a in the following categories: construction and land development item 1.a, plus secured by farm land item 1.b, plus secured by multifamily properties item 1.d, plus secured by nonfarm nonresidential properties item 1.e, plus loans to depository institutions item 2, plus loans to finance agricultural production item 3, plus loans to foreign governments item 6, plus all other loans item 7, plus lease financing receivables item 8, as a percentage of securitized other consumer loans plus all other loans reported on call schedule RC-S item 1, columns e and g plus total loans and leases RC-C item 12, less revolving lines secured by 1–4 family properties 1.c.1, less closed end loans secured by 1–4 family properties item 1.c.2, less loans to individuals on credit cards item 6.a, less other consumer loans item RC-C 6.c, less commercial and industrial loans from RC-C item 4.

Total 30–89 Day Past Due Managed Assets

Dollar amount of all securitized loans and leases 30 to 89 days past due as reported in RC-S, item 4.a, columns a:g plus loans and leases 30 to 89 days past due as reported in RC-N items 1:8 as a percentage of all securitized assets as reported on RC-S item 1, columns a:g plus total loans and leases as reported on schedule RC-C item 12.

90 Plus Day Past Due Managed Assets %

Delinquencies are combined for on-balance sheet and securitized assets.

1–4 Familly Residential Loans

Dollar amount of securitized 1–4 family residential loans 90 plus days past due as reported in RC-S item 4.B column a plus 1–4 family residential loans 90 days past due as reported on RC-N item 1.c.2, column b as a percent of securitized 1-4 Family Residential loans reported on RC-S item 1, column a, plus loans secured by 1–4 family residential real estate as reported on RC-C items 1.c.2, columns a & b.

Home Equity Lines

Dollar amount of securitized home equity lines 90 plus days past due as reported in RC-S item 4.b, column b plus revolving loans 90 plus days past due as reported on RC-N 1.c.1 column b as a percentage of securitized home equity lines reported on RC-S item 1, column b plus home equity lines of credit from RC-C item 1.2.1.

Credit Card Receivables

Dollar amount of securitized credit card receivables 90 plus days past due as reported in RC-S item 4.b, column c plus credit cards 90 plus days past due as reported in RC-N item 5.a, column b as a percentage of securitized credit card receivables reported on RC-S item 1, column c. plus loans to individuals on cards on RC-C item 6.a.

Commercial and Industrial

Dollar amount of securitized commercial and industrial loans 90 plus days past due as reported in RC-S item 4.b, column f plus commercial and industrial loans 90 plus days past due as reported in RC-N item 4 column b as a percentage of securitized commercial and industrial loans reported on RC-S item 1, column f plus commercial and industrial loans from RC item 4.

All Other Loans and Leases

Dollar amount of securitized all other loans and leases 90- plus days past due as reported in RC-S item 4.b, columns e & g plus loans and leases

30 to 89 days past due as reported on RC-N column b in the following categories: construction and land development item 1.a, plus secured by farm land item 1.b, plus secured by multifamily properties item 1.d, plus secured by nonfarm nonresidential properties item 1.e, plus loans to depository institutions item 2, plus loans to finance agricultural production item 3, plus loans to foreign governments item 6, plus all other loans item 7, plus lease financing receivables item 8, as a percentage of securitized other consumer loans plus all other loans reported on call schedule RC-S item 1, columns e and g plus total loans and leases RC-C item 12, less revolving lines secured by 1–4 family properties1.c.1, less closed end loans secured by 1–4 family properties item 1.c.2, less loans to individuals on credit cards item 6.a, less other consumer loans item RC-C 6.c, less commercial and industrial loans from RC-C item 4.

Total 90 Plus Day Past Due Managed Assets

Dollar amount of all securitized loans and leases 90 plus days past due as reported in RC-S, item 4.b, columns a:g plus loans and leases 90 plus days past due as reported in RC-N items 1:8, column b as a percentage of all securitized assets as reported on RC-S item 1, columns a:g plus total loans and leases as reported on schedule RC-C item 12.

Total Past Due Managed Assets

Dollar amount of all securitized loans and leases past due as reported in RC-S items 4.a and 4.b, columns a:g plus loans and leases past due as reported in schedule RC-N items 1:8 as a percentage of all securitized assets as reported on RC-S item 1, columns a:g plus total loans and leases as reported on schedule RC-C item 12.

Net Losses on Managed Assets %

Net losses are combined for each securitized and on-balance sheet

asset category then annualized and expressed as a percentage of the related the related securitized and on-balance sheet assets. The denominator is a five period average.

1–4 Family Residential Loans

Annualized net chargeoffs on securitized 1–4 family residential loans as reported in RC-S column a, item 5.a less 5.b plus net chargeoffs on 1–4 family residential loans as reported in RI-B item 1.c.2, column a less column b as a percent of securitized 1–4 Family Residential loans reported on RC-S item 1, column a, plus loans secured by 1–4 family residential real estate as reported on RC-C items 1.c.2, columns a & b. Denominator is averaged for 5 periods.

Home Equity Lines

Annualized net chargeoffs on securitized home equity lines as reported in RC-S column b item 5.a less 5.b plus net chargeoffs on revolving loans on RI-B item 1.c.1, column a less column b as a percentage of securitized home equity lines reported on RC-S item 1, column b plus home equity lines of credit from RC-C item 1.2.1. Denominator is averaged for 5 quarters.

Credit Card Receivables

Annualized net chargeoffs on securitized credit card receivables as reported in RC-S column c, item 5.a less 5.b plus net chargeoffs on credit cards as reported in RI-B item 5.a, column a less column b as a percentage of securitized credit card receivables reported on RC-S item 1, column c, plus loans to individuals on cards on RC-C item 6.a. Denominator is averaged for 5 quarters.

Commercial and Industrial

Annualized net chargeoffs on securitized commercial and industrial loans as reported in RC-S column f, item 5.a less 5.b plus net chargeoffs on commercial and industrial loans as reported in RI-B item 4, column a less column b as a percentage of securitized commercial and industrial loans reported on RC-S item 1, column f plus commercial and industrial loans from RC item 4. Denominator is averaged for 5 quarters.

All Other Loans and Leases

Annualized net chargeoffs on securitized all other loans and leases 90- plus days past due as reported in RC-S columns e and g item 5.a less 5.b, plus net chargeoffs on other loans and leases as reported in RI-B column a less column b in the following categories: construction and land development item 1.a, plus secured by farm land item 1.b, plus secured by multifamily properties item 1.d, plus secured by nonfarm nonresidential properties item 1.e, plus loans to depository institutions item 2, plus loans to finance agricultural production item 3, plus loans to foreign governments item 6, plus all other loans item 7, plus lease financing receivables item 8, as a percentage of securitized other consumer loans plus all other loans reported on call schedule RC-S item 1, columns e and g plus total loans and leases RC-C item 12, less revolving lines secured by 1–4 family properties1.c.1, less closed end loans secured by 1-4 family properties item1.c.2, less loans to individuals item on credit cards 6.a, less other consumer loans item RC-C 6.c, less commercial and industrial loans from RC-C item 4. Denominator is averaged for 5 quarters.

Net Losses on Managed Assets

Annualized net chargeoffs on securitized loans and leases as reported on schedule RC-S columns a:g item 5.a less 5.b plus net chargeoffs on loans and leases as reported in RI-B items 1:8, column a less b as a percentage of all securitized loans and leases as reported in schedule RC-S item 1, columns a:g plus total loans as reported on schedule RC-C item 12. Denominator is averaged for 5 quarters.

	AVERAGE FOR ALL INSURED COMMERCIAL BANKS					BANKS WITH ASSETS - $MILL 06/30/08		
	06/30/2008	6/30/2007	12/31/2007	12/31/2006	12/31/2005	0-25	25-100	100+
EARNINGS AND PROFITABILITY								
PERCENT OF AVERAGE ASSETS:								
INTEREST INCOME (TE)	6 26	7 51	7 46	7 35	6 33	5 62	6 42	6 21
- INTEREST EXPENSE	2 94	3 38	3 43	2 96	2 06	1 54	2 68	3 05
NET INTEREST INCOME (TE)	3 32	4 13	4 03	4 39	4 26	4 09	3 74	3 15
+ NONINTEREST INCOME	0 60	0 64	0 64	0 69	0 75	5 16	0 59	0 59
- NONINTEREST EXPENSE	3 07	3 07	3 11	3 30	3 17	14 89	3 82	2 79
- PROVISION: LOAN&LEASE LOSSES	0 52	0 24	0 41	0 32	0 30	0 82	0 35	0 60
= PRETAX OPERATING INCOME (TE)	0 29	1 52	1 13	1 58	1 62	-6 46	0 14	0 33
+ SECURITIES GAINS (LOSSES)	0 03	0 00	0 00	0 00	0 00	0 03	0 02	0 03
= PRETAX NET OPERATING INC (TE)	0 33	1 53	1 13	1 58	1 62	-6 44	0 18	0 38
NET OPERATING INCOME	0 19	1 09	0 82	1 10	1 14	-7 26	0 00	0 24
ADJUSTED NET OPERATING INCOME	0 43	1 26	1 07	1 30	1 29	-6 60	0 16	0 52
NET INCOME ADJUSTED SUB S	0 14	0 99	0 74	1 00	1 06	-7 26	-0 10	0 21
NET INCOME	0 19	1 09	0 82	1 10	1 14	-7 26	-0 01	0 24
MARGIN ANALYSIS:								
AVG EARNINGS ASSETS TO AVG ASSETS	93 60	94 21	94 09	94 01	93 92	90 94	93 68	93 57
AVG INT-BEARING FUNDS TO AVG AST	79 15	77 48	77 87	76 56	76 91	44 54	73 17	81 08
INT INC (TE) TO AVG EARN ASSETS	6 68	7 99	7 94	7 83	6 76	6 16	6 86	6 63
INT EXPENSE TO AVG EARN ASSETS	3 14	3 60	3 65	3 16	2 19	1 64	2 86	3 26
NET INT INC-TE TO AVG EARN ASSET	3 56	4 40	4 30	4 68	4 55	4 52	4 00	3 38
LOAN & LEASE ANALYSIS:								
NET LOSS TO AVERAGE TOTAL LN&LS	0 40	0 10	0 23	0 15	0 16	0 39	0 24	0 47
EARNINGS COVERAGE OF NET LOSS(X)	11 92	39 00	20 01	41 97	38 37	2 62	16 89	10 55
LN&LS ALLOW TO LN&LS NOT HFS	1 56	1 36	1 47	1 38	1 39	1 82	1 43	1 60
LN&LS ALLOWANCE TO NET LOSSES(X)	12 78	22 23	13 78	21 71	19 81	5 39	17 51	11 47
LN&LS ALLOWANCE TO TOTAL LN&LS	1 55	1 36	1 46	1 37	1 39	1 56	1 43	1 59
LIQUIDITY:								
NET NONCORE FUNDING DEPENDENCE	30 67	24 85	26 34	23 32	21 40	-97 31	21 67	34 78
NET LOANS & LEASES TO ASSETS	71 95	71 80	71 58	70 38	70 20	34 84	66 57	74 49
CAPITALIZATION								
TIER ONE LEVERAGE CAPITAL	10 21	10 75	10 43	11 05	10 27	43 43	14 34	9 14
CASH DIVIDENDS TO NET INCOME	35 06	27 10	35 94	26 28	25 94	17 50	33 48	37 20
RETAIN EARNS TO AVG TOTAL EQUITY	-1 53	5 95	3 30	6 96	7 19	-6 44	-1 37	-1 73
GROWTH RATES:								
ASSETS	11 12	15 95	14 22	16 51	17 55	1 31	14 83	10 15
TIER ONE CAPITAL	3 08	9 89	6 83	12 17	13 90	-0 45	1 40	3 80
NET LOANS & LEASES	11 72	17 52	15 81	17 14	19 14	3 78	18 70	9 87
SHORT TERM INVESTMENTS	-3 39	42 07	3 47	64 23	81 84	-13 00	-4 51	-2 77
SHORT TERM NONCORE FUNDING	28 96	33 32	25 85	45 80	43 31	35 95	35 25	26 51
NONCURRENT LOANS & LEASES:								
TOTAL LN&LS-90+ DAYS PAST DUE	0 15	0 11	0 19	0 10	0 10	0 13	0 22	0 13
- NONACCRUAL	2 21	0 53	1 05	0 42	0 40	1 23	1 27	2 85
- TOTAL	2 44	0 73	1 34	0 59	0 56	1 35	1 56	3 05
TOTAL ASSETS ($MILLIONS)	274,866	272,508	274,492	273,664	263,109	128	6,027	268,710
EQUITY CAPITAL ($MILLIONS)	29,802	29,858	30,266	29,468	27,453	45	880	28,876
NET INCOME ($ MILLIONS)	853	1,795	2,878	3,438	3,225	-1	3	852
NUMBER OF BANKS IN TABULATION	329	329	327	330	328	7	90	232

UBPR Page STAVG

Summary Information For Banks in State

This page displays statewide peer group averages for Summary Ratio information similar to that found on page 1 of the UBPR.

Four different peer groups appear on this page. First, all banks are combined into a statewide peer group. Then banks are grouped into one of three asset-based statewide peer groups. The asset ranges are: less than $25M, $25M to $100M and over $100M.

Statewide peer group average data is not designed to be a replacement for nationwide peer group information, but as a supplement to provide insight into possible local trends.

The averaging process follows that used for the nationwide peer groups in that banks above the 95th percentile and below the 5th percentile are excluded from the average.

Earnings and Profitability

Percent of Average Assets:

Interest Income (TE)

All income from earning assets plus the tax benefit on tax-exempt loans, leases, and municipal securities, divided by average assets.

Interest Expense

Total interest expense divided by average assets.

Net Interest Income (TE)

Total interest income, plus the tax benefit on tax-exempt income, less total interest expense, divided by average assets.

Noninterest Income

Income derived from bank services and sources other than interest-bearing assets, divided by average assets.

Noninterest Expense

Salaries and employee benefits, expenses of premises and the fixed assets and other noninterest expense divided by average assets.

Provision-Loan/Lease Losses (Percent of Average Assets)

Provision for loan and lease-financing receivables losses divided by average assets.

Pretax Operating Income (TE) (Percent of Average Assets)

Net interest income on a tax-equivalent basis plus noninterest income, less noninterest expenses, the provision for loan and lease-financing receivables losses and the provision for allocated transfer risk, divided by average assets.

Realized Gain/Loss Secs

Pretax net gains for losses from the sale, exchange, retirement, or redemption of securities not held in trading accounts. After December 31, 1993 includes available-for-sale and held-to-maturity transactions divided by average assets.

Pretax Net Operating Income (TE)

Pretax operating income, plus securities gains or losses, divided by average assets.

Net Operating Income

After tax net operating income, including securities gains or losses, (which does not include extraordinary gains or losses), divided by average assets.

Adjusted Net Oper Income

Net operating income after taxes and securities gains or losses, plus the provision for possible loan and lease losses, less net loan and lease losses, divided by average assets.

Net Income Adjusted Sub S

Net income after securities gains or losses, extraordinary gains or losses, and applicable taxes, divided by average assets adjusted for sub chapter S status. Estimated income taxes are substituted for any reported applicable income taxes for banks that indicate sub chapter S status. Estimated income taxes: Federal income tax rates are applied to net income before extraordinary items and taxes plus non-deductible interest expense to carry tax-exempt securities less tax-exempt income from securities issued by states and political subdivisions, less tax-exempt income from leases, less tax-exempt income from other obligations of states and political subdivisions. (See appendix A-3 for tax table)

Net Income

Net income after securities gains or losses, extraordinary gains or losses, and applicable taxes, divided by average assets.

Margin Analysis

Average Earning Assets/Average Earning Assets

Year-to-date average of average total loans (net of unearned income) in domestic and foreign offices, lease-financing receivables, obligations of the U.S. government, states and political subdivisions and other securities, assets held in trading accounts, interest-bearing balances due from depository institutions, and federal funds sold and securities purchased under agreements to resell, divided by average assets.

Average Interest-Bearing Funds/Average Assets

Average interest-bearing domestic and foreign office deposits, federal funds purchased and securities sold under agreements to repurchase, interest-bearing demand notes (note balances) issued to the U.S. Treasury, other liabilities for borrowed money, and notes and debentures subordinated to deposits, divided by average assets.

Interest Income (TE)/ Average Earning Assets

Total interest income on a tax-equivalent basis divided by the average of the respective asset accounts involved in generating that income.

Interest Expense/Average Earning Assets

Total interest expense divided by the average of the respective asset accounts involved in generating interest income.

Net Interest Income (TE)/Average Earning Assets

Total interest income on a tax-equivalent basis, less total interest expense, divided by the average of the respective asset accounts involved in generating interest income.

Loan & Lease Analysis

Net Loss to Average Total Loan & Lease

Gross loan and lease charge-offs, less gross recoveries (includes allocated transfer risk reserve charge-offs and recoveries), divided by average total loans and leases.

Earnings Coverage of Net Loss (X)

Net operating income before taxes, securities gains or losses, and extraordinary items, plus the provision for possible loan and lease-financing receivables losses divided by net loan and lease losses.

Loan & Lease Allowance Net Losses (X)

Ending balance of the allowance for possible loan and lease-financing

receivables losses divided by net loan and lease losses. If gross recoveries exceed gross losses, NA is shown at this caption.

Loan & Lease Allowance to Total Loans & Lease

Ending balance of the allowance for possible loan and lease losses divided by total loans and lease-financing receivables.

Liquidity

Net Noncore Funding Dependence

See page UBPR page 10 for definition.

Net Loans & Leases to Assets

Loans and lease-financing receivables net of unearned income and the allowance for possible loans and lease-financing receivables losses divided by total assets.

Capitalization

Tier One Leverage Capital

Tier one capital divided by adjusted average assets. See the description of UBPR page 11A for definitions of tier one capital and adjusted average assets.

Cash Dividends to Net Income

Total of all cash dividends declared year-to-date divided by net income year-too-date. If net incomes less than or equal to zero, NA is shown at this caption.

Retain Earnings to Average Total Equity

Net income, less cash dividends declared, divided by average equity capital.

Growth Rates

Growth rates are calculated for a 12-month period. The percentage

is determined by subtracting the account balance as of the corresponding reporting period in the previous year from the current period account balance and dividing the result by the previous year balance. The following growth rates are displayed:

Assets

Tier One Capital

Net Loans & Leases

Short Term Investments

See definition on UBPR page 10.

Short Term Noncore Funding

See definition on UBPR page 10.

Noncurrent Loans and Leases:

Summation of all categories of loans by past due status, divided by gross loans. See page 8 for specific definitions.

Total LN&LS 90+Days Past Due

Summation of all categories of due loans by past due status, divided by gross loans. See page 8 for specific definitions.

Nonaccrual

Total

Total Assets

Total assets for all banks with in the peer group.

Equity Capital

Total of equity capital for all banks with in the peer group.

Net Income

Total of net income for all banks with in the peer group.

Number of Banks in Tabulation

Number of banks with in the peer group.

FIDUCIARY AND RELATED SERVICES

	06/30/2008			03/31/2008			12/31/2007			
TOTAL FIDUCIARY AND REL ASSETS	($000)	%TOTAL	%MGD	($000)	%TOTAL	%MGD	($000)	%TOTAL	%MGD	%CHG
PERSONAL TRUST AND AGENCY	24,845,996	37.82	94.86	25,684,369	37.88	94.29	27,271,445	38.04	94.79	-14.12
EMPLOYEE BENEFIT DC	8,782,639	13.37	4.02	9,107,523	13.43	3.70	10,153,078	14.16	3.33	-16.04
EMPLOYEE BENEFIT DB	7 989 851	12.16	36.46	7 989 611	11.78	38.37	8 548 868	11.93	39.26	-7.07
OTHER RETIREMENT	3,154,219	4.80	60.94	3,166,521	4.67	61.94	3,465,812	4.83	59.86	-13.23
CORPORATE TRUST AND AGENCY	290,199	0.44	2.59	282,370	0.42	1.87	289,737	0.40	1.79	-39.48
INVESTMENT MANAGEMENT AGENCY	16,927,674	25.76	100.00	18,010,909	26.56	100.00	18,417,730	25.69	100.00	-16.05
OTHER FIDUCIARY	3 711 679	5.65	81.12	3 569 665	5.26	82.11	3 539 937	4.94	80.14	26.64
TOTAL FIDUCIARY ASSETS	65,702,257	100.00	74.13	67,810,968	100.00	74.51	71,686,607	100.00	73.76	-12.63
CUSTODY AND SAFEKEEPING	85,645,298			92,335,236			93,086,903			-5.42
MEMO ACCTS IN FOREIGN OFFICES	0		0.00	0		0.00	0		0.00	N/A
TOTAL FIDUCIARY AND REL ACCOUNTS	(#)	%TOTAL	%MGD	(#)	%TOTAL	%MGD	(#)	%TOTAL	%MGD	%CHG
PERSONAL TRUST AND AGENCY	20,101	59.41	94.74	20,442	59.49	95.47	20,655	59.44	95.75	-5.89
EMPLOYEE BENEFIT DC	1,035	3.06	7.73	1,049	3.05	8.10	1,067	3.07	8.06	-5.48
EMPLOYEE BENEFIT DB	548	1.62	28.10	550	1.60	29.09	549	1.58	30.60	2.62
OTHER RETIREMENT	3,593	10.62	80.10	3,560	10.36	82.42	3,606	10.38	82.45	-6.87
CORPORATE TRUST AND AGENCY	362	1.07	2.21	384	1.12	1.82	425	1.22	1.65	-40.66
INVESTMENT MANAGEMENT AGENCY	7,232	21.38	100.00	7,345	21.38	100.00	7,471	21.50	100.00	-8.06
OTHER FIDUCIARY	962	2.84	47.92	1 031	3.00	50.24	977	2.81	50.56	4.00
TOTAL NUMBER OF ACCOUNTS	33,833	100.00	88.25	34,361	100.00	88.95	34,750	100.00	89.14	-6.66
CUSTODY AND SAFEKEEPING	8,402			8,487			8,501			-2.83
MEMO ACCTS IN FOREIGN OFFICES	0		N/A	0		N/A	0		N/A	N/A
CORPORATE TRUST AND AGENCY	($000)	#ISS	%CHG	$(000)	#ISS	%CHG	$(000)	#ISS	%CHG	
CORPORATE AND MUNI TRUSTEESHIPS	N/A	N/A	N/A	N/A	N/A	N/A	4,082,908	333	-63.33	
ALL OTHER CORPORATE		N/A	N/A		N/A	N/A		185	-82.06	

UBPR Page TRUST 1

Fiduciary and Related Activities

Information on fiduciary and related services is reported by banks on call schedule RC-T. This information is available from December 31, 2001 forward, however several reporting limitations apply. Depending on asset size and the percentage of trust and related revenue to total income, an individual institution may be required to report certain items quarterly, annually or not at all. Please see instructions for the report of condition and income on **www. ffiec.gov** for details. Additionally, all information on fiduciary income as reported on RC-T items 12 through 23 and memorandum item 4 are considered confidential. While confidential information is provided to regulatory users it is not made available on the public UBPR website. Individual banks should contact their respective federal bank supervisor for access to confidential information.

Please note that special trust peer groups are used for purposes of the analysis on trust page 2. These peer groups and the associated averages are only used on the fiduciary activities page 2. Please see section II of the UBPR Users Guide for specifics.

For dollar items on trust page 1 an annual growth rate or percentage change is calculated.

Total Fiduciary and Related Assets

The dollar balance of managed and non-managed fiduciary account is displayed by type. Also the percentage of trust assets by caption is displayed. Additionally the proportion of managed assets to total assets within each category is shown. Finally, the percentage change or growth rate is displayed.

Personal Trust and Agency

Dollar balance of managed and non-managed personal trust and agency accounts as reported on schedule RC-T item 4, columns a & b is displayed. The dollar balance is also displayed as a percentage of total trust assets as reported on RC-T item 4, columns a & b. Finally managed assets as reported on RC-T item 4, column a, is displayed as a percentage of RC-T item 4, columns a & b.

Employee Benefit Defined Contribution

Dollar balance of retirement related employee benefit—defined contribution accounts as reported on schedule RC-T item 5.a, columns a & b is displayed. The dollar balance is also displayed as a percentage of total trust assets as reported on RC-T item 9, columns a & b. Finally managed assets as reported on RC-T item 5.a, column a is displayed as a percentage of RC-T item 5.a, columns a & b.

Employee Benefit Defined Benefit

Dollar balance of retirement related employee benefit—defined benefit accounts as reported on schedule RC-T item 5.b, columns a & b is displayed. The dollar balance is also displayed as a percentage of total trust assets as reported on RC-T item 9, columns a & b. Finally managed assets as reported on RC-T item 5.b, column a is displayed as a percentage of RC-T item 5.b, columns a & b.

Other Retirement

Dollar balance of other retirement accounts as reported on schedule RC-T item 5.c, columns a & b is displayed. The dollar balance is also displayed as a percentage of total trust assets as reported on RC-T item 9, columns a & b. Finally managed assets as reported on RC-T item 5.c, column a is displayed as a percentage of RC-T item 5.c, columns a & b.

Corporate Trust and Agency

Dollar balance of corporate trust and agency accounts as reported on schedule RC-T item 6, columns a & b is displayed. The dollar balance is also displayed as a percentage of total trust assets as reported on RC-T item 9, columns a & b. Finally managed assets as reported on RC-T item 6, column a is displayed as a percentage of RC-T item 6, columns a & b.

Investment Management Agency

Dollar balance of investment management agency accounts as reported on schedule RC-T item 7, columns a & b is displayed. The dollar balance is also displayed as a percentage of total trust assets as reported on RC-T item 9, columns a & b. Finally managed assets as reported on RC-T item 7, column a is displayed as a percentage of RC-T item 7, columns a & b.

Other Fiduciary

Dollar balance of other fiduciary accounts as reported on schedule RC-T item 8, columns a & b is displayed. The dollar balance is also displayed as a percentage of total trust assets as reported on RC-T item 9, columns a & b. Finally managed assets as reported on RC-T item 8, column a is displayed as a percentage of RC-T item 8, columns a & b.

Total Fiduciary Assets

Dollar balance of all fiduciary accounts both managed and non-managed as reported on schedule RC-T item 9, columns a & b.

Custody and Safekeeping

The total balance of custody and safekeeping accounts as reported on schedule RC-T item 10, column b.

Memo: Accounts in Foreign Offices

Dollar balance of fiduciary accounts held in foreign offices as reported on schedule RC-T item 11, columns a

& b. Managed assets as reported on RC-T item 8 column a is displayed as a percentage of RC-T item 11, columns a & b.

Total Fiduciary and Related Accounts

The number of managed and non-managed fiduciary accounts is displayed by type. Also the percentage of number of trust accounts by caption is displayed. Additionally the proportion of the number of managed accounts to total number of accounts within each category is shown. Finally, the percentage change or growth rate is displayed.

Personal Trust and Agency

Number of managed and non-managed personal trust and agency accounts as reported on schedule RC-T item 4, columns c & d is displayed. The number of accounts is also displayed as a percentage of total number of accounts as reported on RC-T item 9, columns c & d. Finally managed accounts as reported on RC-T item 4, column c, is displayed as a percentage of RC-T item 4, columns a & b.

Employee Benefit Defined Contribution

Number of retirement related employee benefit—defined contribution accounts as reported on schedule RC-T item 5.a, columns c & d is displayed. The number is also displayed as a percentage of total number of accounts as reported on RC-T item 9, columns c & d. Finally managed accounts as reported on RC-T item 5.a, column c is displayed as a percentage of RC-T item 5.a, columns c & d.

Employee Benefit Defined Benefit

Number of retirement related employee benefit—defined benefit accounts as reported on schedule RC-T item 5.b, columns c & d is displayed. The number is also displayed as a percentage of total number of trust accounts as reported on

RC-T item 9, columns c & d. Finally managed accounts as reported on RC-T item 5.b, column c, is displayed as a percentage of RC-T item 5.b, columns c & d.

Other Retirement

Number of other retirement accounts as reported on schedule RC-T item 5.c, columns c & d is displayed. The dollar balance is also displayed as a percentage of total number of trust accounts as reported on RC-T item 9, columns c & d. Finally managed accounts as reported on RC-T item 5.c, column c is displayed as a percentage of RC-T item 5.c, columns c & d.

Corporate Trust and Agency

Number of corporate trust and agency accounts as reported on schedule RC-T item 6, columns c & d is displayed. The number of accounts is also displayed as a percentage of the total number off trust accounts as reported on RC-T item 9, columns c & d. Finally managed accounts as reported on RC-T item 6, column c is displayed as a percentage of RC-T item 6, columns c & d.

Investment Management Agency

Number of investment management agency accounts as reported on schedule RC-T item 7, columns c & d is displayed. The number of accounts is also displayed as a percentage of the total number of trust accounts as reported on RC-T item 9, columns c & d. Finally managed accounts as reported on RC-T item 7, column c is displayed as a percentage of RC-T item 7, columns c & d.

Other Fiduciary

Number of other fiduciary accounts as reported on schedule RC-T item 8, columns c & d is displayed. The number of accounts is also displayed as a percentage of the total number of accounts as reported on RC-T item 9, columns c & d. Finally managed accounts as reported on RC-T item 8, column c is displayed as a percentage of RC-T item 8, columns c & d.

Total Fiduciary Accounts

Number of all fiduciary accounts both managed and non-managed as reported on schedule RC-T item 9, columns c & d.

Custody and Safekeeping

The total balance of custody and safekeeping accounts as reported on schedule RC-T item 10, column d.

Memo: Accounts in Foreign Offices

Number of fiduciary accounts held in foreign offices as reported on schedule RC-T item 11, columns c & d. Managed accounts as reported on RC-T item 8, column c is displayed as a percentage of RC-T item 11, columns c & d.

Corporate Trust and Agency

The Balance and number of corporate trust and agency accounts are displayed. Additionally, an annual growth rate in balances between quarters is displayed.

Corporate and Municipal Trusteeships

The number of issues and balance of corporate and municipal trusteeships as reported on RC-T memoranda item 2.a, columns a & b respectively.

All Other Corporate

The number of transfer agent, registrar, paying agent and other corporate agency issues as reported on schedule RC-T item 2.b, column a.

Fiduciary and Related Services Income

The amount of income generated from and expense related to trust activities is displayed. Additionally, each component of income is expressed as a percentage of gross fiduciary and related services income. Note that this information is confidential and as a consequence **WILL NOT** be displayed on the public website. Regulatory users have access to the information. Individual banks should see their respective federal bank supervisor to obtain this information.

Personal Trust and Agency

Total amount of income from personal trust and agency accounts as reported on RC-T item 12. It is also expressed as a percentage of gross fiduciary income as reported on RC-T item 19.

Employee Benefit Defined Contribution

Total amount of income from employee benefit defined contribution accounts as reported on RC-T item 13.a. It is also expressed as a percentage of gross fiduciary income as reported on RC-T item 19.

Employee Benefit Defined Benefit

Total amount of income from employee benefit defined benefit accounts as reported on RC-T item 13.b. It is also expressed as a percentage of gross fiduciary income as reported on RC-T item 19.

Other Retirement

Total amount of income from other retirement accounts as reported on RC-T item 13.c. It is also expressed as a percentage of gross fiduciary income as reported on RC-T item 19.

Corporate Trust and Agency

Total amount of income from corporate trust and agency accounts as reported on RC-T item 14. It is also expressed as a percentage of gross fiduciary income as reported on RC-T item 19.

Investment Management Agency

Total amount of income from investment management agency accounts as reported on RC-T item 15. It is also expressed as a percentage of gross fiduciary income as reported on RC-T item 19.

Other Fiduciary Accounts

Total amount of income from other fiduciary accounts as reported on RC-T item 16. It is also expressed as a percentage of gross fiduciary income as reported on RC-T item 19.

Custody and Safekeeping

Total amount of income from custody and safekeeping accounts as reported on RC-T item 17. It is also expressed as a percentage of gross fiduciary income as reported on RC-T item 19.

Other Fiduciary and Related Services Income

Total amount of income from other fiduciary and related services as reported on RC-T item 18. It is also expressed as a percentage of gross fiduciary income as reported on RC-T item 19.

Gross Fiduciary and Related Income

Gross amount of fiduciary and related income as reported on RC-T item 19.

LESS: Expenses

The total of expenses as reported in schedule RC-T item 20. It is also expressed as a percentage of gross fiduciary income as reported on RC-T item 19.

LESS: Net Losses

Net losses from fiduciary activities as reported in schedule RC-T item 21. It is also expressed as a percentage of gross fiduciary income as reported on RC-T item 19.

PLUS: Intercompany Credits

The total of intracompany income credits as reported on schedule RC-T item 22. It is also expressed as a percentage of gross fiduciary income as reported on RC-T item 19.

Net Fiduciary and Related Income

Net fiduciary and related services income as reported on schedule RC-T item 23.

Memo: Fiduciary Income Foreign

The memo amount of fiduciary and related service income—foreign offices as reported on schedule RC-T item 19.a, It is also expressed as a percentage of gross fiduciary income as reported on RC-T item 19.

Gross Fiduciary Income % Noninterest Income

Total fiduciary income as reported on schedule RC-T item 19, expressed as a percentage of total noninterest income reported in schedule RI, item 5.m.

	06/30/2008				03/31/2008				12/31/2007		
FIDUCIARY INCOME % FID ASSETS	BANK	PEER	PCT	BANK	PEER	PCT		BANK	PEER	PCT	
PERSONAL TRUST AND AGENCY	N/A	0.59	N/A	N/A	0.57	N/A		N/A	0.55	N/A	
EMPLOYEE BENEFIT DC	N/A	0.45	N/A	N/A	0.43	N/A		N/A	0.40	N/A	
EMPLOYEE BENEFIT DB	N/A	0.19	N/A	N/A	0.21	N/A		N/A	0.20	N/A	
OTHER RETIREMENT	N/A	0.42	N/A	N/A	0.42	N/A		N/A	0.45	N/A	
CORPORATE TRUST AND AGENCY	N/A	0.26	N/A	N/A	0.57	N/A		N/A	0.61	N/A	
INVESTMENT MANAGEMENT AGENCY	N/A	0.42	N/A	N/A	0.40	N/A		N/A	0.37	N/A	
OTHER FIDUCIARY	N/A	0.17	N/A	N/A	0.16	N/A		N/A	0.15	N/A	
TOTAL FIDUCIARY ASSETS	N/A	0.40	N/A	N/A	0.38	N/A		N/A	0.35	N/A	
CUSTODY AND SAFEKEEPING	N/A	0.04	N/A	N/A	0.04	N/A		N/A	0.05	N/A	
MEMO FIDUCIARY INCOME FOREIGN	N/A	0.50	N/A	N/A	0.37	N/A		N/A	0.26	N/A	
GROSS FIDUCIARY LOSSES - MANAGED	($000)	%REV	PEER	PCT	($000)	%REV	PEER	PCT	($000)	%REV	PEER	PCT
PERSONAL TRUST AND AGENCY	N/A	N/A	0.69	N/A	N/A	N/A	N/A	N/A	N/A	N/A	0.30	N/A
RETIREMENT TRUST AND AGENCY	N/A	N/A	6.11	N/A	N/A	N/A	N/A	N/A	N/A	N/A	0.11	N/A
INVESTMENT MANAGEMENT AGENCY	N/A	N/A	0.81	N/A	N/A	N/A	N/A	N/A	N/A	N/A	0.30	N/A
OTHER FIDUCIARY	N/A	N/A	105.23	N/A	N/A	N/A	N/A	N/A	N/A	N/A	0.11	N/A
TOTAL GROSS MANAGED LOSSES	N/A	N/A	27.30	N/A	N/A	N/A	N/A	N/A	N/A	N/A	0.23	N/A
GROSS FIDUCIARY LOSSES - NON MGD												
PERSONAL TRUST AND AGENCY	N/A	N/A	0.00	N/A	N/A	N/A	N/A	N/A	N/A	N/A	0.02	N/A
RETIREMENT TRUST AND AGENCY	N/A	N/A	0.00	N/A	N/A	N/A	N/A	N/A	N/A	N/A	0.26	N/A
INVESTMENT MANAGEMENT AGENCY	N/A	N/A	0.00	N/A	N/A	N/A	N/A	N/A	N/A	N/A	0.02	N/A
OTHER FIDUCIARY	N/A	N/A	0.00	N/A	N/A	N/A	N/A	N/A	N/A	N/A	0.62	N/A
TOTAL GROSS NON MANAGED LOSSES	N/A	N/A	0.00	N/A	N/A	N/A	N/A	N/A	N/A	N/A	0.24	N/A
NET FIDUCIARY LOSSES - ALL												
PERSONAL TRUST AND AGENCY	N/A	N/A	-0.31	N/A	N/A	N/A	N/A	N/A	N/A	N/A	0.29	N/A
RETIREMENT TRUST AND AGENCY	N/A	N/A	0.00	N/A	N/A	N/A	N/A	N/A	N/A	N/A	0.26	N/A
INVESTMENT MANAGEMENT AGENCY	N/A	N/A	0.33	N/A	N/A	N/A	N/A	N/A	N/A	N/A	0.30	N/A
OTHER FIDUCIARY	N/A	N/A	1.26	N/A	N/A	N/A	N/A	N/A	N/A	N/A	0.67	N/A
TOTAL NET LOSSES	N/A	N/A	0.56	N/A	N/A	N/A	N/A	N/A	N/A	N/A	0.38	N/A
COLLECTIVE/COMMON TRUST FUNDS	$(000)	%TOTAL	%CHG		$(000)	%TOTAL	%CHG		$(000)	%TOTAL	%CHG	
DOMESTIC EQUITY	N/A	N/A	N/A		N/A	N/A	N/A		N/A	N/A	N/A	
INTERNATION/GLOBAL EQUITY	N/A	N/A	N/A		N/A	N/A	N/A		N/A	N/A	N/A	
STOCK/BOND BLEND	N/A	N/A	N/A		N/A	N/A	N/A		N/A	N/A	N/A	
TAXABLE BOND	N/A	N/A	N/A		N/A	N/A	N/A		N/A	N/A	N/A	
MUNICIPAL BOND	N/A	N/A	N/A		N/A	N/A	N/A		N/A	N/A	N/A	
SHORT TERM/MONEY MARKET	N/A	N/A	N/A		N/A	N/A	N/A		N/A	N/A	N/A	
SPECIALITY/OTHER	N/A	N/A	N/A		N/A	N/A	N/A		N/A	N/A	N/A	
TOTAL TRUST FUNDS	N/A	N/A	N/A		N/A	N/A	N/A		N/A	N/A	N/A	

Page 1A displays an analysis of income and losses on fiduciary accounts. Additionally gross loss, recovery and net loss rates are calculated for each type of account. To provide a basis for analysis of bank information, average ratios are calculated for a peer group of comparably sized banks. Please see section II for details on peer group composition and a description of the averaging process. Finally, a percentile ranking or relative position is developed for each income and loss ratio. Please note that, all fiduciary income and loss data as reported on RC-T items 12 through 23 and memorandum item 4 are considered confidential. While confidential information is provided to regulatory users it is **not** made available on the public UBPR website. Individual banks should contact their respective federal bank supervisor for access to confidential information.

Fiduciary Income % Fiduciary Assets

An analysis of yields by type of fiduciary account is presented. Income generated by a particular type of account is divided by the outstanding account balance. For non-year end dates the income is annualized. Please note that not all banks will report income on RC-T. Please see the call instructions on www.ffiec.gov.

Personal Trust and Agency

Income from personal trust and agency accounts reported on RC-T item 12 expressed as a percentage of personal trust and agency account assets reported on RC-T item 4, columns a & b.

Employee Benefit Defined Contribution

Income from employee benefit defined contribution accounts reported on RC-T item 13.a expressed as a percentage of employee benefit

defined contribution account assets reported on RC-T item 5.a, columns a & b.

Employee Benefit Defined Benefit

Income from employee benefit defined benefit accounts reported on RC-T item 13.b expressed as a percentage of employee benefit defined benefit account assets reported on RC-T item 5.b, columns a & b.

Other Retirement

Income from other retirement accounts reported on RC-T item 13.c expressed as a percentage of other retirement account assets reported on RC-T item 5.c, columns a & b.

Corporate Trust and Agency

Income from corporate trust and agency accounts reported on RC-T item 14 expressed as a percentage of corporate trust and agency assets reported on RC-T item 6, columns a & b.

Investment Management Agency

Income from investment management agency accounts reported on RC-T item 15 expressed as a percentage of investment management and agency account assets reported on RC-T item 7, columns a & b.

Other Fiduciary

Income from other fiduciary accounts reported on RC-T item16, expressed as a percentage of other fiduciary account assets reported on RC-T item 8, columns a & b.

Total Fiduciary Assets

Gross fiduciary income as reported on RC-T item 19 expressed as a percentage of total managed and non managed account assets reported on RC-T item 9, columns a & b.

Custody and Safekeeping

Income from custody and safekeeping accounts as reported on schedule

RC-T item 17 expressed as a percentage of custody and safekeeping accounts as reported on schedule RC-T item 10, column b.

Memo: Fiduciary Income Foreign

Fiduciary and related services income-foreign offices as reported on schedule RC-T item 19.a expressed as a percentage of total managed and non-managed fiduciary accounts held in foreign offices as reported on schedule RC-T item 11, columns a & b.

Gross Fiduciary Losses— Managed

The rate of gross losses on fiduciary accounts is expressed as a percentage of the income generated by type of account.

Personal Trust and Agency

The dollar amount of gross losses on managed personal trust and agency accounts reported on schedule RC-T memoranda item 4.a, column a is displayed. It is also expressed as a percentage of income on personal and trust agency accounts reported in RC-T item 12.

Retirement Trust and Agency

The dollar amount of gross losses on managed retirement trust and agency accounts reported on schedule RC-T memoranda item RC-T item 4.b, column a. It is also expressed as a percentage of income on retirement related and agency accounts reported on RC-T items 13.a, b & c.

Investment Management Agency

The dollar amount of gross losses on managed investment management agency accounts reported on schedule RC-T memoranda item 4.c column a. It is also expressed as a percentage of income in investment management agency accounts reported on RC-T item 15.

Other Fiduciary

The dollar amount of gross losses on managed other fiduciary accounts and related services reported on schedule RC-T memoranda item 4.d, column a. It is also expressed as a percentage of income from corporate trust and agency, other fiduciary, custody and safekeeping and other related services accounts reported on RC-T items 14, 16, 17 & 18.

Total Gross Managed Losses

Total fiduciary settlements, surcharges and other losses on managed accounts reported on schedule RC-T item 4.e, column a. It is also expressed as a percentage of total fiduciary and related services income reported on RC-T item 19.

Gross Fiduciary Losses— Non Managed

The rate of gross losses on fiduciary accounts is expressed as a percentage of the income generated by type of account.

Personal Trust and Agency

The dollar amount of gross losses on non- managed personal trust and agency accounts reported on schedule RC-T memoranda item 4.a, column b is displayed. It is also expressed as a percentage of income on personal and trust agency accounts reported in RC-T item 12.

Retirement Trust and Agency

The dollar amount of gross losses on non-managed retirement trust and agency accounts reported on schedule RC-T memoranda item 4.b, column b. It is also expressed as a percentage of income on retirement related and agency accounts reported on RC-T items 13.a, b & c.

Investment Management Agency

The dollar amount of gross losses on non-managed investment management agency accounts reported on schedule RC-T memoranda item 4.c, column b. It is also expressed

as a percentage of income in investment management agency accounts reported on RC-T item 15.

Other Fiduciary

The dollar amount of gross losses on non-managed other fiduciary accounts and related services reported on schedule RC-T memoranda item 4d, column b. It is also expressed as a percentage of income from corporate trust and agency, other fiduciary, custody and safekeeping and other related services accounts reported on RC-T items 14, 16, 17 & 18.

Total Gross Non-Managed Losses

Total fiduciary settlements, surcharges and other losses on managed accounts reported on schedule RC-T item 4.e, column b. It is also expressed as a percentage of total fiduciary and related services income reported on RC-T item 19.

Net Fiduciary Losses—All

The rate of net losses on fiduciary accounts is expressed as a percentage of the income generated by type of account.

Personal Trust and Agency

The dollar amount of gross losses on managed personal trust and agency accounts reported on schedule RC-T memoranda item 4.a, column a, plus gross losses on non-managed accounts reported on RC-T memoranda item 4.a, column b, less recoveries reported on RC-T item 4.a, column c is displayed. It is also expressed as a percentage of income on personal and trust agency accounts reported in RC-T item 12.

Retirement Trust and Agency

The dollar amount of gross losses on managed retirement trust and agency accounts reported on schedule RC-T memoranda item 4.b, column a, plus gross losses on non-managed accounts reported on RC-T memoranda item 4.b, column b, less recov-

eries reported on RC-T memoranda item 4.b, column c. It is also expressed as a percentage of income on retirement related and agency accounts reported on RC-T items 13 a, b & c.

Investment Management Agency

The dollar amount of gross losses on managed investment management agency accounts reported on schedule RC-T memoranda item 4.c, column a plus gross losses on non-managed accounts reported on schedule RC-T memoranda item 4.c column b less recoveries reported on RC-T item 4.c, column c. It is also expressed as a percentage of income in investment management agency accounts reported on RC-T item 15.

Other Fiduciary

The dollar amount of gross losses on managed other fiduciary accounts and related services reported on schedule RC-T memoranda item 4.d, column a plus gross losses on managed accounts reported on schedule RC-T memoranda item 4.d, column b, less recoveries reported on RC-T item 4.d, column c. It is also expressed as a percentage of income from corporate trust and agency, other fiduciary, custody and safekeeping and other related services accounts reported on RC-T items 14, 16, 17 & 18.

Total Gross Managed Losses

Total fiduciary settlements, surcharges and other losses on managed accounts reported on schedule RC-T item 4.e, column a plus gross losses reported on non-managed accounts reported on RC-T item 4.e, column b, less recoveries reported on RC-T item 4.e, column c. It is also expressed as a percentage of total fiduciary and related services income reported on RC-T item 19.

Collective and Common Trust Funds

The dollar amount of collective and common trust funds is displayed by type of investment vehicle. In addition individual totals are shown as a percentage of total collective and common trust funds. Finally an annual growth rate is calculated.

Domestic Equity

Dollar amount of domestic equity funds as reported on RC-T memoranda item 3.a, column b is displayed. It is also expressed as a percentage of total collective investment funds reported on RC-T memoranda item 3.h, column b.

International/Global Equity

Dollar amount of international/global equity funds as reported on RC-T memoranda item 3.b, column b is displayed. It is also expressed as a percentage of total collective investment funds reported on RC-T memoranda item 3.h, column b.

Stock/Bond Blend

Dollar amount of stock/bond blend funds as reported on RC-T memo-

randa item 3.c, column b is displayed. It is also expressed as a percentage of total collective investment funds reported on RC-T memoranda item 3.h, column b.

Taxable Bond

Dollar amount of taxable bond funds as reported on RC-T memoranda item 3.d, column b is displayed. It is also expressed as a percentage of total collective investment funds reported on RC-T memoranda item 3.h, column b.

Municipal Bond Funds

Dollar amount of municipal bond funds as reported on RC-T memoranda item 3.e, column b is displayed. It is also expressed as a percentage of total collective investment funds reported on RC-T memoranda item 3.h, column b.

Short Term/Money Market

Dollar amount of short term investments/money market funds as

reported on RC-T memoranda item 3.f, column b is displayed. It is also expressed as a percentage of total collective investment funds reported on RC-T memoranda item 3.h, column b.

Specialty/Other

Dollar amount of specialty/other funds as reported on RC-T memoranda item 3.g, column b is displayed. It is also expressed as a percentage of total collective investment funds reported on RC-T memoranda item 3.h, column b.

Total Trust Funds

Dollar amount of total collective investment funds as reported on RC-T memoranda item 3.h, column b is displayed.

Appendix A: Tax-Equivalency Worksheet

This work sheet can be used to replicate the Uniform Bank Performance Report tax-equivalency adjustment.

General Information

This Tax-Equivalency Worksheet is divided into four parts. Part I determines the amount of tax-exempt income that is available for tax benefit by comparing it to taxable income. Part II estimates the tax benefit for this amount of available tax-exempt income by determining the bank's marginal tax rate and multiplying by a percentage based on that tax rate. Part III describes the usage of this estimated tax benefit in the UBPR, in earning ratios, dollar amounts, and asset yield ratios. The "Definition of Preliminary Calculations" section describes the calculation of items for Part I using Report of Income items.

PART I: Determine the Amount of Tax-Exempt Income Available for Tax Benefit

Preliminary Calculations

Calculate the following items according to the definitions in the last section of the Appendix:

i. tax-exempt income (write the amount here and at "Final Part I Calculation," line b: _____ ;
ii. pretax *taxable income:* _____ ;
iii. total pretax income, *including* tax-exempt income: _____ ;
iv. *total* applicable income taxes: _____ ;
v. 100% nondeductible interest expense: _____ .

Alternatives for Part I—(Only *one* alternative is possible for any bank.)

Alternative 1

If the bank does not have any tax-exempt income, the tax-equivalent adjustment equals zero (0) and no further calculations are necessary. Otherwise, proceed to the next alternative. _____

Alternative 2

If pretax taxable income (preliminary calculation ii) *exceeds* tax-exempt income, or if pretax taxable income is greater than or equal to zero (0), write the amount of tax-exempt income here and at "Final Part I Calculation," line a, and proceed from there; otherwise, proceed to the next alternative. _____

Alternative 3

If pretax taxable income (preliminary calculation ii) is less than zero (0) *and* total pretax income (preliminary calculation iii) exceeds zero (0) *and* total applicable income taxes (preliminary calculation iv) is less than zero (0) (e.g., the bank reports tax credits), perform the following calculation; otherwise, proceed to the next alternative.

Multiply the total applicable income taxes (preliminary calculation iv) by negative 1.67 (–1.67). Add the result to total pretax income (preliminary calculation iii). Write the amount here and at "Final Part I Calculation," line a, and proceed from there. _____

Alternative 4

If total pretax income (preliminary calculation iii) is less than or equal to zero (0) and total applicable income taxes (preliminary calculation iv) is less than zero (0), then perform the following calculation; otherwise, proceed to the next alternative.

Multiply the total applicable income taxes (preliminary calculation iv) by negative 1.67 (–1.67). Write the result here and at "Final Part I Calculation," line a, and proceed from there.   _____

Alternative 5

If total pretax income (preliminary calculation iii) is less than or equal to zero (0) and total applicable income taxes (preliminary calculation iv) are greater than or equal to zero (0), then the bank receives no calculated tax benefit. Enter a zero (0) in Final Part I Calculation, line a.   _____

Final Part I Calculation

a. Amount calculated using one of the five above alternatives: _____

b. Amount of tax-exempt income (preliminary calculation I):   _____

  Write the *lesser* of a. or b. here: _____

  Subtract the amount of nondeductible interest expense (preliminary calculation vi):   − _____

          _____

If the result is zero (0) or less, there is no tax-exempt income available for tax benefit. If the result is greater than zero (0), proceed with Part II using that amount.

PART II: Estimate the Tax Benefit for Available Tax-Exempt Income from Part I.

The tax benefit for the amount of tax-exempt income available for such benefit is estimated by: Calculating the annualized amount of net taxable income plus available tax-exempt income; determining the marginal income tax rate for this adjusted income figure; calculating the tax benefit based on the marginal tax rate.

A. Calculating Annualized Taxable Income Plus Available Tax-Exempt Income

  In order to estimate the tax benefit of tax-exempt income, it is first necessary to calculate what the annalized taxable income would be if available tax-exempt income were included. Up to this point, all figures have been on a year-to-date basis. Perform the following calculation to determine annualized taxable income for tax-equivalency purposes:

  1. Add: pretax taxable income (preliminary calculation ii):   _____

     Plus: available tax-exempt income from Part I: + _____

     Equals: year-to-date adjusted income: _____

  2. Multiply the above result by the appropriate annualization factor:

Reporting Period Ending	Annualization Factor
March 31, YYYY	4
June 30, YYYY	2
September 30, YYYY	1.333
December 31, YYYY	1

          X _____

  Equals: annualized amount of taxable income plus available tax-exempt income   _____

B. Calculating Estimated Tax Benefit:

1. Find the appropriate tax benefit factor in the table below, based on the annualized income calculated above.

Tax Rates and Tax Benefit Factors

Annualized Income from Part II A	1986 or earlier		1987		1988 or later	
	Marginal Tax Rate (Percent)	Tax Benefit Factor	Marginal Tax Rate (Percent)	Tax Benefit Factor	Marginal Tax Rate (Percent)	Tax Benefit Factor
up to 25	15	.18	15	.18	15	.18
25–50	18	.22	16.5	.20	15	.18
50–75	30	.43	27.5	.38	25	.33
75–10,000	40	.67	37.0	.59	34	.52
over 10,000	46	.85	40.0	.67	35	.54

2. Enter the available tax-exempt income from Part I here: _____

Multiply by the tax benefit factor from the above table: X _____

Estimated Tax Benefit (year-to-date): _____

PART III: Using the Estimated Tax Benefit in the UBPR

The estimated tax benefit calculated in Part II, which is based on total tax-exempt income, is allocated back to tax-exempt loan & lease income and tax-exempt securities income.

The tax benefit is then added to pretax income and used in earnings presentations and yield ratios in the UBPR.

A. Allocating Tax Benefit to Loans & Leases and Securities:

Assign the estimated tax benefit from Part II back to the two sources of tax-exempt income as follows:

1. Calculate the ratio of tax-exempt loan & lease income to total tax-exempt income:

Tax-exempt loan & lease income (see "definitions of Preliminary Calculations", Paragraph i): _____

Divided by total tax-exempt income (preliminary calculation I): ÷ _____

Equals: ratio of tax-exempt loan & lease income: _____

2. Multiply the estimated tax benefit: _____

By the ratio calculated in 1.: X _____

Equals estimated tax benefit for tax-exempt loan & lease income: _____

3. From the total estimated tax benefit: _____

Subtract: loan & lease tax benefit from 2.: _____

Equals: estimated tax benefit for tax-exempt securities income: _____

B. Using and Presenting Tax Benefits in the UBPR

1. The tax benefits allocated loans and securities allocated in A. above, are also presented separately on UBPR Page 02. For other than December reporting periods, these figures must be de-annualized by dividing by the annualization factor in Part II. Tax benefits are included in various sub-totals that appear on page 2 such as Total Interest Income (TE) and Pre Tax Net Operating Income (TE). Computed tax benefits are reversed or subtracted out to allow after tax net income to reconcile properly. Tax benefits are reversed by including them as Current Tax Equivalent Adjustment in Applicable Income Taxes (TE).

2. The tax-equivalent income amounts, annualized, are used in the earnings ratios that appear on UBPR Page 01.

3. The book and tax-equivalent income figures for loans & leases and securities that appear on page 2 are used in selected yield ratios that appear on UBPR Pages 03 and 12.

Definitions of Preliminary Calculations

i. Tax-exempt Income:

Add:

Tax-exempt loan & lease income:
(Report of Income Memoranda section item 3): _____

Tax-exempt securities income:
(Report of Income Memoranda item 4): + _____

Equals: Total tax-exempt income:

These figures are presented on UBPR Page 02. _____

ii. Pretax Taxable Income
Income (loss) before income taxes, extraordinary items and other adjustments (Report of Income item 8): _____

Plus: Interest expense incurred to carry tax-exempt obligations acquired after August 7, 1986, that is not deductible for federal income tax purposes (Report of Income item M1): + _____

Less: Tax-exempt income (preliminary calculation I.): − _____

Equals: Total pretax taxable income: _____

iii. Total Pretax Income

Tax-exempt income (preliminary calculation I.): _____

Plus: Pretax taxable income (preliminary calculation ii.): + _____

Equals: Total pretax income: _____

iv. Total Applicable Income Taxes:
Applicable income taxes (Report of Income item 9): _____

Plus: Applicable income taxes on extraodinary items and other adjustment (Report of Income item 11a): + _____

Equals: Total applicable income taxes: _____

v. 100% Nondeductible Interest Expense:

Interest expense incurred to carry tax-exempt obligations acquired after August 7, 1986, that is not deductible for federal income tax purposes (Report of Income item M1).

Appendix B: UBPR Data Ordering Information

In addition to the individual bank UBPR, the FFIEC makes data available on DVD. UBPR data is stored on the DVD in delimited format for use with spreadsheets and database software individual UBPR Reports are available on line for viewing and printing at **www.ffiec.gov**. These items are:

UBPR Data Tapes

The types of UBPR data that are available on DVD are:

- R1—Bank-level ratio and dollar values:

  Each tape will contain a record for each insured commercial bank for one data date. Each record will contain approximately 900 ratio or dollar values.

- R2—Peer group averages:

  Each tape will contain a record for each of the UBPR peer groups plus a record for all banks, for all of the data dates for that edition. Each record will contain approximately 330 average ratio values.

- R3—Bank percentile ranks:

  Each tape will contain a record for each insured commercial bank for one data date. Each record will contain approximately 330 percentile rank values.

- R4 and R5—State and state/asset group averages:

  Each tape will contain a record for each state plus a record for all banks. The same tape will also contain a record for each of three asset size groups in each state, plus a record for all banks in each of these asset sizes ($0–25 million, $25–100 million and over $100 million); these size group records are present only for the latest data date for the edition. Each record will contain approximately 33 ratio averages, plus total assets and total net income.

UBPR Data

Requests for or inquiries about UBPR data DVDs should be made to:

Federal Financial Institutions Council
UBPR Coordinator
3501 Fairfax Drive
Room D8073a
Arlington, VA 22226-3550

Phone: 703-516-5732

E-Mail: jsmullen@fdic.gov